book presents a variety of exciting new perspectives on the
perception of risk and the strategies that people adopt to cope with it.
Using the framework of recent social and cultural theory, it reflects the
fact that risk has become integral to contemporary understandings of
selfhood, the body and social relations and is central to the work of
writers such as Douglas, Beck, Giddens and the Foucauldian theorists.
The contributors are all leading scholars in the fields of sociology,
cultural and media studies and cultural anthropology. Combining
empirical analyses with metatheoretical critiques, they tackle an
unusually diverse range of topics including drug use, risk in the
workplace, fear of crime and the media, risk and pregnant embodiment, the social construction of danger in childhood, anxieties about
national identity, the governmental uses of risk and the relationship
between risk phenomena and social order.

Deborah Lupton is Associate Professor in Cultural Studies and
Cultural Policy and Director of the Centre for Cultural Risk Research
at Charles Sturt University, Australia. She has published numerous
books and journal articles in areas such as the sociocultural aspects of
health, sexuality, food, the emotions, HIV and the media.

Risk and sociocultural theory:

new directions and perspectives

Edited by

Deborah Lupton

CAMBRIDGE
UNIVERSITY PRESS

PUBLISHED BY THE PRESS SYNDICATE OF THE UNIVERSITY OF CAMBRIDGE
The Pitt Building, Trumpington Street, Cambridge, United Kingdom, CB2 1RP

CAMBRIDGE UNIVERSITY PRESS
The Edinburgh Building, Cambridge CB2 2RU, UK http://www.cup.cam.ac.uk
40 West 20th Street, New York, NY 1011–4211, USA   http://www.cup.org
10 Stamford Road, Oakleigh, Melbourne 3166, Australia

First published 1999

Printed in the United Kingdom at the University Press, Cambridge

Typeset in Plantin 10/12 pt   [CE]

A catalogue record for this book is available from the British Library

Library of Congress cataloguing in publication data

Risk and sociocultural theory: new directions and perspectives / edited by
Deborah Lupton.
    p.   cm.
ISBN 0 521 64207 8 (hardback). – ISBN 0 521 64554 9 (paperback)
1. Risk – Sociological aspects.
2. Risk perception – Social aspects.
1. Lupton, Deborah.
HM1101.R57   1999
302′.12 – dc21   99–24201   CIP

ISBN 0 521 64207 8 hardback
ISBN 0 521 64554 9 paperback

Contents

Contributors

STEPHEN CROOK is Professor of Sociology and Head of the Department of Psychology and Sociology at James Cook University, Townsville, Australia. His general interests are in the sociology of culture, social theory and the sociology of change. He is the author of *Modernist Radicalism and its Aftermath*, co-author of *Postmodernization: Change in Advanced Society* and editor of *Adorno: the Stars Down to Earth*. His recent research has centred on his role as co-chief investigator in a major research project on 'Environmentalism, Public Opinion and the Media'. In this capacity he is a contributor to, and co-editor of *Ebbing of the Green Tide? Environmentalism, Public Opinion and the Media in Australia*. His current work is focused on the sociocultural regimes through which technological and other risks are managed, and the relation of those regimes to more general patterns of order and change.

MITCHELL DEAN is Professor and Head of the Department of Sociology at Macquarie University, Sydney, Australia. He is the author of one of the first full-length studies of governmentality, *The Constitution of Poverty: Toward a Genealogy of Liberal Governance* (1991), as well as *Critical and Effective Histories: Foucault's Methods and Historical Sociology* (1994). He has written numerous articles on applied and theoretical aspects of governmental and ethical practices and published in European, North American and Australian social science and theory journals. He is the co-editor (with Barry Hindess) of *Governing Australia* (1998) and author of *Governmentality* (1999).

NICK FOX is Senior Lecturer in Sociology at the University of Sheffield, UK. He is the author of *The Social Meaning of Surgery* (1992) and *Postmodernism, Sociology and Health* (1993). He has written extensively on postmodernism and is currently working on a new book on postmodern social theory and research.

STEVI JACKSON is Professor of Women's Studies and Director of the Centre for Women's Studies, University of York, UK. She is the author of *Childhood and Sexuality* (1982) and *Christine Delphy* ('Women of Ideas' Series, 1996). She has co-edited *Women's Studies: A Reader* (1993), *The Politics of Domestic Consumption: Critical Readings* (1995), *Feminism and Sexuality* (1996) and *Contemporary Feminist Theories* (1998). She has also published a number of articles on romance, sexuality and family relationships and is currently working with Sue Scott, Kathryn Milburn and Jennifer Harden researching the impact of risk and adult risk anxiety on the everyday world of children. Forthcoming books include *Concerning Heterosexuality*, and *Childhood and Sexuality Revisited*.

DEBORAH LUPTON is Associate Professor in Cultural Studies and Cultural Policy and Director of the Centre for Cultural Risk Research, Charles Sturt University, Australia. Her research interests are in the sociocultural dimensions of: the body; medicine and public health; risk; sexuality and HIV/AIDS; parenthood; food and eating; the emotions; techno-culture; and the mass media and commodity culture. Her most recent books are *Television, AIDS and Risk* (1997, with John Tulloch), *Constructing Fatherhood* (1997, with Lesley Barclay), *The Emotional Self* (1998) and *Risk* (1999).

EVA MACKEY is a postdoctoral research fellow in the Centre for Cultural Risk Research at Charles Sturt University, Australia. A social anthropologist (PhD, University of Sussex, 1996), her publications include *The House of Difference: Cultural Politics and National Identity in Canada* (1999), and numerous journal articles and book chapters on race, representation, identity and nationalism. Her current research interests include concepts of culture and danger in 'postcolonial' settler nations, and the construction of 'dangerous' populations in colonial societies.

SUE SCOTT is Professor of Sociology at the University of Durham, UK. She was previously at the University of Stirling and the University of Manchester. Her previous research includes the Women, Risk and AIDS Project (WRAP) and she is currently involved in a large study of sex education in Scotland and a qualitative project exploring risk and risk anxiety in the lives of parents and children. Her publications include *Private Risks and Public Dangers* (edited with Gareth Williams); *Body Matters* (edited with David Morgan) and *Feminism and Sexuality* (forthcoming, with Stevi Jackson). She is currently working, with Stevi Jackson, on the importance of gender in feminism and sociology.

JOHN TULLOCH is Professor of Media Communication at Cardiff University, Wales. Previously he was Professor of Cultural Studies,

Director of Research at the Arts Faculty, and Director of the Centre for Cultural Risk Research, Charles Sturt University, Australia. His recent and forthcoming books are: *Science Fiction Audiences* (1995 with Henry Jenkins), *Television, AIDS and Risk* (1997, with Deborah Lupton), *Performing Culture* (forthcoming), and *Watching Television Audiences* (forthcoming).

Introduction: risk and sociocultural theory

Deborah Lupton

One of the most lively areas of theoretical debate in social and cultural theory in recent times is that addressing the phenomenon of risk and the role it plays in contemporary social life and subjectivities. Three major theoretical perspectives on risk emerging since the early 1980s and gaining momentum in the 1990s may be distinguished. The first is offered by the work of Mary Douglas, who began in the early 1980s setting forth an influential perspective on risk, one that adopts a cultural anthropological approach (Douglas and Wildavsky, 1982; Douglas, 1985, 1990, 1992). The German sociologist Ulrich Beck's book *Risk Society*, published in English in 1992, has provided a major impetus to recent sociological examination of risk (for some of his other writings on risk in English see also Beck, 1992a, 1992b, 1994, 1995, 1996a, 1996b; Beck and Gernsheim, 1995). The English sociologist Anthony Giddens (1990, 1991, 1994, 1998), adopting a similar perspective to that of Beck, has also influenced sociological diagnoses of the role of risk in society. A third perspective is offered by the several theorists who have taken up Michel Foucault's writings on governmentality (for example, Foucault, 1991) to explore the ways in which the state and other governmental apparatuses work together to govern – that is, manage and regulate – populations via risk discourses and strategies (Castel, 1991; Ewald, 1991; O'Malley, 1996; Dean, 1997).

I have elsewhere identified these three major approaches respectively as the 'cultural/symbolic', the 'risk society' and the 'governmentality' perspectives (see Lupton, 1999). There are, of course, some differences in the approaches offered by the scholars I have grouped together within these perspectives, but there is clear evidence of similar concerns, foci and epistemological underpinnings in their work. Together they stand in clear contrast to technico-scientific approaches to risk in taking into account the broader social and cultural, and in some cases, historical, contexts in which risk as a concept derives its meaning and resonance. For exponents of the technico-scientific perspective, which emerged from and is expressed in such disciplines as science, engineering, psychology, economics, medicine and epidemiology, risk is largely treated as a taken-for-granted objective phenomenon. The focus of research on risk in these fields is the identification of risks, mapping their causal factors, building predictive models of risk relations and people's responses to various types of risk and proposing ways of limiting the effects of risks. These inquiries are undertaken adopting a rationalistic approach which assumes that expert scientific measurement and calculation is the most appropriate standpoint from which to proceed. Such researchers may be described, therefore, as adopting a realist approach to risk.

For those working within the influential field of psychometric studies of risk, for example, people are largely viewed as responding individually to risks according to various 'heuristics', or frames of perception and understanding that structure judgement. Little attention is paid to the broader social, cultural and historical contexts in which such heuristics are developed and function. In this research, lay people's judgements on risk are typically portrayed as 'biased' or ill-informed compared with 'experts'' more 'accurate' and 'scientific' assessments. The question of how risk might be understood as a sociocultural phenomenon in its own right rarely intrudes into technico-scientific research endeavours. This question, however, propels the analyses of writers adopting the three major social and cultural perspectives referred to above. For exponents of these perspectives, a risk cannot simply be accepted as an unproblematic fact, a phenomenon that can be isolated from its social, cultural and historical contexts. Rather, what are identified as 'risks', by 'experts' as much as lay people, are understood as inevitably the outcome of sociocultural processes. Further, such risks tend to serve certain social, cultural and political functions.

These commentators argue that there are a number of important new features in notions of risk in late modern societies. They have addressed the following aspects of risk: the ways in which risks are conceptualized, in terms of from where they are thought to originate and whom they are seen to affect; how blame is ascribed for risk; the role played by expert knowledges in identifying, mediating and managing risk; the ways in which different perspectives on risk tend to create conflict between social groups based on differing aesthetic, moral and political assumptions; the relationship between the emergence of risk as an important phenomenon and broader social structural trends such as modernization and globalization; and the symbolic use of risk as a means of casting blame upon certain individuals and social groups, distinguishing social groups and establishing cultural boundaries.

The 'cultural/symbolic' perspective proposed by Douglas and her followers has its origins in her earlier work on notions of purity and contamination (Douglas, 1966/1969). In this earlier work, Douglas argued for a view of these notions as serving to construct cultural boundaries – between individual bodies, between social groups within a community and between communities. What is understood to be contaminating or polluting – and therefore as dangerous in the threat it poses to social order – is culturally specific, and works to establish and maintain ideas about self and Other. Douglas' later writings on risk and culture drew attention to the use of the concept of risk as a means in contemporary western societies of maintaining cultural boundaries. She sees risk as acting primarily as a locus of blame, in which 'risky' groups or institutions are singled out as dangerous. A 'risky' Other may pose a threat to the integrity of one's own physical body or to the symbolic body of the community or society to which one belongs. Notions of risk, Douglas argues, are inevitably phrased through cultural assumptions, and thus are shared conventions and expectations rather than individualistic judgements or 'cognitive aids for the individual decision-maker' (1985: 80). Risk acts as a 'forensic resource' in providing explanations for things that have gone wrong or unfortunate events that are foreseen to occur. Risk as a forensic resource has come to dominate in western societies because of its associations with scientific neutrality, while that of 'sin' or 'taboo' continues to dominate thinking about the dangerous Other in non-western societies.

With her collaborator Wildavsky (Douglas and Wildavsky, 1982; Douglas 1992), Douglas developed a functional structuralist analysis of the cultural response to risk in communities and organizations, entitled the 'grid-group' model (where group relates to the degree of group ethos and grid to the presence of other constraints and expectations that shape social relations). High-group and high-grid organizations are hierarchical in nature and conform closely to group norms and responses to risk, placing their trust in institutions. In contrast, low group and low grid organizations are highly individualistic, preferring a self-regulatory approach to risk. While such structuralist models of risk responses may be criticized for their rigidity, they do begin to offer a view on risk that goes beyond a focus on the individual and her or his psychological or cognitive response to risk to an interest in the sociocultural context in which individuals are sited and through which they make judgements about risk.

The 'risk-society' theorists have chosen to focus their analyses largely on macro-structural factors influencing what they see to be an intensification of concern in late modern societies about risks. They argue that the risks produced under the conditions of late modernity have increased in magnitude and become globalized, and are therefore more difficult than in past eras to calculate and therefore manage or avoid. Central to Beck's and Giddens' writings on risk society is the concept of reflexive modernity. This concept incorporates the notion that late modernity is characterized by a critique of the processes of modernity, which are no longer unproblematically viewed as producing 'goods' (such as wealth and employment) but are now seen to produce many of the dangers or 'bads' from which we feel threatened (such as environmental pollution, unemployment and family breakdown). The central institutions of late modernity – government, industry and science – are singled out as the main producers of risk. An emphasis on risk, Beck and Giddens assert, is thus an integral feature of a society which has come to reflect upon itself, to critique itself.

Exponents of the 'risk society' thesis also argue that in late modernity there is a trend towards individualization, or the progressive loss of tradition and social bonds as a means of structuring the life-course and forming personal identity. A major difference, they argue, in the ways in which we conceptualize and deal with dangers compared with individuals in earlier eras is the extent to which individuals are positioned as choosing agents. We now think of ourselves as exercising a high level of control over the extent to which we expose ourselves to danger and therefore as culpable for becoming prey to risk. Risk is primarily understood as a human responsibility, both in its production and management, rather than the outcome of fate or destiny, as was the case in premodern times.

The role played by experts in constructing and mediating discourses on risk would also appear to be a particularly late modern development. Since the sixteenth century, as Foucault and exponents of the 'governmentality' perspective have described, a huge network of expert knowledges has developed, accompanied by apparatuses and institutions built around the construction, reproduction, dissemination and practice of these knowledges. This is an outcome of the emergence of the modern system of liberal government, with its emphasis on rule and the maintenance of order through voluntary self-discipline rather than via coercive or violent means. Risk is understood as one of the heterogeneous governmental strategies of disciplinary power by which populations and individuals are monitored and managed so as to best meet the goals of democratic humanism. Normalization, or the method by which norms of behaviour or health status are identified in populations and by which individuals are then compared to determine how best they fit the norm, is a central aspect of liberal government. Those who are determined to deviate from the norm significantly are typically identified as being 'at risk'. To be designated as 'at risk', therefore, is to be positioned within a network of factors drawn from the observation of others. The implication of this rationalized discourse again is that risk is ultimately controllable, as long as expert knowledge can be properly brought to bear upon it.

Several writers on governmentality have drawn attention to the increasing focus in contemporary neo-liberalism (the political rationale that currently dominates Anglophone countries), on personal responsibility for avoiding and managing risk. They have identified a 'new prudentialism' currently evident in governmental discourses and strategies, which moves away from older notions of social insurance as a means of distributing risks to a focus on individuals protecting themselves against risk (see O'Malley, 1996; Dean, 1997). Like the 'risk society' theorists, therefore, some exponents of the 'governmentality' perspective have drawn attention to the importance placed upon the self-management of risk and the increasing privatization of risk. They have less to say about the ways in which large institutions are singled out as responsible and 'to blame' for risks, a point emphasized in both Douglas' work and that of Beck and Giddens.

While all three theoretical perspectives emphasize the social, cultural and political nature of risk, they each offer somewhat differently nuanced approaches to the phenomenon as socially constructed. Indeed, they may be placed at different points along a continuum, at which a realist approach of the kind offered in technico-scientific approaches is at one pole and a highly relativist constructionist approach is at the other (see Lupton, 1999: chapter 2 for a more detailed model of the risk continuum). The 'risk society' perspective tends to waver between a realist and a weak social constructionist position on risk. Beck in particular tends to move ambivalently between the two positions. Sometimes he suggests that risks are objective phenomena which are proliferating out of control, while at other times he draws attention to their mediation through social and cultural processes. In one of his books Beck explicitly seeks to develop a position that lies between realism and social constructionism. In doing so he puts forward the idea that 'real risks' exist and can be objectively measured through science but also supports the notion that what are considered to be 'risks' are conceptualized differently in different historical and cultural contexts (see Beck, 1995: 76).

The 'cultural/symbolic' perspective is more towards the relativist pole. However, Douglas does emphasize at various points in her writing on risk that she sees the dangers which are identified as risks as 'all too real'. She claims that her interest lies in elucidating the ways in which these 'real risks' are singled out as important compared with other possible risks and how they are used in social and cultural relations: 'this argument is not about the reality of dangers, but about how they are politicized' (Douglas, 1992: 29). The 'governmentality' perspective – taking its cue from Foucault's work on the discursive construction of reality – offers the most relativist position on risk. For writers such as Ewald, 'nothing is a risk in itself; there is no risk in reality' (1991: 199). They are, therefore, not interested in investigating the nature of risk itself, but rather the forms of knowledge, the dominant discourses and expert techniques and institutions that serve to render risk calculable and knowable, bringing it into being.

Surprisingly enough, there has been little examination, hitherto, of the convergences and differences in the insights to risk as a sociocultural phenomenon conducted within the three perspectives. Exponents working within each of the perspectives have tended to refer to each other, effectively ignoring the contributions offered by writers adopting the other perspectives. There is little reference to the work of Mary Douglas, for example, in the writings of Beck and Giddens or the governmentality theorists, even as a critique. It is also surprising that there has been little interaction between areas of inquiry such as media and cultural studies, the sociology of the body, postcolonial theory and gender theory and sociocultural theories of risk. Yet several of their concerns and interests overlap: many commentators writing in these areas address questions of risk and danger as sociocultural phenomena. There is much potential for these literatures to relate to each other more closely than they have in the past in further developing insights into risk.

Further, all three major sociocultural perspectives tend to operate at the level of grand theory, with little use of empirical work into the ways in which people conceptualize and experience risk as part of their everyday lives. There remains much room for investigations addressing these issues which bring together theories on risk with empirical research and go beyond the universal 'risk subject' that tends to appear particularly in the 'risk society' and 'governmentality' perspectives. As critics such as Lash (1993) and Wynne (1996) have argued, responses to risk may be understood to be aesthetic, affective and hermeneutic phenomena grounded in everyday experiences and social relationships. Better understanding is needed of how risk logics are produced and operate at the level of situated experience. To what extent, for example, have people in late modern societies adopted the highly rationalistic reflexive approach to risk claimed for them by exponents of the 'risk society' thesis? How do people singled out as being 'at risk' respond to the imperatives on behaviour and deportment issued forth from expert knowledges and governmental apparatuses? What sorts of information do individuals trust and draw upon in developing their logics of risk? How do the structuring factors of gender, ethnicity, age, social class and so on, and different social contexts such as the workplace versus leisure sites, for example, influence risk logics? What role do the mass media play in contributing to the risk knowledges of their audiences?

The chapters collected in this book begin to address some of these lacunae, adopting some new ways of using or interpreting risk theories and new topics of investigation. The first chapter, by Nick Fox, unpacks the process of risk assessment by problematizing the relationship between risks and hazards. Fox sets out three epistemological positions on risk, ranging along the realist–constructionist continuum I referred to above. In the 'realist' position, as interpreted by Fox, risks map directly on to underlying real hazards. The 'culturalist' position sees hazards as real, while risks are the socially constructed responses to these hazards. A third, highly relativist 'postmodern' position is proposed and preferred by Fox, in which both risks and hazards are regarded as social constructions. From this position, hazards may be understood as the reifications of moral judgements about the 'riskiness' of choices, evoked discursively to support estimations of risk and those assessed to be 'at risk'. Fox examines the life choices made by people in relation to risk using two case studies: the first of health in the workplace and the second of drug use in club culture. He argues that assessing environmental circumstances as 'risks' masks political claims about how people should live, silencing voices which dissent.

The next chapter takes as its point of the departure the topic of fear of crime. John Tulloch argues that fear of crime has received a huge literature. Despite the common positioning in lay and expert cultures of both crime and fear of crime as 'risks', however, few commentators have as yet engaged with contemporary sociocultural theories of risk. Focusing in particular on the role played by the media in constructing notions of crime, Tulloch first outlines the epistemological field in which this work and risk theory more broadly has been positioned. His chapter includes a survey of empirical, cultural-realist and poststructuralist work in the fear of crime field that offers both a methodological and theoretical way ahead. Tulloch concludes with some discussion of an empirical study that examined public perceptions of media and fear of crime among Australians. The findings of this study vividly demonstrate the complex interrelationship of audience members' responses to media with their everyday situated experiences.

As noted above, the theorization of risk has tended to neglect the insights offered by contemporary feminist theory and the sociology of the body in understanding the links between gender, embodiment, subjectivity and risk. In my chapter I draw on popular media accounts of pregnancy as well as empirical research involving interviews with pregnant women to address the topic of pregnant embodiment and the ways in which this body is constructed by various discourses as particularly 'at risk' and also 'risky' to others. I make use of some of the insights of all three major theoretical perspectives on risk I have identified above in the discussion. The 'governmentality' perspective is used to examine the pregnant body as an intensely governed body, both on the part of medicine and on the part of the woman herself as an autonomous, self-regulated citizen seeking her own best interests (and, even more importantly these days, those of the foetus). The 'risk society' perspective provides some explanation at the macro-level for why risk discourses have proliferated around pregnancy, including changes in gender relations, women's participation in work, the move towards individualization and the development and introduction of new medical technologies for assessing foetal wellbeing *in utero*. The 'cultural/symbolic' perspective, particularly the psychoanalytic extensions of Douglas' work put forward by feminist philosophers Kristeva and Grosz, offers a way of thinking about the pregnant body as a cultural anomaly, a liminal body that is therefore conceptualized as risky and dangerous to sociocultural order and requiring sustained surveillance and regulation.

Stevi Jackson and Sue Scott's chapter, in addressing risk anxiety in relation to public concerns about children and childhood, provides a complementary analysis, with particular emphasis on the sexualization of risk. Contemporary constructions of childhood and sexuality, they argue, give rise to very particular anxieties whenever the sexual 'innocence' of children is thought to be endangered. Children are regarded as a 'special' category of people (as particularly cherished and vulnerable yet potentially unruly), while sexuality is constructed as a 'special' aspect of social life (uniquely pleasurable but also dangerous, quintessentially part of 'private life' yet hotly contested in public arenas). These two sets of discourses intersect in the construction of the 'innocent' child. Focusing in particular on some recent much-publicized cases of the murder of children by adults and by other children, Jackson and Scott explore these issues in relation to some key antinomies which have emerged in relation to children and childhood in late modernity: tensions between children's autonomy and child protection and between perceptions of children as 'at risk' and as potentially threatening. They argue that the concept of risk anxiety provides a useful means of analysing contemporary fears about children and childhood and thus may be conceptualized as contributing to the continuing social construction of childhood.

The next chapter differs from the others in adopting a specifically cultural anthropological approach to understanding aspects of risk. Eva Mackey uses postcolonial theory as a resource for understanding issues of cultural identity and the unexpected resurgence of cultural and racial intolerance in the late modern world of de-territorialized and transnational identities. She argues that new forms of 'cultural racism' emerging in western nation-states often depend upon common-sense conceptions of national cultures 'at risk' from dangerous and destructive foreign elements that supposedly threaten the social cohesion of the nation. Multiculturalism, immigration and Aboriginal rights are often constructed as risks to the 'body politic' of the Australian nation. Mackey uses empirical data from original anthropological research on race and the construction of national identity in Canada and Australia to assess the applicability of work by risk theorists representing a range of approaches. In doing so, her goal is to develop a theoretical framework that will help to understand the emergence of new forms of racial intolerance at the end of the twentieth century. There is a particular focus in her discussion on recent Australian political events around the attempts by Aboriginal people to seek title over land traditionally used by their forebears and the emergence of a new right-wing political party in Australia that has sought to marginalize Aboriginal people and deny them their rights to land.

The final two chapters take a meta-theoretical approach, seeking to identify the ways in which risk discourses and strategies operate as part of broader social concerns and social relations. Mitchell Dean compares the approach to risk in the work of Beck and Giddens with that of the 'governmentality' writers. Dean argues that fundamental to the 'risk society' thesis is a sense of the profound limitation and even subversion of the older mechanisms of risk calculation and management. The 'governmentality' approach, by contrast, attends to precisely those forms of rationality by which risk is constructed as a calculable domain and is linked to techniques of government and self-government. Here may be distinguished different types of risk rationality and technology: epidemiological, insurantial, case-management, and incalculable. According to Dean, our present bears witness to both the subversion of certain types of risk management and to the prodigious attempt at the re-managerialization of risk through multiple techniques. These range from the audit to health promotion, population screening to case-management, in relation to concerns as diverse as smoking, policing, unemployment, mental health, traffic control and pregnancy. Dean analyses the use and outcomes of the 'new prudentialism' as it operates in relation to risk discourses and strategies.

Stephen Crook takes as his point of departure the importance, in all societies, of the problem of order. He argues that the relations between risk consciousness, risk management and sociocultural order are at the heart of analyses of risk. Crook reviews the insights offered on social order and risk put forward in 'cultural/symbolic' (the 'sociocultural' account, as he terms it), 'risk society' and 'governmentality' perspectives, as well as that offered by actor–network theory, an approach which emphasizes the interrelationship of human with non-human actors. He contends that the present high levels of anxiety about risk phenomena of all kinds are intertwined with uncertainties about sociocultural order. Specifically, alternative modes of risk consciousness and regimes of risk management can be related to more general and distinct 'orderings': a 'modern' ordering centred on formal institutions, a 'hyper-reflexive' ordering associated with radical individualization, and a 'neo-traditional' ordering working through intense social solidarity. To these orderings correspond 'organized', 'neo-liberal' and 'ritualized' regimes of risk management respectively. Crook claims that the high levels of anxiety about order and risk in contemporary western societies can be related to the eclipse of the hegemony of modern ordering and the inevitable failings of organized risk management. Living with risk, therefore, may involve the acceptance of some degree of uncertainty and instability, however controversial this may seem to we late moderns who are obsessed with control and certainty.

REFERENCES

Beck, U. (1992a) From industrial society to risk society: questions of survival, social structure and ecological environment. *Theory, Culture & Society*, 9, 97–123.

(1992b) *Risk Society: Towards a New Modernity*. London: Sage.

(1994) The reinvention of politics: towards a theory of reflexive modernization. In Beck, U., Giddens, A. and Lash, S., *Reflexive Modernization: Politics, Tradition and Aesthetics in the Modern Social Order*. Cambridge: Polity Press.

✳(1995) *Ecological Politics in the Age of Risk*. Cambridge: Polity Press.

(1996a) World risk society as cosmopolitan society? Ecological questions in a framework of manufactured uncertainties. *Theory, Culture & Society*, 13(4), 1–32.

(1996b) Risk society and the provident state. In Lash, S., Szerszynski, B. and Wynne, B. (eds.), *Risk, Environment and Modernity: Towards a New Ecology*. London: Sage.

Beck U. and Beck-Gernsheim, E. (1995) *The Normal Chaos of Love*. Cambridge: Polity Press.

Castel, R. (1991) From dangerousness to risk. In Burchell, G., Gordon, C. and Miller, P. (eds.), *The Foucault Effect: Studies in Governmentality*. London: Harvester Wheatsheaf.

Dean, M. (1997) Sociology after society. In Owen, D. (ed.), *Sociology after Postmodernism*. London: Sage.

Douglas, M. (1966/1969) *Purity and Danger: an Analysis of Concepts of Pollution and Taboo*. London: Routledge & Kegan Paul.

(1985) *Risk Acceptability According to the Social Sciences*. New York: Russell Sage Foundation.

(1990) Risk as a forensic resource. *Daedalus*, 119 (4), 1–16.

(1992) *Risk and Blame: Essays in Cultural Theory*. London: Routledge.

Douglas, M. and Wildavsky, A. (1982) *Risk and Culture: an Essay on the Selection of Technological and Environmental Dangers*. Berkeley, CA: University of California Press.

Ewald, F. (1991) Insurance and risks. In Burchell, G., Gordon, C. and Miller, P. (eds.), *The Foucault Effect: Studies in Governmentality*. Hemel Hempstead: Harvester Wheatsheaf.

Foucault, M. (1991) Governmentality. In Burchell, G., Gordon, C. and Miller, P. (eds.), *The Foucault Effect: Studies in Governmentality*. Hemel Hempstead: Harvester Wheatsheaf.

Giddens, A. (1990) *The Consequences of Modernity*. Cambridge: Polity Press.

(1991) *Modernity and Self-Identity: Self and Society in the Late Modern Age*. Cambridge: Polity Press.

(1994) Living in a post-traditional society. In Beck, U., Giddens, A. and Lash, S., *Reflexive Modernization: Politics, Tradition and Aesthetics in the Modern Social Order*. Cambridge: Polity Press.

(1998) Risk society: the context of British politics. In Franklin, J. (ed.), *The Politics of Risk Society*. Cambridge: Polity Press.

Lash, S. (1993) Reflexive modernization: the aesthetic dimension. *Theory, Culture & Society*, 10, 1–23.

Lupton, D. (1999) *Risk*. London: Routledge.

O'Malley, P. (1996) Risk and responsibility. In Barry, A., Osborne, T. and Rose, N. (eds.), *Foucault and Political Reason: Liberalism, Neo-Liberalism and Rationalities of Government*. University College of London Press.

Wynne, B. (1996) May the sheep safely graze? A reflexive view of the expert–lay knowledge divide. In Lash, S., Szerszinski, B. and Wynne, B. (eds.), *Risk, Environment and Modernity: Towards a New Ecology*. London: Sage.

1   Postmodern reflections on 'risk', 'hazards' and life choices

Nick J. Fox

Introduction: risk, hazards and modernity

Before the era of modernity, *risk* was a neutral term, concerned merely with probabilities, with losses and gains. A gamble or an endeavour that was associated with high risk meant simply that there was great potential for significant loss or significant reward. However, in the modern period, *risk* has been co-opted as a term reserved for a negative or undesirable outcome, and as such, is synonymous with the terms *danger* or *hazard*. Thus the British Medical Association's (1987: 13) guide *Living with Risk* describes a hazard as 'a set of circumstances which may cause harmful consequences', while risk is 'the likelihood of its doing so'. Furthermore, this hazard/risk differentiation introduces a moral dimension, such that the perpetrators of risk may be held to account in some way or other (Douglas, 1992: 22–5). This chapter explores this dichotomy, and develops a postmodern position that challenges more traditional readings.

The science of risk calculation, assessment and evaluation is emblematic of modernism and its commitments to progress through rationalization: from the actuarial tables of life insurers to the risk analysis of those in the business of risk: the movers and shakers of capitalism (Hassler, 1993). In what might almost be a handbook for such entrepreneurial activity, Johnstone-Bryden (1995: 1), in a monograph sub-titled *How to Work Successfully with Risk*, offers a blueprint for 'how risks can be identified and reduced economically and effectively, before serious damage occurs'. Hertz and Thomas (1983: 1) describe risk analysis as methods which seek a 'comprehensive understanding and awareness' of the risks associated with a given setting.

Risk assessment, we are led to believe by such authors, is a technical procedure which, like all aspects of modern life, is to be undertaken through rational calculation of ends and means (Fox, 1991). Figure 1, based on an illustration of the process of risk assessment in a British government publication, suggests the 'simple, logical sequence of steps'

(Department of the Environment, 1995: 5) to be taken to identify and manage risk. This process of risk assessment has been widely applied to many areas of technology over the past half century (Carter, 1995: 135.) Within such a scenario, all risks may be evaluated and suitably managed, such that all may be predicted and countered, so risks, accidents and insecurities are minimized or prevented altogether (Johnstone-Bryden, 1995: 3; Prior, 1995).

Such accounts fail to problematize risk and its assessment. In response a range of social science analyses have been developed to offer a more critical approach, which address the socially constructed and historically specific character of such conceptualization of risk and its assessment. At the simplest level, we may conclude that 'risk is in the eye of the beholder':

Insurance experts (involuntarily) contradict safety engineers. While the latter diagnose zero risk, the former decide: uninsurable. Experts are undercut or deposed by opposing experts. Politicians encounter the resistance of citizens' groups, and industrial management encounters morally and politically motivated consumer boycotts. (Beck, 1994: 11)

In Beck's typification of contemporary western civilization as a 'risk society' (Beck, 1992, 1994), the proliferation of risks as a consequence of technological innovation has got out of control. The success of modernist instrumental rationality has led to an apparent solution through technology to every problem, ill or need. But alongside the development of technology, and – for those who may earn a living through such innovation – the accumulation of wealth, Beck suggests there is a concomitant accumulation of risks in undesirable abundance as a consequence of working with or consuming technology (1992: 22, 26). But, Beck goes on, risks 'only exist in terms of the (scientific or anti-scientific) *knowledge* about them. They can be changed, magnified, dramatized or minimized within knowledge, and to that extent they are particularly *open to social definition and construction*' (23, original emphases).

Furthermore, some people are more affected by the distribution and growth of risks, and there are winners and losers in risk definitions. Power and access to and control of knowledge thus become paramount in a risk society. This is the issue of *reflexivity* to which Beck alludes: society becomes a problem for itself (Beck, 1994: 8).

In risk issues, no one is an expert, or everyone is an expert, because all the experts presume what they are supposed to make possible and produce: cultural acceptance. The Germans see the world perishing along with their forests. The Britons are shocked by their toxic breakfast eggs: this is where and how their ecological conversion starts. (Beck, 1994: 9)

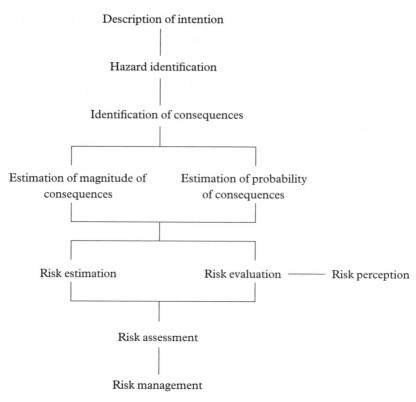

Figure 1: From intention to risk management

This, for Beck (12), is both a crisis for society in the late modern period, an opportunity for social critique, and ultimately for a new emancipation coming in the wake of the failure of socialism to provide a resolution to the inequities of capitalism. Reflexivity challenges the old status barriers of class and control of wealth, creating new possibilities for coalition and organization.

In contrast to this kind of approach, and at the 'cultural' end of the spectrum of social theories of risk, the work of anthropologist Mary Douglas has been influential. In the same way she had explored the apparently irrational behaviour of both 'primitive' and 'civilized' peoples (Douglas, 1966) concerning fears over pollution, she identified

the baffling behaviour of the public, in refusing to buy floodplain or earthquake insurance, in crossing dangerous roads, driving non-road-worthy vehicles, buying accident-provoking gadgets for the home, and not listening to the education on risks, all that continues as before. (Douglas, 1992: 11)

Douglas suggested that the reason such behaviour seems baffling is the failure to take culture into account. Using the typology of cultures developed by herself and Aaron Wildavsky (Douglas, 1996) based on the two dimensions of *grid* and *group* (reflecting degrees of social stratification and social solidarity respectively), she sought to illustrate how the risks one focused upon as an individual had less to do with individual psychology (the discipline informing rational-choice theory and the health-belief model) and more about the social forms in which those individuals construct their understanding of the world and themselves (Douglas, 1992:12). Further,

> if the cultural processes by which certain societies select certain kinds of dangers for attention are based on institutional procedures for allocating responsibility, for self-justification, or for calling others to account, it follows that public moral judgements will advertise certain risks powerfully, while the well-advertised risk will turn out to be connected with legitimating moral principles. (Rayner, 1992: 92)

Three of the four possible combinations of high and low grid and group are identified by Douglas in her most recent work (and developed and explored in Rayner, 1992) as cultural backcloths to risk decisions and perceptions (the fourth – high grid/low group – comprises isolated, alienated individuals). Douglas suggests that the remaining three combinations can be seen in aspects of (late) modern culture. The low-grid/low-group culture is typical of the competitive environment of the entrepreneurial capitalist free-market, in which individuals are untrammelled by restrictive practices or rules. Also found in capitalist institutions are the high-grid/high-group cultures where Weber's 'iron cage' of bureaucracy has regulated and incorporated systems and structures for interaction. The third kind of culture, low-grid/high-group are collectivist, egalitarian groups, which Douglas and others have suggested are found in voluntary groups including the anti-nuclear movement and political and religious cults (Douglas, 1992: 77, Rayner, 1992: 89).

What is considered as a risk, and how serious that risk is thought to be, will be perceived differently depending upon the organization or grouping to which a person belongs or with which he identifies, as will the disasters, accidents or other negative occurrences which occur in a culture (Douglas, 1992: 78). The free-market environment (low grid and low group) will see competitors as the main risk, to be countered by good teamwork and leadership. In the bureaucratic culture (high grid and high group), the external environment is perceived as generally punitive, and group commitment is the main way to reduce risk. Finally, in the voluntary culture (low grid with high group), the risks come from external conspiracies, and group members may be suspected of treachery.

This typology has been developed and related to empirical examples. Thus, for example, Douglas (1992: 102–21) explores the impact of these cultural dimensions of stratification and solidarity upon individual health responses to HIV contagion. The emphasis in this culturalist model of risk perception upon the *social* construction of risk is highly relevant for the explorations that follow.

Three models of the risk/hazard opposition

At the beginning of this chapter, I remarked upon the etymological constructions of *risk* and *hazard* in modernist discourse. Having explored the different positions of realist and culturalist analysts (as exemplified by Beck and Douglas), I now want to look at this in somewhat greater depth to consider the differing perspectives that are possible concerning the ontological relation of a *risk* to a *hazard*. While there is potential overlap between perspectives, for heuristic purposes I shall consider three possibilities, the last of which being what I shall call the *postmodern* position, with its emphasis on the textual fabrication of reality. I shall use two realms as exemplars of the differing positions: discussions of risks associated with the workplace and with illegal drug use.

Position one: A risk maps directly on to an underlying hazard

The first position may be called realist or materialist, given the under-lying ontology of a hazard as real and material. This is the approach identified at the beginning of the chapter as the mapping of a *risk* (that is, the likelihood of an unpleasant occurrence) on to a *hazard* (the circumstances that could lead to the occurrence). Thus the risks for health workers of contracting hepatitis or other blood-related diseases are directly related (amongst other things) to the hazard of working with sharps (hypodermic needles, etc.). The risk of side-effects from using illegal drugs derives from the pharmacological properties of these drugs. Given the existence of sharps in the work environment of a hospital nurse or doctor, or the pharmacological properties of drugs, there are associated probabilities of negative outcomes from working in such environments or using illegal drugs.

This is the position that is generally adopted in risk management and assessment literature, where the objective is risk reduction (for example Wells, 1996: 6; van Leeuwen, 1995: 3). Wells (1996: 1) describes a hazard as something which 'has the potential to cause harm'. Given the presence of the hazard, then, strategies are to be adopted to minimize the likelihood (the risk) that the hazard will be manifested in an unpleasant outcome. The emphasis may be on individual education, individual or population prevention measures or corporate strategy. As such, the position is not inherently political, and may be co-opted to serve any or all of the different interests which may engage discursively with the perceived hazard, although often emphasizing an individualized approach to risk analysis. Thus, Johnstone-Bryden suggests that

People represent the real risk. Human greed, malice and error are the primary threats. It could be argued that almost every risk, perhaps even every risk, relates back to human error, or deliberate human actions. (Johnstone-Bryden, 1995: 57)

While the realist or materialist position may acknowledge that the level of risk offered by a hazard is based on subjective judgement (Anand, 1993), the one-to-one mapping of risk on to hazard means that, while

at no time will all of us agree on a single level of acceptable risk[,] . . . if people can agree upon the way risks are measured, and on the relevance of the levels of risk thus represented to the choices we must all make, then the scope for disagreement and dissent is thereby limited. (British Medical Association, 1987: vii)

Despite the different value perspectives of analysts (for example, from management, trade unions or pressure groups), the realist position establishes the potential for a formal process of scientific analysis of risks. I would suggest that such a claimed consensus over *how* to assess risk also creates the basis for moral judgements concerning implementation of risk-reduction procedures, and implicitly, a culture of blame (although, as Douglas' typology implies, who is blamed may depend on who is the analyst.)

Position two: Hazards are natural, risks are cultural

In the second position, which might be called culturalist or constructionist, risks are opposed to hazards in the sense that while the latter are 'natural' and neutral, risks are the value-laden judgements of human beings concerning these natural events or possibilities. Within social science, this approach to risk has become more prominent. To focus again on Mary Douglas, despite her culturalist analysis which seeks to demonstrate that risks are perceived in a social context, she is keen to note that

the dangers are only too horribly real . . . this argument is not about the reality of the dangers, but about how they are politicized . . . Starvation, blight and famine are perennial threats. It is a bad joke to take this analysis as hinting that the dangers are imaginary. (Douglas, 1992: 29)

This position has been the basis for a corpus of sociological analyses of risk perception. Two main themes emerge, first concerning the differing types of 'knowledge' which inform perceptions of risk, and second, the moral dimension to risk and risk taking.

Concerning the constructed nature of 'knowledge', Thorogood (1995) surveyed patients' reflections on an imagined scenario of attending an HIV-positive dentist. She found patients keen to rely upon the professionalism of the dentist, not only to tell them if the (dentist) was positive for the disease, but also because it was the dentist who possessed the professional knowledge of the risks involved. In return, they judged themselves responsible for reporting to their dentist if they (the patients) were HIV-positive.

Thorogood's study also illustrates the moral character of such judgements. Her respondents made such remarks as '. . . he wears gloves, uses a mask and a sterilizing unit, all you would expect from a good dentist' or '. . . he is a particularly nice dentist, everything is covered up': the moral qualities of the dentist are indicative of her/his hazardousness. Rogers and Salvage (1988: 106) report the other side of the coin, when they describe the stigmatizing by her manager of a nurse who had received a needlestick injury, and was required to use a marked cup, saucer and plate, even prior to a test result for HIV. Failure to abide by societal norms or rules may lead to victim-blaming. As Carter argues

those groups facing danger which can be defined as 'other' often face controls which work in the interests of the powerful 'same'. Thus a range of social practices exist, connected with risk assessment, which historically have often targeted specific groups . . . the effect is to push the group into a space of danger – the place of the 'other'. Here they become a useful repository for our cultural ideas of danger. As long as we are 'good' . . . then danger is elsewhere. (Carter, 1995: 142–3)

Once again, such analyses can incline towards an individualization of risk assessment, and victim-blaming is particularly rife concerning aspects of life deemed societally deviant: for example, in the arenas of sexual behaviour and drug use. This moral dimension to risk assessment affects the allocation of resources within society to reduce the risks of various hazards. Risk reduction has costs attached to it, for society, for government, for industry or for individuals, and judgements must be made about the relative balance between costs and benefits (CCTA, 1994: 16). From the culturalist perspective what is required is a sociologically informed risk assessment, which can overcome the 'naiveté' of the technical scientific evaluation, and take into account the 'real world' of hazards, and how they impinge on the daily working lives of employees. Unfortunately, such a conclusion depends upon discovering an Archimedean spot outside of culture upon which to stand, and such spots are notoriously hard to find!

Position three: Risk perceptions fabricate hazards

In addition to these two readings of the risk/hazard relationship, a third position is possible: the one which I shall call postmodern,[1] and which I wish to explore in this chapter. It moves beyond the culturalist or constructionist model, to argue radically that hazards are *themselves* socially constructed: created from the contingent judgements about the adverse or undesirable outcomes of choices made by human beings. These 'hazards' are then invoked discursively to support estimations of risk, risky behaviour and of the people who take the risks.

The first step in grasping what at first sight may appear counter-factual, comes in recognizing that, as Wells (1996: 6) puts it, the 'materialization of a hazard' is the result of identifying 'undesired or adverse events'. My lesson with advanced driving instructor Alan Oates illustrated that. For Alan, everything on the road was a *hazard*. What I thought was just a milk truck or a pedestrian crossing, turned out to be a hazard. That was the way he thought, and the result was safe – some would say, boring – driving. 'You're a top gear man, you always want to get into top gear even when approaching hazards,' said Alan. 'Safety must be the paramount consideration, even if you have to sacrifice a little time' (Fox, 1984).

To explore this further, let me consider the issue of health workers and infected sharps in some detail. Let us accept that discarded needles and other sharps that may have been infected by blood products exist as real objects. In and of themselves, these objects do not constitute a *hazard*. They become *hazardous* under certain circumstances, princi-pally if conditions arise such that they may come into contact with and pierce the skin of a person in their vicinity. And we know this event is hazardous, not through some 'natural' quality of this event, but because we appraise it as undesired or adverse, based on bodies of knowledge about blood and the risks of infection associated with various blood-borne diseases such as hepatitis B and HIV. This cycle is illustrated in figure 2.

The transformation of an 'inert' object into one possessing *hazardous characteristics* (Wells, 1996) thus occurs only as a result of our evaluations of *risk*, that is, the likelihood of an adverse result from an incident. Such evaluation may be based on anecdote or personal experience of danger or security. More formally, it may be based on a particular 'discourse' (an authoritative body of knowledge): that of risk assessment. Thus it is

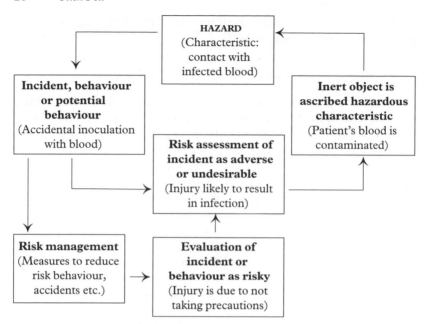

Figure 2: Risk assessment and the construction of hazards: contamination with infected blood

only in the analysis of *risks* that the *hazard* comes into existence: if the risk is assessed as zero or close to zero, the inert object would remain just that (regardless of whether it 'really' does possess hazardous characteristics).

This model of hazard creation is at odds with received wisdom concerning the hazard/risk relationship. In figure 1, hazards are prior to risks. What is argued now is that the selection of various 'inert' objects, procedures or humans as 'hazards' must itself depend upon some prior judgement, otherwise risk assessors would be faced with an insurmountable task of sifting through every element of an environment or context. Indeed, the impossibility of assessing every risk prospectively is reflected in the realities of risk analysis, which is sometimes faced with the consequences of a previously unidentified risk (Suter, 1993: 313). Without some system of prioritization, analysis of risk would be absurdly long-winded, as analysts would forever be suggesting the most far-fetched, though potentially fatal, events to be avoided by safety precautions. Inevitably, risk assessment must begin with some prior knowledge about the world, what is 'probable' and what 'unlikely', what is 'serious', what is 'trivial' or seemingly 'absurd'. Such judgements may derive from 'scientific' sources, or may depend on 'common-sense' or experiential resources; either way, the perception of a hazard's existence will depend on these judgements. How the judgement is made (that is, what is counted as evidence to support the assessment), is relative and culturally contingent.

This process of the construction of hazards can be seen in another study of health workers and contamination by blood, in which Grinyer (1995) explored 'expert' and 'lay' views on the prevention of accidental contact with blood products. While the hospital authorities issued guidelines to staff, needlestick accidents had occurred, and staff were doubtful about how feasible it would be to avoid these incidents based on the guidelines. Grinyer found when she reported some accidents involving sharps and blood products, management denied her data's validity (40). She concluded that such unwillingness to recognize lay knowledge about hazards undermined risk reduction policies.

Not only are risk perceptions multi-dimensional, but, at any given time, people are managing a number of different agendas which may conflict with the official ones and can be contradictory. Official information is only one of a number of different routes through which a hazard is understood. Powerful social forces shape the way in which information is perceived and acted upon . . . which may be underestimated by those responsible for risk assessment. (Grinyer, 1995: 49)

Following Wynne (1992), Grinyer argues that 'expertise' is often held by the lay actors, while expert knowledge is usually based only upon 'scientific evidence', and the latter is often privileged when it comes to what counts as a hazard. In another study of risk assessment (of pesticide manufacture), Wynne suggested that

scientific risk analysis did not avoid, and could not have avoided, making social assumptions in order to create the necessary scientific knowledge. It was *conditional* knowledge in that its validity depended, *inter alia* upon the conditions in this embedded social model being fulfilled in actual practice . . . Each party, both scientists and workers, tacitly defined different actual risk systems. They built upon different models of the social practices controlling the contaminants and exposures. (Wynne, 1992: 285–6, original emphases)

Wynne's argument is that technical or scientific discourses tend to make claims to objectivity while they tell the public how 'stupid and irrational they are' (286). This is not arrogance, but a failure by the 'experts' to recognize the contingency of their own position. Both sociologists and risk analysts have recognized that the credibility of evidence concerning whether an object is hazardous and the perceived 'relevance' of such evidence are weighed differently depending on perspective (Callon, 1986; Suter, 1993: 22, 40). This explains the failure of different groups to agree on risks: not because they interpret the data in different ways (the culturalist position set out earlier), but because they have different data: their differing knowledgeabilities prevent them from agreeing what is to count as evidence of a hazard. It is not just outlooks on *risks* that are dependent on social milieu, but also world views on *hazards* themselves. *Both risks and hazards are cultural products.*[2]

Unlike the previous analyses, in which hazards are assumed to be the 'natural' underpinning of cultural attributions of risk, in this postmodern position the 'risky' quality of the environment is constructed from prospective assessment of the circumstances under which objects become hazardous (see figure 2). Such predictions both establish 'hazards' and may create a subjectivity in people of being 'at risk' (and evaluations of which behavioural choices are 'safe' and which are 'risky'). In the rest of this chapter, I shall use this postmodern understanding of risk and hazard to explore issues of choice, first in relation to health at work and second to the use of the drug Ecstasy. Before that, I shall look in some detail at the issue of 'health' itself, which necessarily underpins any perspective on behaviour in relation to risks to health.

A postmodern perspective on 'health'

Were health an absolute, then the creation of a subjectivity which would tend to encourage 'healthy' living (i.e. behaviour minimizing health risks) could be accepted as non-problematic. However, health is now rarely defined simply as an absence of illness. For the World Health Organization (WHO, 1985), health is a state of 'complete physical, mental and social well-being', while Wright (1982) suggests an anthropological phenomenology of 'what it is to function as a human'. Canguilhem (1989) sees health and illness as positive and negative biological values, and Kelly and Charlton call health a 'neutral idea relating to non-pathological physical functioning and the fulfilment of ordinary social roles' (1995: 83). Illness is a 'notion of increasing dependency' for de Swaan (1990: 220), and Sedgewick identified illnesses as socially constructed definitions of natural circumstances which precipitate death or a failure to function within certain norms (1982: 30).

We saw earlier the moral dimension to attributions of 'risk', which are generally seen as the negative pole of an opposition to a desired state of 'safety'. Such moral positions are political, in that they ascribe rights and responsibilities to those subjected to them, and require actions in line with these rights or responsibilities. The human subject of risk analysis is drawn into a *subjectivity* as 'risky' and perhaps culpable. Similarly, all these definitions of health (be they medical or sociological) have a politics associated with them, all try to persuade us to a particular perspective on the person who is healthy or ill.

Modernism, it has been argued, is a project of *mastery* which begins with a process of definition and then – through reason and via the application of technology – controls and changes a phenomenon (typically, in this case, from 'ill' to 'healthy'). The modernist *responsibility to act* replaces any concern with the justice of the action in and of itself (Bauman, 1989). This responsibility, White suggests, always requires one, at some point, to fix or close down parameters of thought or ignore or homogenize at least some dimensions of specificity or difference among actors (1991: 21).

White goes on to argue for a postmodern politics which substitutes the responsibility to act with a *responsibility to otherness*. By this he means an engagement with others which encourages differentiation rather than prescribing a particular value against which the other should be evaluated. In relation to issues of 'health' and 'illness', a responsibility to otherness suggests a radically different kind of response to others from that entailed by a biomedical or even biopsychosocial notion of health. Differentiation and transformation are involved, so rather than a static notion of human 'being', this kind of engagement is concerned with potential: with 'human becoming'. I have coined the term *arche-health* (Fox, 1993) and elaborated on its features (Fox, 1995, 1998) to denote this sense of health as concerned with 'becoming other' or transformation.

Arche-health is a process, not a state, which – in its commitment to 'becoming other' or transformation – resists attempts to impose a unifying identity (e.g. patient, man, foreigner, wife) on a thing or a person. It is most explicitly *not* intended to suggest a natural, essential or in any way prior kind of health, upon which the other healths are superimposed. It is not supposed to be a rival concept of health. Indeed the reason for using this rather strange term is in homage to Derrida's (1976: 56) notion of *arche-writing*, which is not writing but rather the system of difference between concepts which makes language possible.[3] Similarly, *arche-health* refers to the differences and the diversities which enable us linguistically to generate the ideas of 'health' and 'illness', terms which *can* reflect the dynamic, fluctuating character of the organism but which all too often are recruited as static conceptions which codify and evaluate that organism.

As a process of differentiation and transformation, *arche-health* (which is at the same time *arche-illness*) dissolves the opposition health/illness, offering in its place a flux and a multiplication of meaning. *Arche-health* can be seen in the active choice-making behaviour of people as they engage with their bodies, their bodies' functions and the efforts of doctors to normalize those functions. For carers, it is the process of reaching out to others, of opening up possibilities and choices which a disease or disability closes down (Fox, 1995).

In sociological analysis, the notion of choice is unfashionable, perhaps even regarded as politically incorrect and reactionary. Both Marxist and Weberian traditions emphasized the constraints on action to be experienced by agents, while a Foucauldian understanding of the construction of the self has described a human subject seemingly incapable of resistance (Lash, 1991, 1994). Poststructuralist approaches (including those engaging with feminism) have sought to re-introduce discussions of how it is possible to refuse the totalizing effects of discourse (Butler, 1990; Cixous, 1990; Deleuze and Guattari, 1984, 1988), and the notion of *arche-health* as a resistance to stasis, a becoming, articulates with these writings.

Risks – and particularly health risks – are intimately tied up with choices (Hertz and Thomas, 1983: 3). If we acknowledge the constructed nature of 'health', we see how the subjectivity which arises from any definition is based in a partial truth grounded in some claim or other concerning what it is to be a human being, or have a body, or be part of a community, or whatever. This is where choice comes in, although not in an individualistic, rational-actor sense, implying a voluntaristic model of action. Rather, choice may be exerted negatively, in a refusal or resistance, as well as positively in affirmations. Choices may be temperamental or unconscious, or collective, as opposed to rational or individual. But such choosings are processual, and are associated with *arche-health* in that they are a becoming rather than a state of being. I will illustrate this argument concerning risk and choice with two examples.

Health risks and choices at work

Here is an extract from my study of surgical work (Fox, 1992), and the hazards of blood-transmitted infection. A consultant surgeon, Mr T, and I talked during a procedure which, he had indicated, involved risks from the patient's blood.

MR T: Never a month goes by that we don't nick ourselves with a scalpel or other instrument, and I suppose we should be concerned about the risk, but we don't generally do anything.
RESEARCHER: I suppose the gloves offer some protection?
MR T: Yes, once a week I tear a glove, so they may help.
RESEARCHER: Do you take precautions when you have a patient who might be a risk?

MR T: Well, it's only if there is inoculation of blood that it's a problem.
RESEARCHER: What about blood spray into the eyes?
MR T: That can be a danger, I suppose. I often wear lenses (binocular magnifiers) so they have a double use. (Fox, 1992: 29)

Mr T, as with other surgeons studied, seemed quite casual about hazards present in his work environment. He could take various actions to reduce these if he wished but all had costs associated with them (not do the operations, invoke complicated precautions which would inhibit his freedom to operate as he wished). Ultimately he made choices to continue to do a job that he wanted to do, trying to take extra care where he perceived a higher risk. Work for Mr T was not simply something into which he was coerced, it was the result of a series of choices which he and his associates made on a daily basis.

Conversations with an operating department manager added support to this understanding. While nursing students and nursing auxiliaries needed counselling concerning health risks, this informant told me, 'higher-grade' staff were able to cope with risks because of their 'professionalism'. Thus the choices made by grades of nursing staff were based on their different perspectives on their work and responsibilities to others. Similarly, Mr T was *active* in his living out of a set of activities which are called 'work' and which impinged upon certain facets of the continuity of that life called 'health'. He made positive and negative choices concerning how he acted and how he saw himself in relation to his work setting and his associates and patients. His evaluations of hazards were based in these complex choices and perceptions, weighings of costs and benefits, and were part of his continual becoming-other: the *arche-health* of his unfolding life.

For Mr T to be able to define his 'health' in this much broader sense of being free to choose how he lives and works, he re-defined the hazards which his choices might lead him to encounter. His choice to work with patients others might see as 'high-risk' resists the kind of cycle of hazard construction set out in figure 2: he does not wish to accept the judgement that his behaviour is risky, as this would limit his actions. But if he assesses the risks involved as low (perhaps drawing on evaluations of his skill and the use of protection as evidence), the infectious body's hazardous characteristics are minimized, the hazard evaporates and it becomes more-or-less an inert object again (see figure 3).

Risks, choices and the use of Ecstasy

The recreational drug MDMA, commonly known as Ecstasy, E or X, and used world wide by millions of people as a mood enhancer, has

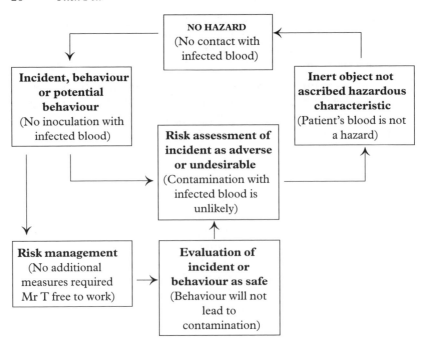

Figure 3: Mr T's re-assessment of the risks and hazards of contamination with infected blood

been associated with a number of fatalities and a range of other less serious health consequences. Its relative newness as a street drug also means that long-term consequences of its use are unknown: it has been linked to chronic changes in neurotransmitter activity and certain other morbidities (Green and Goodwin, 1996). While the death rate from acute effects cannot be easily calculated due to lack of figures about usage, most users will be aware of well-reported cases of deaths following use of Ecstasy. Supporters of the drug counter such stories, arguing that risks are small, and usually associated with the context of ingestion rather than the drug itself. Thus the independent researcher Saunders suggests:

to say that a person died from Ecstasy is never the full story any more than saying that someone died of drink: like alcohol, Ecstasy can be used without any harmful effect. In both cases, death is due to the indirect effects which can be avoided if you are aware of the dangers and look after yourself. The difference is that the dangers of being drunk are well known and recognised, while the dangers resulting from Ecstasy use are far less known. Far from saving young people from harm, much of the so-called drugs education has confused users by trying to scare them, rather than explain the dangers and how to avoid them. (Saunders, 1995)

I am not concerned to debate the 'safety' of Ecstasy, nor with how statistics are used to argue for or against its use. Rather, I am interested to see how users evaluate this evidence, and what affects the choices of hundreds of thousands of people to use Ecstasy on a regular basis. The reason for choosing this example derives from the unequivocal evidence that pure MDMA (that is, Ecstasy which has not been cut with other drugs or toxic substances) produces a highly pleasurable experience. For instance, one respondent on a web site devoted to the study of Ecstasy[4] commented:

The Ecstasy was *unbelievable* and the music was even better. The people there were lovely, the vibe was alive and growing! I spent the night in heaven, meeting people, hugging and dancing my brains out . . . I was moved into such a deep state of trance, the music, the lights, the vibe from the beautiful girl dancing across from me . . . it was perfect!

Ecstasy offers the possibility of a release from the alienation of everyday life.

We were liberated from the chains that bound us for that night. It was an experience of absolute freedom. We danced, talked, laughed and revelled with the world. When we arrived home at night, we gathered in the family room and spoke to the camcorder. The next day when we watched the video we could not believe how different we seemed – so relaxed, happy and natural. Why couldn't life always be like this?

The following responses indicate the kinds of judgements used by those taking the drug for the first time:

I am a 30 year old first time trier, having resisted the influence to do so for all my 20s on the basis that I was too old and it would be unnecessary/dangerous to do so. What bollocks. I stayed up all night with no fatigue and great enjoyment both emotionally, socially, physically and a little spiritually.

I researched this drug before I did it to find out as much as I could about its possible side effects, dangers, other people's experiences, good or bad, every-thing that I thought might help me in my decision, and made a decision to do it. I believe that knowing what I was doing and going into it with a positive outlook and in an environment that I was comfortable in helped this to be the transforming experience that it was for me.

The night that we took the E, I was feeling very stressed out and in a bad mood. I had told my older brother and wife what I was planning to do, and they had some very harsh criticisms to offer as they felt that it was dangerous. I personally did not know much about E, but I trusted my boyfriend S who had done a lot of research on the topic and was careful about what he put into our bodies.

These comments could be read as lay risk assessments, and in a sense, that is what they are. Gillian Taberner's research (personal communication) supports the premise that what is happening here is an active choice-making concerning the possibilities facing these users: each is weighing the desirable outcomes of taking the drug against negative consequences. Her informant Andrew said:

People are becoming more open-minded about it because a lot of people are taking it. Virtually everybody knows someone who takes Ecstasy or has taken it and they're still alive, still having a good time.

Such choices are processual, continually re-thought. Another respondent, Zoe, wondered:

Do you think when you get older you get, like I think I'll get more concerned about my body as well. It feels like when you're young it's OK because you've got control over most things but when you're older you think . . .

When the risks outweigh the attractions, Ecstasy becomes a *hazard*, while for those respondents who decide to take the drug, its possible hazardousness is side-lined, and the drug is seen as an opportunity to experience a desired state.

In the previous section I discussed the surgeon's *arche-health*: the becoming-other which resulted from his active choice making. Similarly, we can see the choices made by these users of Ecstasy as a manifestation of their *arche-health*. Ecstasy is an integral part of the lives of many young people (Power, Power and Gibson, 1996: 78) and to take it is to experience a highly desired set of consequences. The choices of people to use E reflect a desire to incorporate the experiences available through using the drug, or to affirm particular facets of users' self-identity (Beck and Rosenbaum, 1994). To perceive Ecstasy as a hazard is not part of the world view of those positively inclined toward its psychological effects: instead it is a means to a highly rated objective. The bias of pro-Ecstasy commentators in assessing the evidence of risk reflects this differing world view: one in which the spiritual and psychological highs of Ecstasy use far outstrip the risks identified by medical researchers (Rushkoff, 1994; Jordan, 1995). Buchanan's research on teenagers' perceptions of drugs supports this. Notions of harm or illegality are relatively insignificant for many users: 'whether or not drug use is harmful, and/or whether it is against the law, the more important and overriding concern for those at high risk appears to be the issue of individual choice' (Buchanan, 1991: 330–1).

Those who would control the use of Ecstasy must therefore recognize the impact that it has upon the subjectivity of users, and how far the psychological, emotional and spiritual attractiveness of a drug counters perceived risks (Amos *et al.*, 1997). This point is important, because while the decision by a surgeon to operate despite objective assessments of risk from infection may be seen as altruistic and laudable, the decisions of people to use substances which have risks associated with them is more likely to be judged as foolhardy and culpable. In both cases, this analysis suggests a perspective which emphasizes choice, but in the case of Ecstasy use, this kind of analysis is less likely to be favoured. My point, however, is the same for both situations: that people's behaviour must be seen not as based upon differential judgements of risk, but within the context of world views which may deviate very greatly from that of the 'expert' risk assessor.

Discussion: risks and opportunities

I have used two disparate examples in this chapter to unpack the constructed nature of hazards. They were chosen to illustrate the active process of becoming which is part of human lives in settings which may seem very different: comparing the relatively constrained arena of work with the relatively unconstrained leisure context of illegal drug use.

The intention has been to suggest a way of thinking about the hazard/risk dichotomy which is not supplied in either the 'realist' or 'culturalist' perspectives. While building on the insights of the culturalist position (that risks are culturally constructed), it moves beyond what might thus be seen as a culture/nature opposition. In the 'postmodern' position, risks are not absolutes, but neither are the 'hazards' which are supposedly the circumstances which constitute risks. It turns out (in this position) that nature is constructed through the lens of culture. This position bears some resemblance to Woolgar's (1988) argument that even such 'natural entities' as subatomic particles and the continent of America are 'invented' rather than 'discovered' inasmuch as the concepts are produced in a social process and satisfy certain cultural requirements in order to be accepted as real. The position developed from poststructuralism, with its emphasis on *textual* construction of reality, is more sceptical about a direct relationship between cultural contexts and the natural entities which are constructed, acknowledging the intertextual character of such reality construction, which is both complex and always an unfinished project (Curt, 1994: 36).[5] What is hazardous is often likely to be highly contested, and the kinds of situations concerning hazard assessment explored by Wynne (1992) bear this out.

If the very character of the environment in which we live (and this includes our bodies) is constructed in texts, and these texts are contested between different 'authorities', risk analysis is a deeply political activity. The identification of hazards (and the consequent definition of what is a risk), can easily lead to the valorization of certain kinds of living over others. In a 'risk society', notions of health and work will be – in part – dependent upon what is seen as a risk or a hazard. Social perceptions of health and work will in turn contribute to the on-going construction of 'risk' itself. We implicitly evaluate certain actions or situations in terms of the consequences for others or ourselves and label these actions or situations as more or less threatening to our physical, psychological or moral integrity.

'Risk', like 'health' is a concept which contributes to how we think about modern life. These concepts are tied up with the values of a culture and the moral rights and responsibilities of members of that culture, and as such are implicated in how people understand themselves as reflexive, ethical subjects. Because these conceptions are contingent, the subjectivities which are created around risk, health and work are also relative: if this means that we are constrained by cultural constructions of subjectivity, it also means we can resist. The analysis which has been offered in this chapter offers a perspective on 'risk taking' as the active process of choosing as life unfolds: a *becoming-other* and a resistance to discourse. In a somewhat different context, concerning the rights of old people in care, the group Counsel and Care have argued that because a person is living in a protective environment, that does not diminish the human right to take risks (Counsel and Care, 1993: §2, 1). Of course, such a notion of a human right is essentialist, but it may be argued similarly that the autonomy of the human individual – within or without the workplace – cannot be simply denied because she or he is apparently behaving in a way judged to be risky. The implications of such a position are that it is neither sufficient to point to phenomena and claim they are hazardous (because such claims are always dependent upon the partial evidence deemed relevant by the claimant), nor to assume that by making such claims one is necessarily acting in the interests of those whom one may be trying to assist.

In conclusion, I have been concerned in this chapter to establish a basis upon which people may resist authoritative statements about how humans should behave. This postmodern perspective on risks and hazards is not intended to challenge the critiques of industrial production as often injurious to the bodies, minds and spirits of individuals. However, it does suggest that 'health' should be understood as constituted in the unfolding lives of individuals with their own choice-making agendas for living and dying. The *becoming-other* of body, mind or spirit is processual: differently formulated and in the right circumstances, a *risk* to 'health' can be an *opportunity* for transformation and renewal.

NOTES

1 Poststructuralism (and its more political cousin, postmodernism) are approaches which theorize the social world as created through the interplay of multitudinous 'texts' (that is, symbolic systems which are communicative of meaning, may or may not be authoritative 'bodies of knowledge', and may be actual written texts or any other set of signs – including social practices). The work of construction never ends, is continually subject to challenge and re-interpretation, and is the realm within which power is manifested. The association between power and knowledge has been variously explored by poststructuralists including Derrida, Foucault and Lyotard and has been applied influentially in feminist scholarship. For an evaluation of these positions in relation to sociology and health, see Fox (1993).

2 What I am saying here is not that bad things do not happen as a result of certain incidents. However, I feel it is necessary to emphasize this contingency of what is to be considered hazardous. Suter (1993) points out that human health cannot be taken as the 'gold standard' for environmental risk analysis, as this assumes that human health equates with biological protection more generally. Even if human health is taken as a standard, its applicability is not absolute: for the executioner, the lethal characteristics of electricity or narcotics are not *hazards*, they are the functional characteristics to be exploited. In such circumstances, a lethal outcome is not adverse or undesirable for all concerned: the incident is 'real', its hazardousness depends upon point-of-view.

3 Saussurean linguistics suggests that concepts only have meaning (identity) because they can be contrasted with what they are not. Efforts to establish meaning without recourse to difference are doomed, because one concept always leads to another (a kidney is 'bean' shaped, a bean is 'kidney' shaped), *ad infinitum*. Because identity depends on difference, it can never be an absolute or final, but must exist in dynamic relationship with other elements in a system.

4 These responses may be found at web site address: http://obsolete.org/index.html

5 Intertextuality is a key concept in poststructuralist theory, concerning the 'play of one text on another'. Reading a text is not a passive process but an active one of transformation: in effect, a re-writing. The social world is constructed from the collision of myriads of texts: as they collide they alter each other, and there is never a final absolute reading. This perspective explains both the indeterminacy of the continually re-interpreted social world, and the possibility to resist (to re-write) authority.

REFERENCES

Amos, A., Gray, D., Currie, C. and Elton, R. (1997) Healthy or druggy? Self-image, ideal image and smoking behaviour among young people. *Social Science & Medicine*, 45(6), 847–58.
Anand, P. (1993) *Foundations of Rational Choice under Risk*. Oxford: Clarendon.

Bauman, Z. (1989) *Modernity and the Holocaust*. Cambridge: Polity Press and Basil Blackwell.

Beck, J. and Rosenbaum, M. (1994) *Pursuit of Ecstasy: the MDMA Experience*. Albany, NY: State University of New York Press.

Beck, U. (1992) *Risk Society: Towards a New Modernity*. London: Sage.

— (1994) The reinvention of politics: towards a theory of reflexive modernization. In Beck, U., Giddens, A. and Lash S., *Reflexive Modernization: Politics, Tradition and Aesthetics in the Modern Social Order*. Cambridge: Polity.

British Medical Association (1987) *Living with Risk*. Chichester: John Wiley.

Buchanan, D. R. (1991) How teens think about drugs: insights from moral reasoning and social bonding theory. *International Quarterly of Community Health Education*, 11(4), 315–32.

Butler, J. (1990) *Gender Trouble*. London: Routledge.

CCTA (1994) *Management of Project Risk*. Norwich: HMSO

Callon, M. (1986) Some elements of a sociology of translation: the domestication of the scallops and St Brieuac fishermen. In Law, J. (ed.), *Power, Action and Belief* (Sociological Review monograph 32). London: Routledge & Kegan Paul.

Canguilhem G. (1989) *The Normal and the Pathological*. New York: Zone Books.

Carter, S. (1995) Boundaries of danger and uncertainty: an analysis of the technological culture of risk assessment. In Gabe, J. (ed.), *Medicine, Risk and Health*. Oxford: Blackwell Publishers.

Cixous, H. (1990) The laugh of the medusa. In Walder, R. (ed.), *Literature in the Modern World*. Oxford University Press.

Counsel and Care (1993) *The Right to Take Risks*. London: Counsel and Care

Curt, B. C. (1994) *Textuality and Tectonics*. Buckingham: Open University Press.

Deleuze, G. and Guattari, F. (1984) *Anti-Oedipus: Capitalism and Schizophrenia*. London: Athlone.

— (1988) *A Thousand Plateaus*. London: Athlone.

Department of the Environment (1995) *A Guide to Risk Assessment and Risk Management for Environmental Protection*. London: HMSO.

Derrida, J. (1976) *Of Grammatology*. Baltimore, MD: Johns Hopkins University Press.

Douglas, M. (1966) *Purity and Danger: an Analysis of Concepts of Pollution and Taboo*. London: Routledge & Kegan Paul.

— (1992) *Risk and Blame: Essays in Cultural Theory*. London: Routledge.

— (1996) *Natural Symbols*. (New Edition) London: Routledge.

Fox, N. J. (1984) L of a time with the advanced drivers. *In Camera*, 3 (December), 8.

— (1991) Postmodernism, rationality and the evaluation of health care. *Sociological Review*, 39(4), 709–44.

— (1992) *The Social Meaning of Surgery*. Buckingham: Open University Press

— (1993) *Postmodernism, Sociology and Health*. Buckingham: Open University Press.

— (1995) Postmodern perspectives on care: the vigil and the gift. *Critical Social Policy*, 15(3/4), 107–25.

— (1998) The promise of postmodernism for the sociology of health and medicine. In Scambler, G. and Higgs, P. (eds.), *Modernity, Health and Medicine*. London: Routledge.

Green, A. R. and Goodwin, G. M. (1996) Ecstasy and neuro-degeneration. *British Medical Journal*, 312, 1493–4.

Grinyer, A. (1995) Risk, the real world and naive sociology. In Gabe, J. (ed.), *Medicine, Risk and Health*. Oxford: Blackwell Publishers.

Hassler, J. (1993) Variations in risk – a cause of fluctuations in demand? Seminar Paper 532. Stockholm: Institute for International Economic Studies.

Hertz, D. B. and Thomas, H. (1983) *Risk Analysis and its Applications*. Chichester: Wiley.

Johnstone-Bryden, I. M. (1995) *Managing Risk*. Aldershot: Avebury.

Jordan, T. (1995) Collective bodies: raving and the politics of Gilles Deleuze and Felix Guattari. *Body & Society*, 1(1), 125–44.

Kelly, M. and Charlton, B. (1995) The modern and the postmodern in health promotion. In Bunton, R., Nettleton, S. and Burrows, R. (eds.), *The Sociology of Health Promotion*. London: Routledge.

Lash, S. (1991) Genealogy and the body: Foucault/Deleuze/Nietzsche. In Featherstone, M., Hepworth, M. and Turner, B. S. (eds.), *The Body*. London: Sage.

Leeuwen, C. J. van (1995) General introduction. In Leeuwen, C. J. van and Hermes, J. L. M. (eds.), *Risk Assessment of Chemicals*. Dordrecht: Kluwer Academic Publishers.

Power, R., Power, T. and Gibson, N. (1996) Attitudes and experiences of drug use amongst a group of London teenagers. *Education, Prevention and Policy*, 3(1), 71–80.

Rayner, S. (1992) Cultural theory and risk analysis. In Krimsky, S. and Golding, D. (eds.), *Social Theories of Risk*. Westport, CT: Praeger.

Rogers, R. and Salvage, J. (1988) *Nurses at Risk. A Guide to Health and Safety at Work*. London: Heinemann.

Rushkoff, D. (1994) *Cyberia*. London: HarperCollins.

Saunders, N. (1995) The Leah Betts Story. Published at WWW address: http://obsolete.org/index.html.

Sedgewick, P. (1982) *Psychopolitics*. London: Pluto.

Suter, G. W. (1993) *Ecological Risk Assessment*. Chelsea, MI: Lewis Publishers.

Swaan, A. de (1990) *The Management of Normality*. London: Routledge.

Thorogood, N. (1995) 'London dentist in HIV scare': HIV and dentistry in popular discourse. In Bunton, R., Nettleton, S. and Burrows, R. (eds.), *The Sociology of Health Promotion*. London: Routledge.

Wells, G. L. (1996) *Hazard Identification and Risk Assessment*. Rugby: Institute of Chemical Engineers.

White, S. (1991) *Political Theory and Postmodernism*. Cambridge University Press.

WHO (1985) *Targets for Health for All*. Geneva: World Health Organization.

Woolgar, S. (1988) *Science: The Very Idea*. Chichester: Ellis Horwood.

Wright, W. (1982) *The Social Logic of Health*. New Brunswick, NJ: Rutgers University Press.

Wynne, B. (1992) Risk and social learning: reification to engagement. In Krimsky, S. and Golding, D. (eds), *Social Theories of Risk*.Westport, CT: Praeger.

2   Fear of crime and the media: sociocultural theories of risk

John Tulloch

Fear of crime has received a huge literature (for recent surveys, see Hale, 1996; Tulloch *et al.*, 1998a), much of the work in the media area circulating around Gerbner's 'cultivation thesis' (Gerbner, 1970, Gerbner and Gross, 1976, Gerbner *et al.*, 1978; Gerbner *et al.*, 1980). Researchers' ongoing preoccupation with Gerbner and associates (hereafter 'Gerbner') is not surprising, given, as Hale notes, that one major tendency in fear of crime discourse has been the positioning of fear of crime 'as having no grounding in reality but being merely the product of sensational and selective news coverage and lurid dramatisation' (Hale, 1996: 109).

Gerbner's work took its general position theoretically and politically among the hegemonic analyses of the media and late modernity during the 1970s, one of the many 'social control' approaches to the role of the media and society that marked that period. In particular it extended the 'TV violence' debate within a 'power and ideology' framework, challenging both the linear 'effects' model of American communication theory (which was much exercised by that debate), and the somewhat individualized 'normative' frame it was directed at. Whereas debate about television violence had been based on the assumption that its effects were likely to be anti-normative and thus disruptive, Gerbner began from the 'critical theory' view of the media as vehicles of the established sociocultural and industrial order. By way of symbolic demonstrations of who in society wins and who loses, who is validated to use violence and who is not, and especially by the under-representation (except as victims) of women, ethnic minorities and older people in television drama, and the over-representation of law enforcers and legal institutions, there was a cumulative cultivation of adherence to the dominant beliefs and values of society. Thus the media, in Gerbner's view, serve to strengthen rather than subvert dominant sociocultural norms.

Despite this engagement with critical theory and media studies, most of the studies which have responded to Gerbner and his colleagues have been more psychological, quantitative and empiricist than cultural. This is in part because cultural and media studies were already moving into an era of 'resistance' and 'subcultural' analysis, leading to an 'active audience' approach much less interested in the more pessimistic 'hegemonic' critical theory approaches; and partly because Gerbner's own focus on their 'mean world' and 'violence in society' indices encouraged critics to focus on this 'individual effects' (rather than social control) aspect of the thesis. Here, Gerbner argued that people with a heavy diet of television (especially of violent action genres) tended to a 'mean world' perception of the occurrence of crime and violence in society. Much of the debate around their cultivation thesis was, as a result, methodological (about statistical control of variables, replication, his distinctions between heavy and light viewers, and so on). Other major quantitative research studies, such as Gunter (1987), argued that the relationship between fear of crime and television viewing might be the opposite to Gerbner's hypothesis, insofar as selective perception and selective viewing by anxious personalities could account for the heavy viewing of certain kinds of television programme. Overall, Gunter favoured a notion of 'circularity' in his fear of crime and television analysis. 'Greater fear of potential danger in the social environment may encourage people to stay indoors, where they watch more television, and are exposed to programmemes which tell them things which in turn reinforce their anxieties' (Gunter, 1987: 88).

Little of this debate has been within cultural and media studies (Gunter's interest, for example, was primarily on the relationship between individual/psychological level responses and categorical cultural descriptors like age, gender and class); and none of it has embraced recent risk theory, especially its focus on situated analysis of 'lay knowledgeability'. This chapter describes recent research which did draw on these aspects of 'risk' debate to look again at the field by way of fieldwork with three generations of respondent (teenagers; parents of teenagers; and seniors) in a number of Australian centres (Tulloch et al., 1998b). Here a team of researchers from the Centre for Cultural Risk Research (CCRR) at Charles Sturt University undertook in 1997 a main fear of crime research study and two substudies, one of the latter focused on fear of crime and the media, and one on fear of crime and public transport. The media study consisted of focus-group discussions and long interviews with respondents in each of the three generations surveyed, and in each of three geographical regions: city (Sydney); tourist/commuter belt (the Blue Mountains region close to Sydney); and rural urban (the small inland town of Bathurst in New South Wales, some 250 kilometres from Sydney). In all there were nine focus groups (of 6 to 13 people) and eighteen long interviews in the media substudy.

I will begin with a survey of the epistemological fields in which fear of crime analysis (and risk theory more broadly) is currently positioned, indicating the 'absences' vis-à-vis media analysis that these various epistemological positions reveal. I will conclude with brief discussion of our own theoretical frame and findings. For convenience in this epistemological 'mapping' exercise, I will draw on Nick Fox's distinction (this volume) of three epistemologies of risk: what he calls the realist or materialist; second, the culturalist or constructionist; and third, a postmodern position. Except that I would prefer to call empiricist what Fox describes as a 'realist' or 'materialist' position (since some of the more powerful 'left realist' theory in criminology is both culturalist and materialist by his definition), this is a useful initial framework for our survey.

Empiricist paradigms

Typically empiricist paradigms of risk operate, as Fox says, within a simplistically materialist ontology: risk is the probability of a material hazard circumstance occurring. Because of this 'probability' emphasis within empiricist perspectives, there is generally a methodologically quantitative and 'expert'-driven research focus contrasting 'real' risk and public perceptions of risk. So although reliance on 'expert' rather than 'lay knowledgeability' has become a major target of current risk theory (e.g. Wynne, 1996), it is still quite dominant in both fear of crime and risk/media policy analysis (Sparks, 1992). The problem with top–down 'expert' (and invariably quantitative) empiricist methodologies lies in their probabilistic comparisons of crime statistics with various groups' perceptions of crime. 'Fear of crime' thus becomes the 'mistaken impression' (among women, older people, etc.) about the real probability of their being victims of crime. An implicit juxtaposition of notions of the rational against 'irrationalities' can then very quickly lead to a conventionally gendered (i.e. women as emotional) and aged (i.e. old people as like children) devaluation of the emotions, pleasures, fantasies and so on in this or any other area of risk.

From this perspective the media are at best neutral, at worst 'sensationalist' vehicles for the top–down facts of empiricism. As Sparks (1992), Handmer (1995) and others argue, top–down risk-management approaches are so concerned to persuade people to adopt self-protective behaviour that they can be blind to the many different legitimate ways in which people view risk via the media. In the assumption of top–down 'scientific' views, risk specialists are needed to counteract the 'dysfunctional' role of a 'sensationalist' media and an 'irrational' public. But, as

Handmer says, this can only be seen to be 'reasonable in the context of a communication model where all the worthwhile knowledge is seen to be held by specialists' (Handmer, 1995: 88).

It is these 'expert' methodologies (and their 'accusations of irrationality', while relying on official statistics as an adequate base for research or policy) that have been most subject to critique in sociocultural risk theory. From an alternative ('below–up') perspective, as Sparks (1992) has argued, what this misses is media inevitably engaged with audiences who are situating the symbolic within everyday social practices. In addition, in the broader field of cultural and media theory, the empiricist tradition (particularly of communication 'effects' theory) has been criticized for its tendency to 'divorce . . . processes of empirical generalization from their theoretical context', giving rise 'to a research practice emphasizing the goal of establishing direct correlations among variables at the expense of understanding the social and psychological mechanisms involved' (Tudor, 1995: 85). More profoundly, even when top–down 'effects' research did seek social or psychological mechanisms, its equally top–down social ontology tended from stimulus–response models at one extreme ('the Skinnerian Actor') to the over-socialized, normatively determined individual at the other ('the cultural dope'). 'Variability in meaning construction and heterogeneity of culture and social practice were thus effectively excluded from consideration' (87).

The simplistic belief in 'mass culture' legitimating a belief in 'strong effects' underpins a considerable amount of empiricist work in the risk communication field, as well as in the fear of crime area. And, Tudor argues, even where foundational media/fear of crime researchers like Gerbner rejected the traditional normative/individual models of social consensus for one based on conflict, power and symbolic manipulation, he still resorted to the single-identity 'socialized' actor. No less than in 'effects' research, this respondent was 'at the receiving end' of broad processes of sociocultural constraint. 'The heavy television viewers central to Cultivation Analysis remain victims of culture rather than parties to the constant construction and reconstruction of their cultural environments' (88).

Culturalist paradigms

The very problem critics have raised with top–down empiricist assumptions of consensus-building around the 'rationality' of science and the irrationality of those who do not adhere to its statistics, becomes the focus of the culturalist position; and the issue of 'expert' versus 'lay' knowledge has become a key theme in current debate. Especially because of the emphasis on individuals as choosing agents in current risk theory, there is a focus on disputes among experts (between which individual members of the public must choose; as in Giddens, 1994), and an emphasis as well on the value of contingent, 'lay' knowledge (Wynne, 1996).

'Lay' actors – the very same women and older people that top–down accounts and statistics find to be irrational or suffering from 'mistaken impressions' – are now, in a culturalist model, assumed to have special expertise, because only they have access to the fine grain of their personal and cultural experience. Fear is no longer 'extraneous, excessive, generated by something other than its ostensible objects and thus irrational' (Sparks, 1992: 8). In this model, the separation of public and private spheres (and between 'reason' and 'emotion') is challenged (4). In this culturalist perspective, the media are not locked into the straightjacket of being either neutral (i.e. 'scientific') or else 'dysfunctional' (e.g. 'sensationalist') communication vehicles. Rather the media are processual players and negotiators in the cognitions and also the emotions of risk and fear.

Risk communication

Despite the fact that the field of risk communication still remains predominantly empiricist in its main centres and journals, there are significant signs that the anti-technicist, culturalist focus Sparks is advocating has gained a toe-hold in this influential area, with significant methodological implications. Because of the centrality of risk analysis to this field, I will give some attention to it, even though it has not focused as yet on fear of crime. Handmer, Brown, Campbell and others have argued for a 'negotiation' oriented approach to risk methodology via high stakeholder interaction. A key emphasis in culturalist approaches to risk communication policy is, as Handmer puts it, 'to search through negotiation for solutions that have broad-based support and therefore may be sustainable' (Handmer, 1995: 88). It is partly because of the emphasis on political sustainability in culturalist risk communication that there is such a major focus on 'stakeholder partnership' research methodologies (e.g. Brown and Campbell, 1991 clearly prefer focus groups and planning cells to leaflets or attitude surveys). And this is also why the emphasis on 'active' and differentiated audience interpretations current in mainstream media and cultural studies has taken on such a pragmatic dimension in risk communication.

Thus a new version of risk management is developing which is more culturalist in orientation, drawing in part on Mary Douglas' influential work on risk, but more substantially on the critique among risk theorists of the normative control embodied in 'normal scientific epistemic commitments' (Wynne, 1996: 70). In Handmer's formulation, the emphasis on 'expert' versus 'lay' perceptions of risk is mapped across quite specific differences of understanding of both uncertainty and ignorance. In relation to uncertainty, for example, Handmer points to the difference between probabilistic data which indicates that there is a very low chance of commercial airliners being involved in fatal accidents and a different kind of 'lay' uncertainty which may be caused by media reports: say, of alcohol abuse by pilots or of major health risks associated with airline advice to pilots to save on fuel costs by cutting back on fresh air circulation. To 'achieve shared meaning we need to be aware of different perspectives on ignorance (uncertainty and irrelevance) – and we need to look at the attributes considered important by the major stakeholders . . . In summary, ignoring the different meanings stakeholders ascribe to risk guarantees the failure of risk communication programmes' (Handmer, 1995: 90–1).

In this emerging culturalist/pragmatic tradition of risk communication, the emphasis on research methodologies has increasingly been both qualitative (since these methodologies are deemed to give better access to the 'different meanings stakeholders ascribe to risk'), and processual (because of the emphasis on multiple perspectives and negotiation with stakeholders). In our own fear of crime research it was this risk communication emphasis on stakeholder input which influenced both our initial research proposal and some of our methodology. The public transport substudy, for example, included focus-group interviews with a wide range of stakeholders: not only various age groups of users, but also New South Wales State Rail management, employees (including train guards and drivers), bus drivers, etc. It was via the 'triangulation' of these different respondents, for example, that we were able to break down (during the focus group interviews with management) their familiar empiricist emphasis on a gap between 'real' crime (as demonstrated by statistics) and the public's 'irrational' fear of crime, and were also able to engage with their familiar scapegoating of a 'sensational' media (see Tulloch et al., 1998b: 207–9, 321).

Left realism

There has been little work on fear of crime and the media as such stemming from the culturalist risk communication tradition. This is not the case with the most important culturalist/materialist tradition within the fear of crime field, 'left realism'. Because of its sociostructural emphasis, left realism has a much less sanguine view than risk communication theorists like Handmer and Brown, either in terms of their trust in conflict resolution or the belief in the 'procedural fairness' (Handmer, 1995: 94) of a 'co-operative' stakeholder approach. Indeed, the gap between risk-communication approaches and the left realist tradition replicates in some key areas the debate within criminology itself between crime prevention or social justice approaches (see for example, Sutton, 1994: 5–20; O'Malley, 1994: 21–4; Chan, 1994: 25–9).

We need to be clear, here, that realist epistemology, in the context of the left realists' analysis of fear of crime, differs fundamentally from Nick Fox's (this volume) use of 'realist' for the naive materialist/ empiricists. In fact, realist epistemology has quite another meaning in cultural materialist (as in the work of Raymond Williams, 1989) and some feminist literature (as in Terry Lovell's work), and these can certainly be equated with parts of what Fox calls 'culturalist or constructivist' approaches to risk. Lovell, for example, distinguishes empiricism, whose 'world . . . exists at the level of sense data, generated through observation and experiment', from realism whose 'propositions of theory relate to the deep ontological furniture of the universe, rather than at the surface [of appearances] at which experience is located. Experience, properly interpreted, gives us access to that deep ontological layer because it is causally connected to it' (Lovell, 1940: 19). Similarly Tudor (1995: 99, 98) in media theory and Pawson and Tilley (1994: 292) in criminology argue for a philosophical realism that constructs explanations by seeking to identify the 'underlying causal mechanisms' that sustain patterned activity.

While deriving much of its emphasis (on notions of ontological depth, surface appearance and the causal mechanisms which link these two layers) from philosophers of science like Bhaskar, this critical realism has drawn much of its inspiration in the area of media and textual analysis from Raymond Williams, from the European materialist theorists who influenced him (such as Lukacs and Goldmann) and from the cultural materialist tradition which grew out of his early work. For example, the critical realist contrast between the surface of appearances and the 'underlying' causalities and 'mechanisms' of everyday experience led Raymond Williams to his central distinction between naturalism and realism in his critique of a new 'left formalism' in screen, media and literary theory. And with a similar epistemological commitment, but a slightly different focus, left realist criminologists have critiqued the 'left idealism' of 'moral panic' media theorists (who tend to portray 'panics' as simply media instigated rather than rational responses to underlying conditions of living) because they ignore under-pinning structural constraints and mechanisms.

At best, critical realist criminologists and media theorists have em-bedded their media analysis on the one hand in 'thick' descriptions of the everyday lives of media professionals or audiences (see for example Schlesinger *et al.*, 1992); and on the other in sociostructural and historical analysis. Valuable recent examples of this kind of culturalist/realist research in the area of fear of crime include Ian Taylor's ethno-graphic studies of fear of crime, the media and other circuits of communication in suburban Manchester. Drawing on an impressively broad yet integrated range of quantitative, qualitative and critical realist methodologies, Taylor conducts:

> ethnographic 'thick description' of various circuits of communi-cation – corner-shop gossip, school-children's narratives of risk as told to parents, local media, etc. – within one affluent, 'rural'-nostalgic south Manchester suburb;
>
> discursive analysis of the local media, and of a local word-of-mouth campaign against a particular pub landlord – both of these in relation to the representation of the local community 'under siege' from 'city Others' who supposedly bring drugs, ram-raids and break-ins; and,
>
> comparative analysis globally of post-industrial cities' attempts to reposition themselves as 'headquarter' sites for world-wide multinational corporations (e.g. Manchester's upgraded international airport, new light transit system, 'twenty-four-hour city' promotion, Olympic bids, etc.).

Taylor (1995) is then able to position contradictions within specific local community groups (e.g. opposing the new Manchester runway but supporting the safer twenty-four-hour streets strategies) as well as contrasting fear of crime 'structures of feeling' (Raymond Williams' term) between an international 'headquarter' post-industrial city like Manchester, and an old industrial city in decline like Sheffield. Here 'causal mechanisms' (such as the shift towards multinational 'head-quarters city' status in one postindustrial conurbation, and not in another) underpin the structures of feeling which explain different representations and fears of crime in these different areas.

Postmodern paradigms

Media analysis as part of a culturalist/realist account of modernity and fear of crime, such as Taylor's, is important, but here media texts are often in the background and deeply embedded in 'thick description' of the local milieu. Within a postmodernist paradigm, however, textual media analysis tends to come to the forefront; in part because of an emphasis on 'reality' as constructed by discourse (including media languages).

Thus for Fox, risk assessment, in so far as it is consensually accepted as 'objective', depends on Foucault's power-knowledge: i.e. the knowledgeability which constructs objects discursively and in doing so asserts the authority of the person claiming this knowledge. For Fox, the media (both 'expert' like scientific journals, and popular) are important because they routinely circulate, via countless discourses, our sense of who we are and how we should behave. Fox focuses on one particular hegemonic discourse that circulates in these media sites – that individuals have become at risk from themselves. 'Hazard' and 'risk' are thus discursively circulated via these contingent knowledgeabilities in scientific journals and popular magazines, as they construct subjectivities 'balanced' between the 'controlling self' and the 'risky self'. In particular, Fox's position is postmodernist because he is opposing what he calls the modernist enterprise of 'mastery' which is still evident in this discourse of 'controlling self' and 'risky self'.

A powerful postmodern account of fear of crime that focuses on media texts directly, and the failure of modernist attempts to master signification and representation, is Alison Young's article 'In the frame: crime and the limits of representation' (1996). She analyses the media in the Jamie Bulger case (the little boy abducted from a shopping centre and murdered by two older boys in northern England). Young focuses on the 'scenes of representation – that is, the ways in which the crime is staged as a problem in and of cultural representation' (82). Lacking both a represented content of abduction which could be called upon with any certainty (as evidenced by the eye-witnesses' 'faulty' memory of seeing a child with his family or friends), and a form of representation (since the shopping mall video camera captured no images of the abduction), there could be no guarantee of meaning in the Bulger case. Thus the media necessarily constructed the crime as not only unthinkable, but also as unrepresentable. 'The event – both seduction and death – is held to exceed the limits of representation and as such represents for us the borders of what can be imagined' (94–5).

Richard Osborne describes fear of criminality as perhaps 'the perfect metaphor for postmodernism', and Young's analysis is symptomatic of this. As Osborne sees it, 'media narratives encode crime and disorder as the representations of fragmentation rendered coherent' (Osborne, 1995: 27–8). In his account, and in Young's, the 'obsessive . . . and hysterical replaying of the possibility of being a victim and staving it off'

(1995: 29) has become systemic in the media's attempt to institutionalize a postmodern condition that eludes mastery.

Yet, plausible though it is at one level, Young's kind of analysis loses touch completely with situated understandings of the media. A new (postmodern/culturalist/textualist) 'expert story' has replaced that of empiricism. But Brian Wynne's multidimensional and adaptive 'lay knowledgability' is nowhere to be found. On the other hand, Richard Sparks' (1992) mix of culturalist and postmodernist approaches does offer (without actually delivering) current risk theory's emphasis on lay understandings, even while adopting a primarily textualist position. Like Fox and other postmodernist theorists of risk, Sparks' particular emphasis is on the construction of 'reality' via narratives, discourse frames and rhetorics of crime in everyday (particularly media-everyday) life. In addition, from a poststructuralist position, Sparks refuses to privilege a rationality/emotionality duality, and emphasizes in his media and fear of crime theory the intuitive, the emotional, the non-rational and the pleasurable aspects of negotiating with risk.

One methodological approach to this problem, Sparks argues, is to consider the ways in which the underlying preoccupations of fear, danger, reassurance and retribution are encoded, diffused and received in networks of communication. This is not automatically to assume a powerful direct influence of media representations over the consciousness and beliefs of audiences as in Gerbner. Like Taylor, Sparks emphasizes networks of local 'talk' in relation to these representations. But unlike Taylor, Sparks does still look at textual forms, at 'crime and punishment as cultural forms: things which interest people and sometimes give them pleasure' (3).

Like Fox, Sparks emphasizes the discursive construction of both subjectivity and of risks. Thus he asks the question: to what sources of information, reassurance or distraction do people turn in seeking to cope with fear? Sparks' own analysis focuses on television crime genres. The (valued) emotional experience of media representations of crime (according to genre, narrative, iconography, scheduling, etc.) becomes his major focus, rather than the empiricist 'disparity' thesis, tied down to media 'sensationalism'. However, though Sparks insists that 'criminological work should be attentive to the ways in which images of crime, law enforcement and punishment are caught up in the fine grain of cultural and personal experience' (5), his book does not perform the kind of qualitative empirical audience research that would allow him to do this. Sparks asks the question, for example: 'what are the pleasures that people take in the shock/reaffirmation of cop shows?', but relies on theoretical rather than empirical audience-research answers.

The CCRR's 'Fear of Crime and the Media' research

Our own research commitment was to an empirically focused, cultural-materialist and poststructuralist position which is close to current feminist/poststructuralist positions which emphasize feeling (as well as reason) as part of an agentive identity: viz.,

Poststructuralist theory turns the equation between rationality and agency on its head. In understanding the discursive construction of self one is liberated from the burden of a rationality which controls, dominates and negates feeling, the concrete and the real in favour of the abstract and a notion of the good which is . . . coercive and judgemental of those who are not powerfully located in dominant discourses . . . Agency is never freedom from discursive constitution of self but the capacity to recognise that constitution and to resist, subvert and change the discourses themselves through which one is constituted . . . The model of the person being developed here is of an embodied speaker who at the same time constitutes and is constituted by the discursive practices of the collectives of which they are a member. (Davies, 1991: 50–1)

Drawing on Taylor's emphasis on situated research in specific time/place co-ordinates; on Sparks' questions about the public's situated, daily routine responses (emotional as well as rational) to media representations of crime; and on feminist poststructuralist accounts of agency, structure and an 'ethnography of storytelling' (see Ang, 1996) in recognizing that meaning is plural, the CCRR research approached its 'audience'.

There is little space in this chapter to do more than indicate the direction of this research by way of a few of its 'stories', briefly described. The CCRR's *Fear of Crime Fieldwork Report* contained a main study (using both qualitative and quantitative methods) led and written by Deborah Lupton; and two substudies (of fear of crime on public transport; and fear of crime and the media) led and primarily written by myself. The case studies which follow come from these two substudies.

Agency and structure: a 'fear of crime on trains' case study

Very early in our study, it became evident that one of the most significant time/space co-ordinates for fear of crime in New South Wales was train travel. If the 'time' of fear was very specifically at night, the 'space' of fear was primarily trains travelling through specific 'landscapes of fear' as represented in the media: areas such as Redfern (an inner-city, disadvantaged Sydney suburb with a high number of Aboriginal residents); and 'the western suburbs' (mainly lower-middle- and working-class areas, with a high migrant population) like Cabramatta, Mount

Druitt, Penrith and Parramatta. In addition, private-school male teenagers living in the 'North Shore' of Sydney (regarded as an elite
professional and middle-class area) felt significantly threatened (and
targeted) at their own railway stations by 'home boys' or 'homies' (also
called 'townies' in the UK: viz. 'gangs' of youths dressed in 'Los
Angeles' basketball-gear style). Most generational groups (teenagers/
parents/seniors) who lived outside these spatial co-ordinates (e.g. residents in the commuter and tourist area of the Blue Mountains) tended
to feel that the trains there were safer 'once we've passed through the
western suburbs'.

The following narrative of one Blue Mountains mother of teenage
daughters, Pam, needs to be considered as a 'situated story' within this
broader context. 'Pam's story' reveals clearly the way in which different
circuits of communication operate within a mobilized framework of
'structure' and 'agency'.

Pam had always felt that the Mountains trains were 'different' and
safer than suburban trains, simply because they passed through but did
not stop at stations in the western suburbs of Sydney. When asked
whether there was a point in her biography when she began to fear
public transport more, Pam initially said it was after an incident with her
children on the train. However, she then paused, recollected, and told a
more nuanced tale, with four distinct moments of reported or experienced crime on the trains. It is the accretion of these four moments
together which now constitute Pam's powerful memory: 'fear of train
travel'.

The first of these moments was a news report of a man being stabbed
on the Blue Mountains train two years ago. 'That one stood out in my
mind – like normally a stabbing wouldn't stand out in my mind – but
that one did because I thought "That was a Mountains train!" . . .
There's almost that distinction, like we're safe because we all come from
the Mountains.' Second, this news report was followed within a couple
of months by a story from a friend about a group of drunks on the
Mountains train who were fighting until one cried out he had been
stabbed. 'The guard came out and he was this puny little man, and the
passengers were saying "Have the police been called?" – they must have
been able to hear him calling on his intercom. And then, she said, they
were all sitting there absolutely petrified and when they pulled into [the
next station] she said there was no one there, no police or anything. She
said it was just terrible.' Third, this anecdote was followed within a few
months by Pam's personal experience of a terrible fight with chains and
knives when she was travelling with her husband and two daughters on
the train in the western suburbs of Sydney. In this case two young

people got on the train and began to taunt other passengers with 'I'm a dinkum [authentic] Aussie. I'm an Aussie. What are you?' A fight began with 'Lebanese migrants'. Her husband intervened, and she pulled him away fearing he would be stabbed. 'It was quite traumatic because it involved the whole family and we talked about it for days. You know, "Oh wasn't it terrible?" and "Oh, what about Dad?" and "What about her?". Because the twist in the whole thing was that the most aggressive of the young people who we thought was a bloke wasn't a bloke at all . . . It was a girl doing that!'

Fourth, the worst incident of all for Pam happened just before our interview with her (indeed, Pam sought us out to tell us her tale, hoping that our research would 'make things better for other mums'). As a result of the previous experiences Pam did not let her daughters travel on the train, even with older friends. However, a school trip to Sydney was arranged, and her younger, eleven-year-old daughter was allowed to go. The first problem was that although a carriage was booked for the children, when they got on it was already occupied by adults who refused to move when asked to do so by the teacher, even resisting moving their bags off the seats. No rail staff were available to help, so the teacher had to fit in the children wherever she could, scattered throughout the double-decker carriage. Pam's daughter Tracy got a single seat at the top of the stairs facing a seat which had only a bag on it. Once the teacher had returned to her seat, Tracy found herself confronted by a man opposite her. He began to intimidate her by staring at her, then looked at her through his fingers, and finally took his coat off, put it over his shoulder and began to masturbate under his coat.

She's only eleven and she knew she wasn't comfortable, but she didn't know quite how to cope with it, and the teacher had told them all that once they were sitting down they weren't to get up. So she didn't want to get up, but she did go to the toilet and she said she tried to make that last as long as she could. But then she went back and sat down and he had a denim shirt with press studs buttons, and she said he popped all the buttons open and just sat there with his chest all exposed to her, and then he was undoing and doing up his pants. There was a young girl across from her who could see what was going on and called Tracy over and took her back to her teacher. This [older] girl felt that he was actually directing it at her, and Tracy felt like he was directing it at her.

The teacher couldn't get to the guard and finally spoke to the train driver. At a western-suburbs railway-station staff got on and removed the man. However, despite the fact that he was apparently not travelling with a ticket, no documentation was prepared, the police were not called, and the only reason that official action was taken was because the school was required, by its own regulations, to inform the Department of Community Services (DOCS). The police were informed not by the rail staff but by DOCS. Pam followed up herself by ringing the relevant stationmaster. 'He was nice, but flippant. You know, like "I don't know why these people travel on trains", and it seemed to be like "Well, that's part of the culture of travelling on trains". That was the message I got from him.'

Fixed in her seat by the authority of the teacher and the selfishness of adult passengers, sexually harassed by one of these passengers, unprotected by the rail authority, Tracy was then (as a result of school and DOCS regulations) exposed to a series of after-the-event and too-late authority moves, like being asked if she could identify her abuser out of a mass of shouting men at the police station. Her mother Pam, who had tried to be agentive in preparing her daughter after the earlier incidents by telling her to 'try and move to somewhere where you feel safer if you see something that you don't feel is quite right', now feels trapped by all these authorities and procedures, none of which seems to be catching the culprit. Not only is her agency in preparing her children for train travel now completely compromised, but so too is her timetable for discussing sexual matters with her daughter, since she feels she was forced to talk about what the man was doing and why under duress. 'I don't know in the long run how it's going to affect her, and I'm going through all this dilemma, like would we have been better just to forget the whole thing and pretend it didn't happen? But now, because it was a referral and it's got to go through this process, I'm thinking "Oh, is this really worth it?"'

Many interweaving structures – of the mass media, school, State Rail, the police, DOCS – have trapped Pam and her daughter in the site-specific issue of fear of crime on the train. But, at the same time, many different circuits of communication – many different 'stories', both 'lay' and 'expert' – have been interweaving in Pam's attempt at a meta-narrative as she tries (but fails) to control her child's experience by way of her own 'representational order' (Ang, 1996: 77). Pam's stories (and those of her daughter and friends) have entered 'the uneven, power-laden field of social discourse' (76). At the same time, we can see how Pam's use of the media is itself part of what Ang calls a 'never-ending flux' of other circuits of communication.

Fear as mode of experience and perception: media case studies

Following the theoretical directions suggested by both Taylor and Sparks, our 'Fear of Crime and the Media' substudy was concerned to:

examine the way in which differently fearful people draw on
   media (and other) 'heuristics' as narratives for ordering and
   understanding their concerns and feelings;

understand the media as one among the many circuits of
   meaning that people are exposed to;

assess the degree to which particular images, stories, rhetorics
   and political narratives are used, tested, elaborated or found
   wanting within the broader nexus of discursive contexts in
   which people live;

discover which generic sources of information, reassurance or
   distraction differently located people turn to in seeking to
   cope with their fears.

In particular, Sparks believes that because in cop series first, the
'"good", for the most part, continue to end happily, and the "bad"
unhappily', (1992: 39); and second, the scheduled routines of viewing
may reproduce 'the established cosmological and political order . . . as a
self-evident and natural order which goes without saying and therefore
goes unquestioned' (50-1), this particular highly popular television
crime genre needs investigating in its relationship with other circuits of
discourse in determinate settings.

(i) The 'heuristics' of differently fearful people

Lisa is a sixteen-year-old living with her mother and stepfather in Rose
Bay, an affluent Harbour-side Sydney suburb. Before her mother's
second marriage Lisa lived in Bondi, a less affluent but still middle-class
beachside suburb. Her natural father is English, and his first wife
(before Lisa's mother) was a drug addict. As a younger teenager Lisa
had been mugged for her Reeboks shoes at Bondi station, had first-hand
experience of the sexual interference of a close female friend by her
stepfather, had her house at Bondi robbed, and the family car broken
into several times. Also close friends were mugged in the street, and Lisa
and a female friend were sexually harassed by a man in the school posing
as a doctor. Lisa is worried by 'real-life' crime incidents shown on the
TV news, and does not like watching them alone. She talks with her
family about them if she can, to calm her and 'write them off'. 'Funny'
cop shows like Australian police series *Good Guys, Bad Guys* 'kind of
lighten' her fears about crime, but the news makes her feel worse
'because they show you how much of it is actually happening, and so
you've got a bigger chance of it happening to you'. In Lisa's case, the
reiterated quality of television actually increases her fears. Thus cop
series narratives do not work for her, as Sparks predicts, as routinized
forms for both hooking an audience and then assuaging their crime

anxieties (as the 'good guy' wins). In fact, police series featuring real crimes like *Australia's Most Wanted* have increased her fears because they convince her that the police are 'dumb'. 'It's brought the little hidden thought at the back of my mind right to the front'.

Sara is a 'near-seventy' retired woman living in a housing estate in Bathurst, a country town in New South Wales. It is eighteen months since her farmer husband died, and since then she has made her home a fortress with multiple locks everywhere. She locks the front door when she is in the backyard, and locks the back door when she is in the front garden. She says her neighbours are as fearful as she is. Above all 'I don't like it when I see things on TV like home invasions'. She adds that the home-invasions material that she has seen showed attacks on older people, people who are on their own, and 'people who can't defend themselves'. Sara qualifies on all three counts. 'It makes you wonder why they have to attack old people. That's what frightens me. When you're on your own, you wonder if you might be the next one.' Because of her fear of home invasion, Sara refuses to watch any cop shows: 'You can see what happens and it frightens you.' She uses television promotions to decide what not to watch. 'I watched the shorts last night and they had a big stick that I don't know whether they used or not. But those sort of things frighten me. I didn't watch it to know how it happened . . . I don't watch *The Bill* (a British police series) or any of those . . . I watch *The Thin Blue Line* (a British sitcom starring Rowan Atkinson) . . . but that's a comedy and I know that's all right. No, I don't like any of those sort of shows that's got violence in, it frightens me.' As for Lisa, but in a different way, Sparks' prediction about cop series does not work for Sara.

Julie is a lesbian mother in her early forties living in a tough western suburb of Sydney. As a child she was regularly beaten 'to the wall and back' by her father when he was drunk. Nevertheless, her father's radical Left politics have stayed with Julie, strengthened and adapted in her twenties by a feminist group which taught her 'there is no safety anywhere, anytime, so you may as well live your life and not let the fear control you'. As a union organizer and demonstrator she has handled a 'rogue cop' who had injured her female colleague. As a night-time train traveller in areas that most woman fear, the western suburbs, she walks through the train to talk with women who are travelling by themselves. With her partner (who boxes), and her daughter, she has faced out a group of men planning to rob a drunken older woman on the train. Julie says she gives out 'don't mess with me' as she moves about in public places. Yet she, too, has her television fears: she will not watch films or television programmes with stalking themes. She would not watch

Millennium (an American drama) after the first episode because 'the fellow's wife and child were threatened . . . Violence towards women and children bothers me a lot. I don't watch the sorts of murder/horror things where women are being stalked'. Julie argues that she has been 'super sensitive' to cues of male violence since she was a child. Consequently she feels this sensitivity can actually disempower her as a woman if she watches stalking themes where men control women via the gaze of the camera. She will not watch any police series ('I was brought up in a communist household, totally anti-authoritarian – "Cops are somebody not to be trusted"') except *The Bill*, which she enjoys watching 'mainly for the tough female cops'. Again, we have a specifically situated response of pleasure and risk to Sparks' prediction about cop-series narratives.

Angela is a very small woman in her forties living in the Blue Mountains. She is quite poor, having lost her professional position during downsizing (as a result, she believes, of her union activities). Fifteen years ago she ran away from home (with her child) because of her violent husband, and was too frightened of him to press for a fair divorce settlement. Yet, despite this background, Angela is a battler and is not easily scared. For example, she tends not to visit Redfern (one of many people's 'landscapes of fear' because of the high numbers of disadvantaged Aboriginal people living there), but not because of anxiety. 'I see no reason why there shouldn't be Aboriginal territory there. So unless I'm with Aboriginal people or have some real reason to be there, I don't see why I should go there. It would be provocative.' Angela is not made fearful by anything she sees on television, but she is outraged about exploitation, especially of children. 'The Dunblane Massacre [in Scotland] affected me more than any of them because I worried about the bizarre attraction to injure, kill a group of little children. Again there was the attack in Cairns on the little O'Shane boy [nephew of a leading Aboriginal woman judge] . . . So I worry about children. I was outraged and worried.' She enjoys watching *The Thin Blue Line* 'because I like the comic aspect of the police force', and *The Bill* where 'the good guy doesn't always win'.

These were some of the media fears and pleasure of four women among our story-tellers; all of whom had their own situated fears about crime; and all of them complicated Sparks' prediction about the pleasurable emotional effects of cop series. Three of them had been subject to extreme violence or to sexual exploitation and mugging. The woman who (as far as we know) had not been subject to these things was easily the most fearful. But each – and the emphasis on their individual agency here is important – had her own strategies to help her manage her fear.

These related to their gender, their age, their situated identities, their media pleasures, and to other circuits of communication than television cop series.

(ii) The media and other circuits of communication

Sparks argues that we need to focus on 'the study of talk [rather] than . . . the study of texts'; and Lisa would agree with him, particularly in relation to cop series. She said that she does not regularly watch cop shows where the 'good guys' win all the time, because that is boring. 'It's not real. It's OK if the whole thing is meant to be funny, but if it's meant to be serious and then at the end the good guy wins, it's just stupid and ruins the whole thing.' She does enjoy one police series, *Good Guys, Bad Guys*, but that is because in this show the 'good guys are bad guys. The police in *Good Guys, Bad Guys* are all evil, sort of – they're all corrupt. But in *The Bill* they're all sweet, lovely.' *Good Guys, Bad Guys* is 'just TV stories, TV characters'. In contrast, *The Bill* (which she watches, if at all, for its 'English accents' – with her mother and stepfather) pretends to be real, but fails because the good guys (police) usually win. 'Good doesn't always win in real life.'

Lisa says she has plenty of experience of this. A friend is married to a policeman who bashes her; another friend has been hassled by police because of her short skirt while in Lisa's company; another girlfriend who was attacked and her purse stolen on Bondi Beach got a very delayed response from the police (the station was only three minutes away); and she has seen police harass her busker friends at Circular Quay, a popular Sydney 'strolling' site for residents and tourists, with many small shops and entertainers. The Bondi police, she says, 'are just evil!'

Turning neither to television nor to actual police for her 'good guys', Lisa does know the power of talk. She talks with her parents about worries she has over the TV news. She talks with a girlfriend about her fear over seemingly 'normal people' who commit terrible crimes. So she converts major TV crime events like the Oklahoma bombing, the Port Arthur massacre or the serial killings around Perth, Western Australia, much publicized in the Australian news media, where the murderer still has not been caught, into discursive logics where she talks with her friends about the right and wrongs of punishing or releasing threatening male criminals. When a younger teenager at Bondi, she also talked with people about her personalized fears (of being raped or murdered in her home) because these neighbours were frequently subject to break-ins too.

Unlike Lisa, Sara is deprived of talk as a result of her age and her domestic isolation. 'Being on your own, it's a big thing. If you've got somebody to talk to, it gets it out of your system. You bottle it up when you're on your own.' She does not even feel able to talk with her married children about her fear of crime, nor about her concerns for her grand-children. And her family has not felt like talking with her about her crime worries, either. She says that she guesses they know how fearful she is when they see all the locks on the doors. Sara only talks with neighbours, and these older people are, she says, equally fearful. This verbal and physical isolation makes her fear much worse. 'It's all right when you've got someone near. But when you're on your own, every little creak and you think somebody's getting in. You get frightened, you see. That's what it is, it's the fear. I think it builds up. You know, you see these things and think that could happen to me.' Sara does use other circuits of communication in this situation. She is, for example, an assiduous reader of local newspapers. But, as we will see, this only tends to make her fear worse.

Julie talks with other women a lot:

I don't demonstrate any more. But I talk. I talk to individuals, I talk in groups at work, conversations, seminars at lunch time and work time. Once I did some work around my own childhood violence. I figured out what my survival tactics were; and I took that survival tactic and brought it into my present life in a more conscious way. So I use it instead of it just being an unconscious thing.

She also talks with her partner and her work colleagues about societal violence. One of Australia's worst gun massacres had occurred nearby at the Strathfield shopping plaza in the early 1990s. She and a number of women from work shopped there. They talked a lot about it; but this talk was

more like a testing out of my feelings about the situation. It wasn't like all of a sudden I became too scared to go to Strathfield shopping centre. It created a lot of discussion. Some of the other women were expressing fear, usually I provided a reality check. I have that role. It probably helps me a bit too, but more like a getting rid of the sadness and the grief of it rather than getting rid of the fear of it, because the fear becomes negligible.

But Julie says she is deprived by the media of the information to make her talk more effective. She does, she says, learn a bit from crime fact and fiction on television: reports about one particular case of a mur-dered woman taught her, for example, to be personally more observant of things around her when she walks alone. But most of the time the national media are too sensational to be very useful, and she tends to learn 'negatively' from them (e.g. about how women shouldn't behave – like screaming in tense situations!). 'It's good to have an awareness of crime - information keeps fear in check'. Her free local newspaper is able to give her more factual information than the monopolized national papers. But she still finds that the local papers give little sustained information. For example, her neighbour warned her not to leave her decrepit car on the front grass, because of local kids who might burn it (she noticed then that nobody in the street left their cars on the road outside). And the local paper also reported two cars being burned in her suburb. But Julie complained that it was only a two-line report, with no real information or context. In this particular case of potential crime, various circulating 'textual' clues – neighbours' gossip, brief newspaper reports, and the visual cue of streets empty of cars – were generating 'local crime wave' fears for her. But she felt that lack of 'sustained' circulating information left her unable to properly negotiate these different 'heuristics'.

I couldn't fully assess that and make a personal judgement about what level of worry I should have about it. Sometimes a lack of information can be worse than sensationalism because it leaves you with questions that can play on your mind. I think a lot of the problem with authority in general is that they feel like people can't make personal judgements, so they don't give information. I would rather make a judgement for myself – give me the information so that I can assess it.

Angela, like Julie, talks with people a lot, and they talk to her a lot, particularly young people in difficulties (we recall Angela's outrage over children being abused and killed).

I intervened in the train when there was an Asian boy from one of the local schools suffering racist attacks, no-one else wanted to intervene; also a car being attacked in the car park with the occupant in it and the children crying, no-one wanted to intervene; and there was a boy came to us on the train in Rooty Hill [in the western suburbs] and asked us if he could stay with us for protection because he was being harassed by other boys. It worries me that there's a tendency now in society for people to pretend they don't see, pretend things aren't happening and often it just needs another presence there. So in that case I tend to be fairly active, but I don't do enough in a structured way – I don't write letters to the editor, I'm not a member of Neighbourhood Watch and I certainly wouldn't be part of any vigilante type group. If a situation occurs, then I react, but I've noticed lots of other people don't – so I'm active in a reactive way.

Angela also feels that there are things on television (like the exposure of police corruption) which give her 'a greater sense of control of her situation'. Despite saying that she likes 'the idea of there being law and order', this is not a conservative position. 'If corruption is exposed then I am more likely to find law and order.' Her main pleasure in cop shows is thus not the Sparks/Bourdieu repetition of the taken-for-granted world of 'natural' police justice (Sparks, 1992: 50), but rather 'down-to-earth documentaries' which 'exposed' and 'probed' police corruption.

Similarly, she enjoys 'comic' television series which young people watch, like *Frontline* (an Australian series parodying current affairs personnel) and *Good News Week* (an Australian wisecracking, politically critical and irreverent current-affairs/quiz show) that 'send up tabloid television' or 'are using humour to capture the interest especially of young people and encouraging them to probe, to look behind the superficial. And there are comic females on the radio who encourage girls to reject sexist society and female roles, encourage the girls to explore more areas.'

Angela's 'critical realist' position (enjoying shows which 'probe' beneath the 'surface of appearances') and her belief that aspects of the media increasingly are helping us to probe and not hide corruption helps her, she says, 'to handle issues of crime and fear of crime'. She picks her way across television's genres, a 'bricoleur' who tactically enjoys this comic show here, that documentary there because they make her feel more empowered.

(iii) Images, stories, rhetorics, genres and political narratives: reassurance or distraction?

It is clear which aspects of the media Angela 'uses, tests, elaborates or finds wanting' (Sparks, 1992). Like Julie, Angela is on the Left politically, and both these women have a strong suspicion about police and other 'authorities'. Julie, for example, enjoys most science fiction and fantasy series which emphasize 'government conspiracy':

I really like the government conspiracy ones. I especially like [the American] *The Pretender* – nasty government agency doing all sorts of funny experiments on children. One of them grows up and escapes and is being chased by the agency. It's the fear of authority getting at you, but the fear more of what they're doing out there than what they're doing to me; and I like the aspect of escaping from authority and getting even with them. I really, really like that aspect of *The Pretender*.

Angela, in contrast, is more reassured by the politics of watching probing documentaries and comedy shows which encourage young people to question violence, racism and conservative government. Sara, on the other hand, can find no reassurance anywhere in the media. Even her favoured *A Current Affair* (an Australian nightly current-affairs programme) 'often looks at drugs'. Sara is a very anxious viewer; and like Sparks, Gunter has argued that 'the anxious viewer should find comfort and relief in drama because it ultimately reduces their anxieties by projecting a just world . . . [via] the ultimate triumph of justice' (Gunter, 1987: 92). This is clearly not the case with Sara. Rather, she now reinterprets the same police shows she watched before her husband died, finding them more 'realistic' and therefore more frightening now she is alone: 'That's the trouble, they're getting too much like what's happening out on the streets.'

But Sara's information about what is happening in the streets outside is derived mainly from newspapers. She goes out seldom, and never after dark. But she does read the local newspaper and also the Sydney tabloid the *Daily Telegraph*, which are describing to her a world out of control – not just in Sydney (which she says she will not visit), but in her country region too. In particular, she reads the local court cases scrupulously. Nine out of ten cases, she says, are about drugs. Her logic-in-use relates reports of drug taking to her main fear: home invasion. She believes that unemployment and drugs are the main reason for young people increasingly breaking into homes nowadays. It also seems to be the 'home invasion' connected stories that most catch her attention in the local paper. She could not recall, for example, a front-page news item in the local newspaper a couple of months previously of an armed robbery at a local betting office in the shopping centre only a couple of blocks from her home! Yet she did remember, and was obviously disturbed by, TV news coverage at the same time of the bashing of an old man. Though this was in Sydney, and the armed robbery was almost next door, the home attack on an older person was much closer to her.

Sixteen-year-old Lisa, unlike the much older Sara, is still looking to TV for ways to help manage her fears, although, as she gets older she looks at television less, because 'You experience more, whereas television kind of trivializes. You realize it's not like that at all, as they show it on TV shows.' Though Lisa fears items on the news, she doesn't believe this genre helps her with her own personal experiences. TV, she says, goes for the ratings. You do not see the 'ordinary events' (e.g. sexual molesting within the family) but rather 'the big paedophile rings'. The fears she has experienced – sexual abuse in the family, mugging, a drug-addict mother – are imaged on TV, but in genres Lisa dismisses as 'not believable' like cop series. Meanwhile, the 'real' genres like the news, which she does take notice of, do not cover them to her satisfaction.

In these media case studies I have been exploring (via 'talk' rather than 'texts') Sparks' agendas:

> What are the pleasures that people take in the shock/reaffirmation of cop shows? This varies from Sara's total rejection to Julie's pleasure in the occasional representation of good-looking but tough female cops; from Lisa's dissatisfaction with the 'real' to Angela's 'probing' of police corruption to 'find law and order'.
> How can we address the issue that TV helps build consensual images of 'landscapes of fear' – eg the city and its 'risk'

suburbs – and yet these are 'read' differentially by different social groups? Here we can compare Sara's total 'country' rejection of Sydney with Lisa's differentiation of Rose Bay/ Bondi, with Julie's confidence everywhere in the city – except when she went to 'race riot' cities in the USA! (See Tulloch *et al.*, 1998b: 237–8.)

Does TV crime such as police series address us as fearful privatists? Yes in Sara's case (but then she doesn't allow it to address her at all); no (news does) in Lisa's; and quite the contrary for the 'lefties' Julie and Angela.

Do its narrative devices commonly 'hook' an audience? Sara does prefer the 'good guy' to win, but this certainly doesn't hook her; the others are too cynical about Australian police to believe the police are good guys.

Do TV crime series, as Sparks suggests, routinely reproduce the cultural salience of social anxiety about crime and law enforcement? It is rather news and current-affairs material about police corruption which has done this in Australia in recent years; though we found that older people used some drama series nostalgically to argue for a return to 'bobbies on the beat'.

Overall, in my very brief outline here of our 'train' and 'media' studies, I have tried to give a flavour of the key concepts used in our situated analysis of fear of crime. These were:

negotiation of meanings as personal/social practices;

place as situational context (landscapes of fear);

time (biographical/locational/historical);

everyday routine (including the routine management of fear via media, local gossip, talk, etc.);

agency/structure;

judgements (perceptions) of fear;

values (competing priorities);

emotions (and outrage);

behaviours (not just avoidance but also individual agency in controlling fear);

circulating rhetorics and hermeneutics (media/ local);

gender/age/class/ethnicity/sexual preference;

knowledgeability ('expert/lay').

In a research programme so strongly oriented to an 'ethnography of storytelling', this can only be a very partial account. I have focused here on women's 'stories'; to encounter others (of ethnicity, sexual preference, class, etc.) – and also the reflexivity of our own 'representational order' – the reader is encouraged to consult our two main reports (Tulloch *et al.*, 1998a, 1998b).

Conclusion

In this chapter I have drawn attention to the long-term dominance in the media and fear of crime area of Gerbner's 'cultivation' and 'mean-world' theories; and to the fact that very little of the debate in this area has been taking place in relation to sociocultural theories of risk. Via a brief 'mapping' of the epistemologies of risk theory (and its media theory implications) I then pointed to some of the strengths and weaknesses of media-related work in these different fields. Finally, I drew on some of the more valuable of the culturalist and textualist work in the fear of crime and media area – particularly concepts from Ian Taylor and Richard Sparks – to indicate (via our own research project) ways in which risk theory's emphasis on 'lay knowledgeability' could throw new light on an old debate. Our own 'representational order' (Ang, 1996) was profiled as calling for a reintegration of empirical work with theory, of cultural materialist and poststructuralist 'storytelling', and of analysis of the production of texts with the production of daily circuits of communication.

REFERENCES

Ang, I. (1996) *Living Room Wars: Rethinking Media Audiences for a Postmodern World*. London: Routledge.
Brown, J. (ed.) (1989) *Environmental Threats: Perception, Analysis and Management*. London: Bellhaven Press.
Brown, J. and Campbell E. (1991) Risk communication: some underlying principles. *International Journal of Environmental Studies*, 38, 297–303.
Chan, J. (1994) Crime prevention and the lure of relevance: a response to Adam Sutton. *Australian and New Zealand Journal of Criminology*, 27, 25–9.
Gerbner, C. (1970) Cultural indicators: the case of violence and television drama. *Annals of the American Association of Political and Social Science*, 338, 69–81.
Gerbner, G. and Gross, L. (1976) Living with television: the violence profile. *Journal of Communication*, 26(2), 173–99.
Gerbner, G., Gross, L., Morgan, M. and Signorelli, N. (1980) The mainstreaming of America: violence profile. *Journal of Communication*, 30(11), 10–29.
Gerbner, G., Gross, L., Morgan, M., Signorelli, N. and Jackson-Beech, M. (1978) Cultural indicators: violence profile. *Journal of Communication*, 29(9), 176–207.
Giddens, A. (1994) Living in a post-traditional society. In Beck, U., Giddens, A.

and Lash, S., *Reflexive Modernization: Politics, Tradition and Aesthetics in the Modern Social Order*. Cambridge: Polity Press.

Gunter, B. (1987) *Television and the Fear of Crime*. London: John Libbey & Co.

Hale, C. (1996) Fear of crime: a review of the literature. *International Review of Victimology*, 3(3), 211-33.

Handmer, J. (1995) Communicating uncertainty: perspectives and themes. In Norton T., Beer, T. and Dovers, S. (eds.), *Risk Uncertainty in Environmental Management*. Canberra: Australian Academy of Science.

Lovell, T. (1980) *Pictures of Reality*. London: British Film Institute.

O'Malley, P. (1994) Responsibility and crime prevention: a response to Adam Sutton. *Australian and New Zealand Journal of Criminology*, 27, 21–4.

Osborne, R. (1995) Crime and the media: from media studies to postmodernism. In Kield-Hewitt, D. and Osborne, R. (eds.), *Crime and the Media: the Postmodern Spectacle*. London: Pluto.

Pawson, R. and Tilley, N. (1994) What works in evaluation research? *British Journal of Criminology*, 34(3), 291–301.

Schlesinger, P., Dobash, R. E., Dobash, R. P. and Weaver, C. K. (1992) *Women Viewing Violence*. London: British Film Institute.

Sparks, R. (1992) *Television and the Drama of Crime: Moral Tales and the Place of Crime in Public Life*. Buckingham: Open University Press.

Sutton, A. (1994) Crime prevention: promise or threat? *Australian and New Zealand Journal of Criminology*, 27, 5–20.

Taylor, I. (1995) Private homes and public others: an analysis of talk about crime in suburban South Manchester in the mid-1990s. *British Journal of Criminology*, 35(2), 263–85.

Tudor, A. (1995) Culture, mass communication and social agency. *Theory, Culture and Society*, 12, 81–107.

Tulloch, J., Lupton, D., Blood, W., Tulloch, M., Enders, M. and Jennett, C. (1998a) *Fear of Crime, Volume I: Audit of the Literature and Community Programmes*. Canberra: Attorney General's Department.

(1998b) *Fear of Crime, Volume II: The Fieldwork Research*. Canberra: Attorney General's Department.

Williams, R. (1989) *The Politics of Modernism*. Oxford: New Left Books.

Wynne, B. (1996) May the sheep safely graze? A reflexive view of the expert–lay knowledge divide. In Lash, L., Szerszynski, B. and Wynne, B.(eds.), *Risk, Environment and Modernity: Towards a New Ecology*. London: Sage.

Young, A. (1996) In the frame: crime and the limits of representation. *Australian and New Zealand Journal of Criminology*, 29(2), 99–101.

3 Risk and the ontology of pregnant embodiment

Deborah Lupton

Introduction

In an article in a weekend newspaper supplement, entitled 'Mother love gone wrong', Elizabeth Bellamy writes of her experience of what was professionally diagnosed as Obsessive-Compulsive Disorder. She has suffered from this twice in her life – both times when she was pregnant. The disorder first manifested itself when she was five months pregnant with her first child as an extreme worry that something she ate or did would harm her foetus: 'I came to believe that *every* familiar object was contaminated in some way – food, crockery, cutlery, clothes, sheets, books, and so on. The world was swarming with harmful bacteria that I couldn't control or eradicate' (Bellamy, 1998: 16, original emphasis). In the first episode of this state of anxiety, Bellamy was admitted to a psychiatric hospital ward for five weeks. She recovered completely when her baby was born healthy. 'As I had tried to explain to the doctors, I was only concerned about the health of the baby. I didn't give a damn about me' (16). After much deliberation, Bellamy and her husband decided to have another child. This time, she dealt with her fears not by attempting to discount them, but by giving in to them. She washed her hands repeatedly and only ate food that she prepared herself. As a result, she was able to cope with her anxieties about the foetus' health and did not require psychiatric treatment. Again, her anxieties and obsessions vanished with the birth of her baby.

This woman's experience is clearly extreme. It was treated by professionals and represented by the woman herself as an individual's psychiatric disorder, a rare pathological response to pregnancy. But what Bellamy describes may also be interpreted as an exaggerated outcome of the intense focus on the pregnant woman's body in contemporary western societies and the emotional states and impetus towards self-regulatory behaviour that this provokes. At the end of the twentieth century the pregnant woman is surrounded by a complex network of discourses and practices directed at the surveillance and regulation of her body. No longer a single body, but one harbouring the potentiality of another human, the more obviously pregnant a woman becomes, the more she is rendered the subject of others' appraisal and advice. Risk is a central discourse among those that surround the pregnant woman. Much of the appraisal and advice she receives is directed at containing risks, both those threatening her own health, but even more intensely, those threatening the wellbeing of the foetus that she carries.

It is a commonplace in sociological, anthropological and philosophical discussions of human embodiment to argue that we tend not to be highly aware of our bodies unless we are in illness or pain, or experiencing hunger, thirst, sexual desire or other pressing bodily needs. Leder (1990), for example, describes the body as ontologically 'absent' in this state of lack of consciousness of embodiment. This assumption of bodily absence, however, may be challenged for its universality, its presentation of embodiment as lacking a gender. As many feminist commentators have pointed out, women have traditionally been positioned as embodied subjects in ways that men have not, and their inherent embodiment – their supposed emotional and physical lability – has been used as evidence of their inferiority to men. Women's appearance, their deportment of their bodies, are subject to continuing surveillance and control, both on the part of women themselves and of others. Many women in contemporary western societies find it difficult to forget their bodies, whether in public or alone. They are constantly aware of the appraising gaze of others of their appearance. They take vigilant steps not to let such female bodily processes as menstruation and the hot flushes of menopause come to others' attention, and attempt to contain the fleshy, female parts of their bodies, rendering them hard and taut (Bordo, 1993; Heywood, 1996).

In pregnancy, the woman's embodiment is brought even more to the fore. Young argues that the pregnant woman goes into 'aesthetic mode': 'that is, we become aware of ourselves as body and take an interest in its sensations and limitations for their own sake, experiencing them as a fullness rather than a lack' (1990: 165). This attendance to the body and the changes that are wrought through pregnancy, she argues, is not experienced as alienation from the body, as the experience of illness tends to promote. As she writes of her own experience of the pregnant body: 'I merely notice its borders and rumblings with interest, sometimes with pleasure, and this aesthetic interest does not divert me from my business' (165). As this suggests, Young's portrayal of pregnant embodiment, first written some years ago, presents only its pleasurable or interesting aspects. It does not take into account those bodily sensations or signs that may cause anxiety, fear or ambivalence in a woman who is pregnant because of her heightened awareness of risk, her concern about her own health and the normality and wellbeing of her foetus.

This chapter discusses issues of the ontology of the pregnant body as it is constructed and experienced through the discourses, knowledges and strategies of risk. In doing so, various sociocultural theorists' writings on risk will be employed to explore dimensions of risk at various levels of meaning, from the social structural to the cultural and symbolic. The insights of these theorists will be complemented by a focus in the chapter on popular representations of risk in pregnancy and discussion of pregnant women's lived experience of risk. The latter is achieved via a review of previous empirical research on risk and pregnancy and by drawing upon data from an empirical study exploring aspects of first-time motherhood.[1] In this longitudinal study, twenty-five Australian women were interviewed several times, beginning from just before the birth of their first child to three years after the birth. The data here discussed come from the first interview with the women, when they were in the last days of their pregnancy.

Risk discourse and the government of pregnancy

For scholars drawing on Foucault's work on governmentality (see, for example, Foucault 1984, 1991), the centrality of risk discourse in relation to pregnancy can be linked to apparatuses of 'biopolitics' in neo-liberal societies, efforts on the part of the state and other agencies to discipline and normalize citizens, to render them docile and productive bodies. One of these apparatuses, that of normalization, involves gathering information about populations and subpopulations and subjecting it to statistical analysis. Through normalization, individuals may be compared to others, their attributes assessed according to whether they fall within the norm or outside it. If found to fall outside the norm, people are routinely encouraged (or sometimes coerced) to engage in practices that bring them closer to the norm. Risk is a pivotal discourse in strategies of normalization, used to gloss the potential for deviations from the norm. To be designed 'at high risk' compared with others is to be singled out as requiring expert advice, surveillance and self-regulation.

A central aspect of governmentality in neo-liberal societies is the idealized figure of the autonomous, self-regulated citizen. Such individuals voluntarily seek to maximize their life opportunities and minimize the risks to which they are exposed. They police their own behaviour and need only guidance and advice from 'expert' knowledges to engage in activities that serve their best interests (Gordon, 1991). This emphasis on self-regulation is strongly evident in discourses on health and risk emerging from public health institutions (Lupton, 1995; Petersen and Lupton, 1996). A focus on self-responsibility for health states began to emerge as a governmental strategy in the eighteenth century. Health became 'at once the duty of each and the objective of all' (Foucault, 1984: 277). Foucault claims that from the middle of the eighteenth century, the family unit became a particularly important element for governmental surveillance and disciplinary purposes, developing into 'the most constant agent of medicalization' (280). The problem of 'the child' was constructed through discourses on the regulation of the family, with parents – and in particular, mothers – charged with the responsibility of monitoring and facilitating their children's development, growth and health. Since then, women have been constructed as active citizens not through participation in the public sphere, as is the case with men, but rather predominantly through their responsibilities in caring for the health and wellbeing of others, particularly as wives and mothers. Their efforts in fulfilling these responsibilities are aligned with those of the state through risk and public health discourses (Petersen and Lupton, 1996: chapter 3).

In the late twentieth century, the concern with the health of the child has reached back to even before its conception, via the introduction of new technologies, such as ultrasound. Such technologies produce visual images of the foetus that represent it as a separate being from the mother, floating serenely in amniotic fluid. As a result, the notion of the foetus as contained to 'inside' the woman's body, of pregnancy as an 'interior' experience has been disrupted (Petchesky, 1987: 65). The foetus has moved from the realm of private experience, the sensations and emotions felt by the pregnant woman, to the status of the 'public foetus', the object of externalized mechanisms of surveillance and regulation. Pregnant women's views of their experiences no longer primarily construct medical notions of their foetus' health, wellbeing and growth. Rather, medical technologies of visualization, laboratory test results and written reports about the foetus, to which the woman has no access except through expert intervention and interpretation are the dominant source of knowledge (Weir, 1996: 376).[2]

Through such technologies and knowledges, the foetus has become invested with an individual identity apart from that of the mother. As the emphasis on the health and wellbeing of the foetus has intensified, the pregnant woman has become portrayed predominantly as the 'maternal environment' in which the foetus grows (Rothman, 1994: 114). This shift towards foetal risk has had significant implications for the experience of pregnancy. As Weir puts it, 'As the main object in the population-based risk management of pregnancy, the foetus has become implicated in a remoralization of pregnancy' (1996: 373). Despite the discursive separation of foetus from woman's body, the pregnant woman remains positioned as responsible for the foetus' wellbeing. Her body, therefore, is constructed as doubly at risk and she is portrayed as doubly responsible, for two bodies. Her unborn child is typically represented in expert discourses as fragile, highly vulnerable, its development susceptible to a multitude of threats.

Contemporary knowledges and discourses on risk emerge from both expert and lay sites, but it is the experts who hold most sway because of the assumed 'scientific' and 'neutral' character of their knowledges. Expert knowledge on pregnancy has proliferated throughout the century, with the recent emergence of such specialities focused on the foetus as foetal medicine and genetic counselling. Expert concepts of risk as they are applied to pregnancy relate to two types of risk knowledges: clinical risk and epidemiological risk. These approaches serve to render the risks attendant upon pregnancy as calculable and governable, thus bringing them into being as problems that require action. Clinical risk is based upon the characteristics of case studies of individuals observed by experts. Epidemiological risk is calculated through the observation of patterns in anonymous populations of disease and the identification of associated risk factors (see Dean, this volume). Both types of risk knowledges are normalizing, locating the individual woman within a framework of comparisons to many other women. The collective results of diagnostic tests on populations establish a norm against which a particular pregnant woman's health and the development and growth of her foetus may be compared. Any major deviation from the norm is defined as 'abnormal', evidence of 'high risk' that requires further medical intervention. In the case of foetuses, this medical intervention often takes the form of therapeutic abortion.

It would be difficult for a pregnant woman not to become drawn into the discourses of risk that surround her. Most medical and many lay discourses tend to represent the pregnant body itself as inevitably deviating from the norm, as vulnerable and susceptible to a range of ills and risks. Recent media and other popular accounts of infertility, particularly that which may be suffered by women who delay childbearing until they are in their 30s, tend to foster this sense of contingency, of being unable to trust one's own body. Where once bourgeois Victorian women were warned that their luxurious lifestyle might lead to infertility, contemporary middle-class women who delay childbearing are told that they might find themselves too old to reproduce when they eventually make the attempt (Shuttleworth, 1993/1994). As one Australian magazine article about women suffering infertility put it:

You can try pencilling in the diary – January stop Pill, April get pregnant, but at thirtysomething and unless you're very lucky, Nature is unlikely to oblige by fitting in with your busy schedule. Fertility is a percentage game – the odds against conceiving lengthen with the years – and though late goals are possible, you may need to do an awful lot of running up and down the field to score. (Wheatley, 1993: 32)

Women are advised by health experts to take special steps in preparing their bodies for motherhood and to maximize the chances of conception. They are encouraged to have a gynaecological checkup, to maintain a good diet, exercise regularly (but not too strenuously), to avoid alcohol and other drugs and take daily folic acid vitamin supplements to prevent the risk of their foetus developing spina bifida or a cleft palate. After pregnancy is confirmed, the risks associated with pregnancy itself come to the fore. Pregnant women are encouraged to be highly vigilant in their policing of their bodies so as to ensure that the health of their foetus, is not compromised by their own actions. Tobacco and alcohol are represented as highly toxic to the foetus, and women are strongly advised not to smoke or drink alcohol at all during their pregnancy, and to avoid situations where they might be exposed to passive smoking.

The risks of the deportment of the pregnant woman extend even as far as her emotional state. In the Victorian era, women were advised by medical experts and in maternity handbooks to avoid strong emotions during pregnancy, for fear of affecting the temperament and physical constitution of the child. Some contemporary handbooks for pregnant women espouse similar ideas, warning women that any ambivalence they feel about their pregnancy may be conveyed to the foetus, leading to a greater likelihood of difficult birth and a child with physical and behavioural problems (Shuttleworth, 1993/1994). A recent Australian newspaper article reported the findings of one study (extrapolating from research with sheep) that suggested that the foetuses carried by women who were exposed to high stress in the first trimester of pregnancy were more likely to develop high blood pressure as adults. The researcher was quoted as advising that 'pregnant women under stress should count to 10 in high-stress situations' (*Sydney Morning Herald*, 8 May 1998). As Shuttleworth notes, such exhortations to women to control their emotional states for the sake of the foetus may have a counter-productive effect, for they 'necessarily engender the very state of emotional agitation that they are warning against' (1993/1994: 38).

Contemporary handbooks for mothers-to-be make it clear that the responsibility for a good pregnancy and production of a normal infant remains with the mother, tending to highlight the most extreme views in medical discourses on the risks that might affect a foetus. In one best-selling handbook for pregnant women, the American *What to Expect When You're Expecting* (Eisenberg, Murkoff and Hathaway, 1997), women are told that as well as avoiding any consumption of alcohol and tobacco (and illicit drugs such as marijuana and cocaine), they should avoid spending time in rooms with people who smoke, give up tea, coffee and cola drinks, avoid certain sugar substitutes, not take spa baths, ensure that their microwave ovens do not leak potentially harmful microwaves, not use electric blankets, avoid having diagnostic x-rays, be careful in using household cleaning products and insecticides and not take prescription or over-the-counter therapeutic drugs (even headache pills) if possible. Readers are advised to embark on a careful diet that maximizes vitamins, protein and minerals and avoids all sugary and fatty foods, which are only 'empty calories'. As the authors of this handbook counsel:

You've got only nine months of meals and snacks with which to give your baby the best possible start in life. Make every one of them count. Before you close your mouth on a forkful of food, consider, "Is this the best bite I can give my baby?" If it will benefit your baby, chew away. If it'll only benefit your sweet tooth or appease your appetite, put your fork down. (Eisenberg, Murkoff and Hathaway, 1997: 74)

In such handbooks, women are also told that they must be highly careful about food hygiene, for bacteria and parasites causing illnesses such as listeria and toxoplasmosis may cause foetal abnormality and miscarriage. To prevent this, women are advised that they should ensure that they wash their hands thoroughly before cooking and eating, wash all fruit and vegetables carefully (ideally with detergent) and avoid touching raw meat and eating meat that is not thoroughly cooked.

Pregnant women are expected to attend regular antenatal checks, undergoing a series of urine and blood tests and internal examinations. Their weight and blood pressure are regularly checked. Other medical tests, such as the maternal serum or triple test (involving a blood sample from the woman that is screened for various components indicating the normality of the foetus), amniocentesis (tests on a sample of amniotic fluid drawn from the uterus by a needle, used to diagnose chromosomal defects such as Down's Syndrome), chorionic villus sampling (CVS, also a test used to detect chromosomal defects, using tissue taken from the uterus) and ultrasound (magnetic resonance imaging of the foetus) are directed solely at the foetus. In Australia and many other western countries, the information gained from antenatal checks is entered into a card, which the pregnant woman takes with her to each visit. This card becomes the repository of the woman's risk factors, designating her as being at 'high' or 'low risk'. This designation may mean that the woman is at risk herself from a negative health outcome from the pregnancy, or that her foetus is at risk, or both. Even the woman deemed to be 'low risk' remains subject to a high level of expert surveillance and is expected to exert a continuing self-surveillance of her body. In reality, therefore, there is no such thing as 'no risk' in pregnancy, for the potential is ever present for danger to threaten foetal wellbeing, particularly if a woman should let her guard down.

The proliferation of risk discourse around pregnancy and the accompanying assumption that women should take care to avoid risk as much as possible has had the effect of rendering pregnancy as a perilous journey, requiring eternal vigilance on the part of the woman travelling through it. As Tsing observes, 'pregnancy, childbirth, and child rearing are no longer seen as easy and "natural" routes to womanhood, but as fraught with sacrifices, perils, and challenges that women must surmount' (1990: 282). The implications of risk discourse in relation to pregnancy is that the woman who fails to heed expert advice is portrayed as posing a risk to her foetus. Tsing points to the intensification of discourse around 'monster mothers' in the mass media at the end of the twentieth century, or those mothers who are charged with causing harm to their children. Such stories, she claims, are demonstrative of a new public agenda on motherhood, in which foetuses and children are represented as requiring protection from their own mothers and the female body is represented predominantly as a source of danger for foetuses. Tsing notes how women who give birth without medical assistance are now typically portrayed in the American media as 'monster mothers' regardless of the reason why they did so. Such women, who typically are members of marginalized or disadvantaged social groups, are seen as calculating, callous criminals who have little concern for the welfare of their children.

The societal response to these women springs from a number of assumptions, including that responsible pregnant women should seek close supervision and assistance from medical practitioners and that healthy babies can only be delivered under medical supervision. While it may be considered irresponsible and lazy for individuals to neglect their own health care, it is considered criminal for pregnant women to avoid continuing prenatal care and medical care at birth, as they are seen to be placing the health of their foetus at risk. In the United States, women can now be charged with 'prenatal child abuse' or 'foetal abuse' for such actions as using medically unauthorized drugs (including legal drugs such as alcohol) while pregnant or disregarding doctors' orders or giving birth vaginally when ordered by the court to have a caesarean section (Tsing, 1990; Handwerker, 1994). Tsing argues that the new perinatal vigilance calls attention to an agenda that 'isolates female reproductive experience from every other aspect of women's lives, requiring that pregnancy be a transcendent moment that can carry every woman outside the complexity of her particular history' (1990: 297).

The emphasis placed on risk in pregnancy and childbirth is itself part of a broader development in contemporary subjectivity: that which presents one's life and self as a 'planning project', requiring constant work and attention on the part of the individual (Beck and Beck-Gernsheim, 1995; Beck-Gernsheim, 1996). This project of the self (see also Foucault, 1988), involves planning and rationalization, and depends upon individualization, or the progressive freeing of the life course from traditional norms, beliefs, expectations and social relations that has emerged in the wake of industrial society. This version of subjectivity brings with it, as Beck-Gernsheim notes, both new possibilities and new burdens: 'on the one hand, that means an expansion of the radius of life, a gain in terms of scope and choice. Life becomes in many respects more open and malleable. But it also means that new demands, controls and obligations fall upon the individual' (1996: 140). Because people are now viewed as taking more responsibility for life outcomes, negative events come to be seen as their 'fault'.

Beck-Gernsheim points to a number of social changes over this century that have resulted in increasing emphasis being placed on parents' intervention into their children's life chances. The expert-knowledge systems of medicine, psychology and child education have focused on the opportunities for avoiding or ameliorating mental or physical problems in children. Family sizes have become much smaller, so that many children have only one sibling or are only children, meaning that they are the object of less divided attention from their parents.[3] Children have become viewed as 'a "scarce resource", whose success must be ensured' (Beck-Gernsheim, 1996: 143). The child has been invested with meaning as a source of emotional authenticity and personal fulfilment for its parents, its success reflecting parental achievement (Beck and Beck-Gernsheim, 1995: chapter 4). Nippert-Eng (1996: 203) refers to the discourse of the 'sacred child', in which children are represented as 'precious entities entrusted to adults' care, deserving the very best from us'. The quest for the 'perfect child' means that any flaws perceived in children are viewed as targets for intervention, preferably to be prevented before they are even able to manifest themselves. Parents – and particularly mothers – are charged with the primary responsibility of maximizing the potential of their children. It is assumed that there is a great deal of agency on the part of the parent to do so. The emphasis placed on reducing risk in pregnancy is part of the greater goal of creating the 'best possible' child.

Changes in women's opportunities for participation in the labour market and expectations about their societal role are also influencing the intensification of discourses of risk in relation to pregnancy. Many women, particularly those with high levels of education and professional careers from which they derive a high level of personal satisfaction, no longer see their lives as devoted solely to the family. Rather, they position themselves as bourgeois, autonomous entrepreneurs, seeking to achieve success and recognition in the workplace. Because of the inherent structural and symbolic contradictions between paid labour and motherhood, however: 'having children is today *the* structural risk of a female wage-earning biography: indeed, it is a handicap, measured by the yardstick of a market society' (Beck-Gernsheim, 1996: 146, original emphasis). If having a normal child is a handicap, then having a disabled child is even worse in terms of a woman's prospects in the paid workplace and capacity for autonomy and self-improvement.

Living risk: the embodied experience of pregnancy

From the moment of conception the social management of pregnancy and birth imposes a contradictory sense of omnipotence on a mother. She is in other people's hands, yet feels herself to be responsible for producing a healthy baby with a good birth experience. To herself, she is both huge and horribly small. She can experience a wonderful plenitude coexisting with terror of emptiness, loss and fear of failure. (Parker, 1997: 32)

The introduction of new technologies for determining the 'normality' of foetuses has resulted in pregnant women being forced to deal with risk statistics in making decisions about whether or not to have a test and what to do should the test suggest a foetal abnormality. In Australia, women over the age of thirty-five in some states, and thirty-seven in others, are offered amniocentesis or CVS to check for chromosomal abnormalities in the foetus. In deciding whether to take the test, they must weigh up the risk of the test itself causing a spontaneous abortion (estimated at about 1 in 100 for CVS and 1 in 200 for amniocentesis) and the risk of an abnormality (which for many conditions increases with the mother's age). Many women are now offered the 'triple test' as an alternative to the more invasive amniocentesis and CVS. The triple test, however, although it does not pose a risk to the foetus, is not very sensitive, failing to pick up abnormalities in some foetuses and returning false positives to other women. These women must then decide whether to undergo amniocentesis, with its attendant risks, to determine whether their foetus does definitely have the abnormality. Nonetheless, the 'triple test' is being accepted by a rapidly increasing number of pregnant women. In some states in Australia, it is offered to all pregnant women and most of them take it, and in the United States it is also routinely administered to pregnant women (Rothman, 1994: 263). In Australia, terminations of foetuses with Down's Syndrome have risen sharply since the introduction of this test (Eccleston, 1996).

The more such tests are introduced, the more intensified the discourses of risk that surround the pregnant woman and the more choices she is faced with making. The new possibilities of action embodied in the introduction of technologies such as prenatal diagnosis of chromosomal and other defects in foetuses makes for often difficult choices for women and exerts a subtle pressure to conform to expectations about undergoing such tests and aborting the foetus should they prove to give a negative result (Beck-Gernsheim, 1996: 147). Should the test be taken? How should the results be interpreted? What course of action should be taken if the findings suggest an abnormality? Some critics have seen the proliferation of prenatal testing technologies as evidence of a 'new eugenics' discourse that represents more and more genetic and other 'defects' as detracting from perfection and not to be tolerated. Stanworth (1987: 32) questions, for example, whether such technologies might not come to overwhelm attempts to improve the prospects of people with disease and disability and serve to create an environment in which human variability is not allowed to flourish. Others have criticized what they see as the unnecessary monitoring of women using such technologies as ultrasound, the long-term effects of which on the foetus have not yet been tested, and the increasing medicalization of pregnancy they see as being the outcome of the expanding use of prenatal screening (Oakley, 1987).

Because such technologies as amniocentesis and ultrasound exist, a woman may now be held personally accountable for her baby's disability if she decides not to undergo the tests. An American woman interviewed for a study on prenatal screening noted the burden of control that had now been laid upon her to produce the 'perfect' baby:

I was hoping that I'd never have to make this choice, to become responsible for choosing the kind of baby I'd get, the kind of baby we'd accepted. But everyone – my doctor, my parents, my friends – everyone urged me to come for genetic counseling and have amniocentesis. Now, I guess I'm having a modern baby. And they all told me I'd feel more in control. But in some ways, I feel less in control. Oh, it's still my baby, but only if it's good enough to be our baby, if you see what I mean. (quoted in Rapp, 1988: 152)

At the time in the pregnancy when diagnosis of disorders or abnormalities are made by amniocentesis and ultrasound (around eighteen to
twenty weeks' gestation), most women would have begun to feel foetal
movements and have seen the ultrasound image of their foetus. Those
women who are faced with the decision of whether or not to terminate
their foetus because of an abnormality often find it very difficult and
highly emotionally distressing. As one woman interviewed for a magazine article who had chosen to terminate a foetus diagnosed with
Down's Syndrome said: 'it was the hardest thing I've ever done . . . I
kept trying to make excuses, I didn't want to go through with it. But
even though I knew I had to do it, it was still harder in the actual doing
than I had expected . . . Let's not gloss over it. I killed my baby.'
Another woman with the same diagnosis decided to continue with the
pregnancy, commenting that: 'Whatever the decision we would feel
some guilt . . . If we terminated we'd feel guilty about not giving him a
chance because he was less than perfect' (both quoted in Eccleston,
1996).

Prenatal screening technologies have the potential to shape the emotional responses of a pregnant woman and her partner to the foetus. The
point at which the foetus becomes a 'real' entity, or at which the
pregnancy is accepted as 'existing' and 'normal' may be altered through
the experiences of undergoing tests and waiting for their results. Different tests may have opposing consequences: 'ultrasound makes the foetus
more our baby, while the possibility of abortion [related to undergoing
such tests as the triple test and amniocentesis] makes us want to keep
our emotional distance in case the pregnancy isn't going to end up with
a baby after all' (Hubbard, 1984: 335). Rothman (1994) refers to the
'tentative pregnancy' as that experienced by women who wait for
reassurance from prenatal tests before allowing themselves to feel happy
and optimistic about the pregnancy. For many of the women who
undergo prenatal tests, however, particularly for those who eventually
receive a favourable result, far from feeling victimized, distressed or
rendered passive by the technology, it is viewed as a very positive
experience, assuaging their fears and anxieties about the foetus' normality and creating a feeling of intimacy with the foetus. As Petchesky
notes: 'like amniocentesis, in-vitro fertilization, voluntary sterilization
and other "male-dominated" reproductive technologies, ultrasound
imaging in pregnancy seems to evoke in many women a sense of greater
control and self-empowerment than they would have if left to "traditional" methods or "nature"' (1987: 72).

Women's responses to discourses of risk and prenatal testing are
therefore highly variable. As commentators such as Rapp (1988, 1990),

Handwerker (1994) and Rothman (1994) have pointed out, for example, the meanings of 'normality' and 'disability' vary depending on the sociocultural context and the meanings of the pregnancy in a woman's life. Such aspects as whether a woman became pregnant easily or experienced years of infertility before achieving a pregnancy, her previous experiences of pregnancy or miscarriage, how old she is, her beliefs about abortion, her ethnicity and social class and her partner's and family members' attitudes to her pregnancy may structure the way in which she responds to the risk discourse around prenatal screening. A clear social class and ethnicity distinction is evident, for example, in some studies. Rapp's (1990) study of women in New York City who had been offered an amniocentesis test because of their age (over thirty-five) found that white, middle-class women were more likely to agree to have the test and to have an abortion if the foetus was found to have Down's Syndrome. Women from less privileged backgrounds or who were of non-Northern-European ethnicity tended to have a more accepting attitude of the disability or made the decision to trust in fate or God's will and not take the test. For the middle-class women who postpone motherhood in favour of their careers, 'individual self-development looms large as a cultural goal' (Rapp, 1990: 39). Motherhood and the attendant risks of having a child with a defect offers more problems for such women, for it challenges their sense of having control over their lives and undermines their desire to have as 'perfect' a child as possible.

It would seem, however, that most pregnant women feel anxious about the possibility of having an abnormal foetus, and that many of them actively seek out prenatal testing as a means of alleviating their fears. A study of women who had recently given birth at a major hospital in Melbourne sought to identify the extent of the sense of risk they felt during their pregnancy (Searle, 1996). Using a questionnaire and one-to-one interviews, the study revealed an extremely high level of anxiety and fear in the women during their pregnancy, centred on the wellbeing of their foetus. Although most women judged the risk of having a baby with an abnormality to be far less than official statistics estimate, the majority said that they sometimes or often felt anxious about having an abnormal baby themselves. This high level of anxiety was found across sociodemographic groups, but was particularly the case of women having their first child, or those who knew of someone who had had an abnormal baby. More than half the participants also reported feeling anxious sometimes or a lot that their pregnancy would be abnormal, with most worried about it resulting in complications that might place the foetus at risk rather than being concerned about their own health.

The women were worried that they would be blamed for a defect in the foetus, and expressed fears about how they would be able to cope with a disabled child. They were extremely positive about the ability of routine prenatal screening tests to offer them some reassurance and reduce their fear and anxiety while pregnant, even though while waiting for the results they were highly worried about the possibility of the tests showing an abnormality.

In our own study on first-time motherhood, the women who participated were not directly asked about risk in pregnancy. They were, however, encouraged to give a detailed account of their experience of pregnancy, and these accounts often raised risk-related issues. Many of the women noted, for example, that when they first discovered that they were pregnant they did not want to tell any others (apart from their partners) about their condition, because of their fears that the pregnancy would miscarry. Dianne, for example, didn't tell anyone outside her immediate family until twelve weeks into the pregnancy:

because I know that there is a higher risk of miscarriage in those first few weeks, so having to tell people and then if anything had gone wrong in those first few weeks, you'd be upset. Which has just happened to a friend of mine actually, who's just told everyone at six weeks [into the pregnancy] and at eight weeks she's just miscarried. So she's still got people coming up and saying "Congratulations!". She's quite upset.

Melissa, who had been trying to fall pregnant for about a year before it happened, talked about her body in terms of it not having the capacity for pregnancy because of assorted medical problems (including an irregular menstrual cycle, an ovarian cyst earlier in her life that required an operation and serious back problems) and too much stress at work. She had had many different medical tests and treatments in attempting to deal with her infertility. When she finally did become pregnant, she and her partner also made the decision not to tell anyone else about the pregnancy for some time, because her previous health problems had made her feel uncertain that the pregnancy would be successful:

I guess just 'cause I'd had all the cyst problems and the health problems and the back problems and everything else, we just wanted to be sure and didn't want to tell the whole world and then lose the baby or something. And we reached a point then when we thought, 'Well, we'll tell the people who we would tell if we had a miscarriage.' So you know, then I think we told family and just told them to keep quiet for a few weeks.

The twelve- to thirteen-week gestational stage of the pregnancy, Melissa said, was an important milestone for her because she could feel more confident that she would not have a miscarriage. So too was the twenty-seven- to twenty-eight-week stage, because she knew then that the foetus would have some chance of surviving should it be born prematurely. Melissa had started feeling 'really safe' at thirty-six to thirty-seven weeks' gestation because she thought that if the foetus was born it would only be a little premature and would have a very good chance of survival and good health.

Sarah had experienced a bad pregnancy, with many health problems, including severe back pain. The pregnancy was unexpected. As someone who valued control and order in her life, she said that she found becoming pregnant and the health effects of pregnancy distressing. However, she was worried about passing on her negative feelings to her foetus, and did her best to work upon her emotions so as not to do this:

I read some books, but nobody warns you about the real negative aspects and how awful nausea can really be . . . I mean, there were times when I could just couldn't move all day, just constant nausea and dizziness and I couldn't – I had to force myself to drag myself away from the couch . . . I tried to blame it on the pregnancy not on the child, separate the two hopefully. Because I also reckon your negative emotions can be packed on the foetus too, so I thought I better not . . . I thought this isn't fair, it just isn't fair, it's hard enough as it is and you still have to be positive about it too, you must be kidding.

Sarah underwent an amniocentesis because the triple blood test indicated that there could be something wrong. She described the worry she felt following the test about the possibility of losing the foetus: 'You know, even though they say your risk is only 1 in 150 to 200 of having a spontaneous abortion after the amniocentesis, you think, "I'm going to be that one" so you never really relax.' Because of this concern, and the possibility that the foetus would be found to have an abnormality, she and her partner did not tell anyone about the pregnancy until after the results of the amniocentesis came through (about eighteen weeks into the pregnancy).

This woman's anxiety was compounded by her knowledge about another couple's loss of a baby, which she thought had made her feel tentative about her own pregnancy:

When I was working in a different job, my boss's wife went into labour. It was their first child and they were both in their late thirties. It was a boy, and he died at the birth. I think he had asphyxiated, strangled himself on the umbilical cord. And it was a very big experience, and I still remember it very clearly. So maybe that's why I don't think so much about motherhood, I wait until things happen. 'Cause you can't take anything for granted any more, I don't think.

Julie had been told by doctors that it would be very unlikely that she would become pregnant. After years of trying to fall pregnant and several medical tests, doctors told her that her infertility was caused by her body producing antibodies to her partner's sperm. When Julie did become pregnant, therefore, she was overjoyed. During her pregnancy she took great care to eat well, avoid putting on too much weight and drink plenty of fluids. She worried, however, that her baby would be born with brain damage, noting that her sister was born 'mentally retarded' and her husband's brother had been deprived of oxygen at birth and was 'a little bit retarded' and therefore 'I wanted to make sure that everything was all right with [my baby]'. Julie and her partner had also attended genetic counselling, as one of her cousins had had a Down's Syndrome child. As she was only thirty, it was advised that she need not have an amniocentesis, but only an ultrasound, which she subsequently underwent. The couple didn't tell anyone about the pregnancy for four months until they felt sure from the ultrasound results that the foetus was all right.

Various embodied experiences may incite high anxiety because of the threat of miscarriage. Rowena experienced vaginal bleeding twice, once at eleven weeks' gestation and again at twelve weeks. She was also hospitalized for a week for high blood pressure at nineteen weeks and again for a few days at twenty-two weeks. These events had made her feel concerned about the foetus:

I had two lots of bleeding, and thought, you know, 'What if this baby doesn't come through or what if this baby is harmed because the placenta's been damaged because of what's gone on?' And you know, I was sort of going, 'What if, what if?' at that stage. So I'd already had one scare and then at nineteen-weeks when my blood pressure was so high and I was hospitalized, I thought, 'Oh no, my baby's not big enough to survive yet!'

Rowena was particularly concerned about the risk to the foetus at the nineteen-weeks stage, because after having the ultrasound she was thinking about it as a real person:

I think the ultrasounds really make it real, because you can see that there's something in there and hear the foetal heart beat . . . I think when earlier, at eleven, twelve weeks, I was sort of going, 'Well, if [miscarriage] happens, it happens,' you know, 'it's not a real person.' But deep down it really was, it was my baby. And then I went through a stage where I was really quite ambivalent about it. I was feeling great, I wasn't showing and, sort of like, [the foetus] wasn't there for a while. And then it wasn't until after I was in hospital, I got this real sort of feeling that I know there was something there.

Rowena talked about the anxiety engendered by being hospitalized in the High Risk Pregnancy Unit and thus defined as being in a 'high risk' category:

I was transferred to [name of hospital] and it was horrible because for five days I was looking at this sign 'High Risk Pregnancy Unit' and it would have to be the worst sign to have outside a room! . . . It's horrible, and so I sat there watching it for five days as I was on bed rest. Everything was up in the air – what was the cause, why was I sick? It was also unsettling to hear all the other babies at the time, the postnatal wards were overflowing. At the time I was feeling a bit anxious about myself, I think.

The sister of Claire, at the time she was first interviewed, had recently had to undergo a therapeutic abortion at eighteen weeks into her pregnancy because a genetic defect was found. Claire's mother, she said, had been 'somewhat traumatized by my sister's loss . . . And the first four months [of the pregnancy] I got to the point where I didn't want to talk to her about it, because she was raving and ranting about "Oh my God, if you do this you'll lose the baby, if you do that you'll lose the baby! If you don't stop working and take leave, you'll lose the baby!" It's like, well hang on a moment, let's get some perspective!' Claire acknowledged, however, that her sister's experience did have a great emotional impact on her, causing her to worry about the normality of her own foetus. Claire had been told by her doctor that she was in the 'high risk category' because of her sister's experience. As a result, she sought as many tests as possible, in the quest for reassurance: 'I mean I had every blood test that you could possibly think about. And we had two ultrasounds'. She also underwent amniocentesis, noting that she did so because:

I guess I had a phobia about if it was Down's Syndrome. I would never forgive myself for not having the test to determine whether it had Down's Syndrome. So I had the tests done and they were fine. I couldn't justify bringing a child who's – I couldn't deal with it myself, and I don't think [her partner] could either terribly.

These interviews reveal the intense fears and anxieties that may permeate the pregnant experience for women these days, and their heightened consciousness of the manifold risks that appear to threaten the foetus they carry. Under the contemporary discourse of risk, fate has lost the force of its premodern explanatory power for things going well or badly. In its place is human agency – planning and risk avoidance. Risk discourse implies the post-Enlightenment belief that humans can control destiny through the exertion of thought and will, and thus conquer the vagaries of fate (Giddens, 1990: 30). The obsession with the prevention of risk evident in the late twentieth century is built upon 'a grandiose technocratic rationalizing dream of absolute control of the accidental, understood as the irruption of the unpredictable' (Castel, 1991: 289).

In these women's accounts there is evidence of a desire to exert control, an uneasiness with the vagaries of fate they see as being central to the experience of pregnancy. They are highly aware of expert as well as lay understandings of risk in relation to their pregnancies, and seek to contain and control risk as much as possible. These women are reflexive, actively seeking out knowledge about risk and acting upon it. They do so voluntarily, as autonomous, self-regulating citizens, in attempting to achieve peace of mind about the viability of their pregnancy and to maximize the chances of their foetus surviving and being in good health. They also do so as embodied subjects, who sometimes find that despite their best efforts at rational control their bodies let them down, threatening conception or successful pregnancy. Their pregnancies were positioned as tentative not only because of undergoing prenatal screening but also because the women lacked the confidence to 'trust' their body to perform and produce the 'perfect' baby they so desperately wanted. There was a strong sense of lack of control over their bodies and the course of their pregnancies expressed in these women's accounts even as they articulated their desire for greater control.

As these interview data show, in contrast with expert concepts of risk, which rely upon scienticized concepts of probability, concepts of risk for pregnant women forced to deal with them, to make choices about them, are rooted in their life-worlds and emotions. Women draw not only from expert knowledges but from their own experiences, their knowledge of others' experiences and lay concepts of risk that circulate in their cultural context. While expert advice and technologies play an important role in women's notions of risk, both providing reassurance and inciting anxiety, their risk understandings are also grounded in their own bodily experiences. A woman may hold an intuitive feeling about the wellbeing of her foetus or may rely upon her embodied experiences, such as her experiences and feelings of health and wellbeing or her awareness of the movements of the foetus inside her body, to guide her assessment of how much at risk she thinks it is from abnormalities or illness. Women's understandings of risk, therefore, are aesthetic and hermeneutic (Lash, 1993), established via acculturation and feeling, and are not simply rationalistic, or based on cognitive assessment.

Ambivalence and the 'grotesque' maternal body

I was both fascinated and horrified by my body when pregnant. I thought it beautiful, that mound of glistening flesh, but also obscene – a tumour of some kind. Indeed, one had no control over its growth. (Oakley, 1984: 58)

Pregnancy and motherhood are experiences that are fraught with emotional ambivalence (Rich, 1976; Parker, 1995). Even for those women who long to be pregnant and give birth, to be a mother, the emotions of love and hate for the foetus, baby or child tend to co-exist. Because the dominant discourses and cultural representations of motherhood tend to highlight its positive side, it may be very difficult for women to admit to their more negative feelings. Nevertheless, there exist numerous examples – predominantly in literary accounts of motherhood, feminist autobiographical writings (such as the above from Ann Oakley), psycho-analytic investigations and social research studies – of women articulating their ambivalence in ways that reveal the profound nature of the love but also the resentment and hatred they harbour towards their pregnant bodies or their children. Rich, for example, quotes an extract from her journal, written when her children were very young, where she writes that: 'my children cause me the most exquisite suffering of which I have any experience. It is the suffering of ambivalence: the murderous alternation between bitter resentment and raw-edged nerves, and blissful gratification and tenderness' (Rich, 1976: 21).

One aspect of ambivalence felt by women who are mothers, as suggested in the quotation from Oakley above, is the sense of loss of control of the body that may occur in pregnancy. The female body has been consistently represented in medical and popular discourses as subject to chaos due to female reproductive organs and associated hormones. This is particularly the case at key points in reproductive processes. The pre-menstrual, menstrual, pregnant or menopausal body is typically portrayed as more emotionally labile, vulnerable, less capable of reasoned thought and more prone to illness and disorder than are most other types of adult bodies (Ehrenreich and English, 1974; Martin, 1990). Rich has noted the contradictions evident between the cultural ideas of the female body as 'impure, corrupt, the site of discharges, bleedings, dangerous to masculinity, a source of moral and physical contamination' against the mother figure as 'beneficent, sacred, pure, asexual, nourishing; and the physical potential for motherhood – that same body with its bleedings and mysteries – is her single destiny and justification in life' (1976: 34).

The embodied experiences of pregnancy can provoke divergent responses about their sense of body/self for women: 'a mother can feel in harmony with the foetus inside her, or she can feel it as a hostile antagonist; she can experience birth as a splitting apart of her body, and of her mind from her body, or as a flowing process that integrates body and mind in harmonious co-operation' (Cosslett, 1994: 117). Indeed, a woman may harbour several of these emotional responses simultaneously or change between them at various times in her pregnancy. These responses are the product of a complex range of societal structures and

meanings combining with individual life-experiences and psychodynamic processes. For any woman, however, pregnancy will raise questions about her sense of identity and embodiment. Is the foetus part of
one's body/self, or is it separate? Where do I, the woman, begin, and it,
the foetus, end? How much control do I have (if any) over this foetus as
it grows inside my body? How much does it have over me?

Young (1990) argues that the pregnant subject 'is decentered, split, or
doubled in several ways. She experiences her body as herself and not
herself' (160). This is particularly the case when she first feels the
movements of the foetus. While the foetus' movements are those of
another, separate being, they are also 'wholly mine, completely within
me, conditioning my experience and space' (163). The foetus is both
inside and of the pregnant woman's body, so that the distinctions
between 'inner' and 'outer' are elided. Central to the 'risk' of pregnancy,
therefore, quite apart from concerns about the foetus, is the potential
threat imposed by one's own body to a sense of containment, autonomy,
self-control. So too, in its liminal, two-subjectivities-in-one-body state,
the pregnant body comprises a symbolic threat to others. It stands as
Other to notions of acceptable embodiment.

As Mary Douglas (1966/9) has noted, that which is 'in-between',
which crosses conceptual boundaries, is dealt with by societies as
impure, contaminated and risky to their integrity. Pregnancy is a source
of 'social pollution' because it challenges notions about bodily margins:
it is an anomalous bodily state, a body in transition from one state to
another. As such, it is disorderly, inspiring the meanings of fear, danger
and potential contamination. The bourgeois self that is so valued in
contemporary western societies conforms to that of the 'civilized' body,
which stands in marked contrast to the 'grotesque' body. The 'civilized'
body is that which is self-contained, tightly regulated, dry and proper,
kept apart from others and the outside world. It is a cultured body,
distinct from the natural. The 'grotesque' body, in contrast, is that
which is unregulated, its boundaries liquid, liable to bursting open and
transgression between 'inside' and 'outside', closer to 'nature' than to
'culture'. Women's bodies tend to be culturally classified as 'grotesque'
rather than 'civilized' because of their supposed leakiness, their propen-
sity to be ruled by their reproductive organs and their emotions rather
than their reason, their openness to the world (Theweleit, 1987; Grosz,
1994).

One of the most unsettling features of the feminine body is its capacity
to reproduce itself, to take in semen and to generate it, in the dark
interior of itself, into another human. This capacity may inspire not only
awe but fear: 'it is the woman's fertilizable body which aligns her with

nature and threatens the integrity of the patriarchal symbolic order' (Creed, 1993: 50). The pregnant body is a phenomenon beyond social control, a burgeoning of flesh ending in a violent scene of individuation of the one body into two that has its own rhythms that cannot be externally regulated. The pregnant woman, simply by becoming pregnant, announces herself as a penetrable object, a body that has been entered and possessed first by her sexual partner and his semen and then by the foetus. She is a monstrous being, because she has entered a liminal state in being a body with another body inside it, and thus disrupts notions of the ideal body being autonomous and singular, confounding subject and object. Her burgeoning body, with its fleshly swellings and ever-present potential to open and release fluids and another human, confounds the 'civilized' ideal of containedness, tightness and dryness.

The latent anxieties about the monstrous-feminine body, the body that reproduces itself, harbours within it other monsters, find one of their most potent expressions in the horror film genre. The *Alien* film series, for example, is constructed around the notion of the female monster that is able to penetrate human bodies (both male and female) and breed within them, bursting forth from their stomachs in a terrifying parody of human birth. As Creed (1993: chapter 2) points out, the *Alien* films are replete with images and symbols of maternity and female fecundity, beginning with the opening scenes of the first film, *Alien*, which show the crew members of the spaceship waking from their protected sleep in womb-like pods by the ship's computer, called 'Mother'. The alien monster reproduces itself rapidly, laying eggs prolifically as well as breeding inside humans, and is voracious in its appetites, including that for the flesh of humans. Creed observes that the *Alien* films (and many other horror films) draw on the ages-old mythology of the archaic mother, the Mother-Goddess who is omnipotent in her fecundity and single-minded dedication to procreation, outside of morality and the law. It also evokes the fear harboured by women that their bodies will produce monstrous creatures rather than 'normal' babies. In the latest instalment in the *Alien* series, *Alien Resurrection* (1997), the monster has incorporated the genes of the female hero, Ripley, and gives birth to a horrible humanoid hybrid of human/alien which sees Ripley as its mother. Ripley is both drawn to, and repelled by, her creation.

The French psychoanalytic writer Julia Kristeva has built upon Douglas' writings on purity, defilement and body boundaries to explore the unconscious dimension of responses to the maternal body, the body that provides our first food. Kristeva has developed the notion of the 'abject' or that which is liminal in its status, that which is neither 'self' nor 'other', neither 'inside' nor 'outside'. The abject inspires horror, anxiety, disgust and fear for its capacity to overwhelm us, to dissolve boundaries between itself and us. What causes abjection is 'what disturbs identity, system, order. What does not respect borders, positions, rules. The in-between, the ambiguous, the composite' (Kristeva, 1982: 4). We seek to expel the abject from ourselves so as to render our selves 'clean and proper', to re-establish and confirm the limits of our body/self boundaries. Try as we might, however, the abject always remains part of us: 'it is something rejected from which one does not part, from which one does not protect oneself as from an object. Imaginary uncanniness and real threat, it beckons to us and ends up engulfing us'. The abject is at the borderline of meaning, straddling boundaries, and thus cannot fully be imagined but rather is responded to at the subconscious level, with both dread and fascination.

As Kristeva argues, the maternal body is the archetypal abject body in its ambiguous ontological state of one/two bodies. It is a threshold between nature and culture – in reproducing humanity it is nature, but it is also the site at which individuation of the self is constructed, and thus has a symbolic cultural meaning. For Kristeva, abjection is 'a revolt of the person against an external menace from which one wants to keep oneself at a distance' (135). She claims that the notion of the abject develops in earliest infancy, when the infant begins to differentiate itself from the maternal body with which it has felt as 'one'. The infant, in its undeveloped state, perceives the mother's body as omnipotent, and therefore threatening as well as nurturing. The maternal body is constructed as an external menace because of the psychodynamic processes of individuation that infants must go through to separate themselves from it, as bodies and subjects.

Some writers have taken up the object relations perspective to examine the psychodynamics of the ways in which the mother responds to the infant. They argue that ambivalence on the part of the pregnant woman towards her foetus is inevitable, partly because she is seen as reliving the early emotionally intense relationship she had with her own mother, including the struggle for individuation from her mother that she experienced in infancy. For some women, the experience of pregnancy may be unsettling or disturbing, creating a feeling of alienation from or dislike of their bodies. While expert discourses construct the pregnant woman as posing a potential risk to her foetus, the pregnant woman may conceptualize the foetus as a symbolic threat to her sense of individuality and autonomy. She may fear the ambivalence she feels towards pregnancy and impending motherhood. Just as the infant

projects both good and bad feelings upon its mother as part of individuation, the pregnant woman may project unconscious emotions upon
the foetus, identifying it with her own destructive feelings and perceiving
it as 'bad', devouring, voracious, out to destroy her autonomy and sense
of individuation from others (Parker, 1995). Foetuses and infants may
be phantasized as devouring their mothers, invading their bodies like
aliens or sucking their life's energies out of them (Cosslett, 1994).
Alternatively, the mother may invest the foetus with those qualities of
herself that she considers to be positive, and begin to fear that she will
be a danger to this vulnerable, 'good' baby. These feelings about the
foetus may fluctuate over the course of the pregnancy, becoming more
or less manageable at different times (Parker, 1995: 203–4).

From the symbolic and psychodynamic perspectives, therefore, pregnant embodiment is risky in two dimensions. It is potentially fraught
with risk for the woman experiencing it, who undergoes a transformation from the individuated, autonomous, contained body/self to the
divided, two-in-one body/self. The pregnant body is also potentially
risky to others in its abjectness, its liminality and anomalous cultural
status.

Conclusion

In this chapter, the convergence of a number of important factors have
been shown to construct the pregnancy experience as fraught with risk.
At the broader social-structural level, the trend towards individualization, ideas about the malleability of life chances, discourses of the
'perfect' and 'sacred' child, assumptions about individual agency and
autonomy and women's responsibility for the welfare of their children,
the invention and use of new medical technologies and the dissemination of knowledge about the development of the foetus have contributed
to a growing web of expert knowledge, surveillance and regulation
around the pregnant body and the foetus, and an increasing expectation
that pregnant women can and should exert a high degree of control over
the risks to which their foetus may be exposed *in utero*. At the cultural
and symbolic level of meaning, the lability and permeability of the
pregnant body, the blurring of cultural categories and boundaries that
pregnancy entails, produce anxieties about loss of control and challenge
the western ideal of the autonomous, contained body/self.

I have argued that the pregnant body is chaotic, disorderly and therefore highly risky. It is a 'grotesque' body, a body that cultures seek to
control and purify through various rituals and rites. It is little wonder
that in contemporary western societies, expert discourses and strategies

have sought to problematize the pregnant body and render it more calculable and manageable, and that women themselves conform to these attempts at control and ordering. Women's bodies, in their power to generate new life, are threatening and monstrous and powerful enough, but they also have the power to bring monstrous bodies – abnormal, deformed – into the world. Risk discourses and strategies attempt to discipline this process, to regulate the production of monstrous bodies via the body and subjectivity of the pregnant woman.

While pregnant women have probably always felt anxiety and fear about the outcome of pregnancy and the wellbeing of their foetus, more so than ever in the past pregnancy is portrayed as a series of events that are located within a sphere of rationalist control. Producing a 'perfect' infant is seen to be at least partly a result of the woman's ability to exert control over her body, to seek and subscribe to expert advice and engage in self-sacrifice for the sake of her foetus. Her responsibility for the wellbeing of her foetus has intensified. At the same time, however, many aspects of pregnancy and childbirth remain beyond the woman's control, and she must struggle with acceptance of this in the face of her intensified awareness of the risks to which she and her foetus are susceptible and her desire to contain and control these risks.

NOTES

1 The study was funded by the Australian Research Council, which awarded two consecutive grants to my colleague Lesley Barclay and myself. Thanks to Virginia Schmied for her work as interviewer and co-researcher in the study. Recruitment into the study took place progressively between late 1994 and early 1997. Most of the couples (seventeen of the twenty-five) who took part were volunteers attending antenatal classes at a metropolitan Sydney hospital, but limited snowball sampling and other contacts were also used as recruitment strategies. The age of the female participants ranged from twenty-three to thirty-five years, with a mean age of 28.2 years. All of the women in the study had been in paid employment before the birth of their child, with most remaining in their jobs until late in the pregnancy. Fifteen of the women were employed in white-collar occupations such as clerical, administrative, service and health care work. While some of these women held post-school qualifications, none had completed a university degree. The other ten held one or more university degrees: of these, one was a doctoral student, two were speech therapists, one a dietitian, one a research scientist, two were management consultants, two teachers and one a research assistant. All but two of the women (one of whom was born in Brazil and the other of whom was born in Germany) were Australians of British ethnicity.
2 In at least one major Sydney hospital for women, pregnant women's accounts of the date of when their last menstrual period was or when they thought they conceived are no longer accepted as accurate means of estimating the age of

their foetus for the purposes of diagnostic tests. Instead, women are now routinely sent to have an ultrasound to determine the age of their foetus before undergoing a prenatal diagnostic test.

3 In Australia in 1994 the fertility rate was 1.8 children per woman (Australian Bureau of Statistics, 1997).

REFERENCES

Australian Bureau of Statistics (1997) *Australian Demographic Trends 1997.* Canberra: Australian Government Publishing.

Beck, U. and Beck-Gernsheim, E. (1995) *The Normal Chaos of Love.* Cambridge: Polity Press.

Beck-Gernsheim, E. (1996) Life as a planning project. In Lash, S., Szerszynski, B. and Wynne, B. (eds.), *Risk, Environment and Modernity: Towards a New Ecology.* London: Sage.

Bellamy, E. (1998) Mother love gone wrong. *The Weekend Australian Review,* 21–22 March, 16–17.

Bordo, S. (1993) *Unbearable Weight: Feminism, Western Culture, and the Body.* Berkeley, CA: University of California Press.

Castel, R. (1991) From dangerousness to risk. In Burchell, G., Gordon, C. and Miller, P. (eds.), *The Foucault Effect: Studies in Governmentality.* Hemel Hempstead: Harvester Wheatsheaf.

Cosslett, T. (1994) *Women Writing Childbirth: Modern Discourses of Motherhood.* Manchester University Press.

Creed, B. (1993) *The Monstrous-Feminine: Film, Feminism, Psychoanalysis.* London: Routledge.

Crouch, M. and Manderson, L. (1993) Parturition as social metaphor. *Australian and New Zealand Journal of Sociology,* 29(1), 55–72.

Douglas, M. (1966/1969) *Purity and Danger: an Analysis of Concepts of Pollution and Taboo.* London: Routledge & Kegan Paul.

Eccleston, R. (1996) Death before deformity. *The Australian Magazine,* 20–21 January 1996.

Ehrenreich, B. and English. D. (1974) *Complaints and Disorders: the Sexual Politics of Sickness.* London: Compendium.

Eisenberg, A., Murkoff, H. and Hathaway, S. (1997) *What to Expect When You're Expecting.* (Second edition). Sydney: HarperCollins.

Foucault, M. (1984) The politics of health in the eighteenth century. In Rabinow, P. (ed.), *The Foucault Reader.* New York: Pantheon Books.

   (1988) Technologies of the self. In Martin, L., Gutman, H. and Hutton, P. (eds.), *Technologies of the Self: a Seminar with Michel Foucault.* London: Tavistock.

   (1991) Governmentality. In Burchell, G., Gordon, C. and Miller, P. (eds.), *The Foucault Effect: Studies in Governmentality.* Hemel Hempstead: Harvester Wheatsheaf.

Giddens, A. (1990) *The Consequences of Modernity.* Cambridge: Polity Press.

Gordon, C. (1991) Governmental rationality: an introduction. In Burchell, G., Gordon, C. and Miller, P. (eds.), *The Foucault Effect: Studies in Governmentality.* Hemel Hempstead: Harvester Wheatsheaf.

Grosz, E. (1994) *Volatile Bodies: Toward a Corporeal Feminism*. Sydney: Allen & Unwin.

Handwerker, L. (1994) Medical risk: implicating poor pregnant women. *Social Science and Medicine*, 38(5), 665–75.

Heywood, L. (1996) *Dedication to Hunger: the Anorexic Aesthetic in Modern Culture*. Berkeley, CA: University of California Press.

Hubbard, R. (1984) Personal courage is not enough: some hazards of child-bearing in the 1980s. In Arditti, R., Klein, R. and Minden, S. (eds.), *Test-tube Women: what Future for Motherhood?* London: Pandora.

Kristeva, J. (1982) *Powers of Horror: an Essay on Abjection*. New York: Columbia University Press.

Lash, S. (1993) Reflexive modernization: the aesthetic dimension. *Theory, Culture & Society*, 10, 1–23.

Leder, D. (1990) *The Absent Body*. Chicago, IL: University of Chicago Press.

Lupton, D. (1995) *The Imperative of Health: Public Health and the Regulated Body*. London: Sage.

Martin, E. (1990) The ideology of reproduction: the reproduction of ideology. In Ginsburg, F. and Tsing, A. (eds.), *Uncertain Terms: Negotiating Gender in American Culture*. Boston, MA: Beacon Press.

Nippert-Eng, C. (1996) *Home and Work*. Chicago, IL: University of Chicago Press.

Oakley, A. (1984) *Taking It Like a Woman*. London: Flamingo.

(1987) From walking wombs to test-tube babies. In Stanworth, M. (ed.), *Reproductive Technologies: Gender, Motherhood and Medicine*. Cambridge: Polity Press.

Parker, R. (1995) *Torn in Two: the Experience of Maternal Ambivalence*. London: Virago.

(1997) The production and purposes of maternal ambivalence. In Hollway, W. and Featherstone, B. (eds.), *Mothering and Ambivalence*. London: Routledge.

Petchesky, R. (1987) Foetal images: the power of visual culture in the politics of reproduction. In Stanworth, M. (ed.), *Reproductive Technologies: Gender, Motherhood and Medicine*. Cambridge: Polity Press.

Petersen, A. and Lupton, D. (1996) *The New Public Health: Health and Self in the Age of Risk*. Sydney/London: Allen & Unwin/Sage.

Rapp, R. (1988) Chromosomes and communication: the discourse of genetic counseling. *Medical Anthropology Quarterly*, 2(2), 143–57.

(1990) Constructing amniocentesis: maternal and medical discourses. In Ginsburg, F. and Tsing, A. (eds.), *Uncertain Terms: Negotiating Gender in American Culture*. Boston, MA: Beacon Press.

Rich, A. (1976) *Of Woman Born: Motherhood as Experience and Institution*. New York: W.W. Norton and Company.

Rothman, B. (1994) *The Tentative Pregnancy: Amniocentesis and the Sexual Politics of Motherhood*. (Second edition, revised and expanded). London: Pandora.

Searle, J. (1996) Fearing the worst – why do pregnant women feel 'at risk'? *Australian and New Zealand Journal of Obstetrics and Gynaecology*, 36(3), 279–86.

Shuttleworth, S. (1993/1994) A mother's place is in the wrong. *New Scientist*, 25 December/1 January, 38–9.

Stanworth, M. (1987) Reproductive technologies and the deconstruction of motherhood. In Stanworth, M. (ed.), *Reproductive Technologies: Gender, Motherhood and Medicine*. Cambridge: Polity Press.

Theweleit, K. (1987) *Male Fantasies. Volume 1: Women, Floods, Bodies, History*. Cambridge: Polity Press.

Tsing, A. (1990) Monster stories: women charged with perinatal endangerment. In Ginsburg, F. and Tsing, A. (eds.), *Uncertain Terms: Negotiating Gender in American Culture*. Boston, MA: Beacon Press.

Wheatley, J. (1993) Trying times. *HQ*, July/August, 31–8.

Weir, L. (1996) Recent developments in the government of pregnancy. *Economy and Society*, 25(3), 372–92.

Young, I. (1990) *Throwing Like a Girl and Other Essays in Feminist Philosophy and Social Theory*. Bloomington, IN: Indiana University Press.

4   Risk anxiety and the social construction of childhood

Stevi Jackson and Sue Scott

Introduction

The theorization of risk and risk anxiety has, so far, paid scant attention to issues of gender and generation. In particular, there has been little work on childhood in this area, despite the pervasiveness of public anxiety about risks to children. In our everyday world generalized risks, of the kind Beck (1992) associates with the democratization of risk, are deemed more pernicious when they threaten children's wellbeing. This is evident in responses to a range of 'risks' from concerns about food contamination and disease transmission to the threat of violence. The intensity of public anxiety about dangers to children is most marked in extreme and dramatic circumstances, as in the media response to the shooting of sixteen children in the Scottish city of Dunblane in March 1996. Yet the reaction is equally intense when threats come *from* children, for example when a child commits a violent crime. This is not as paradoxical as it seems for, as we will argue in this chapter, it is not only children who are perceived as being 'at risk' but the institution of childhood itself. Childhood is increasingly being constructed as a precious realm under siege from those who would rob children of their childhoods, and as being subverted from within by children who refuse to remain childlike. Our focus here is on risk and risk anxiety in relation to children and, more specifically, on the sexualization of risk and the consequences of this for children's daily lives.

We take it as axiomatic that childhood is socially constructed and that central to this construction is the imputation of 'specialness' to children (as particularly cherished beings) and childhood (as a cherished state of being). Because children are thus constituted as a protected species and childhood as a protected state, both become loci of risk anxiety: safeguarding children entails keeping danger at bay; preserving childhood entails guarding against anything which threatens it. Conversely, risk anxiety helps construct childhood and maintain its boundaries – the specific risks from which children must be protected serve to define the characteristics of childhood and the 'nature' of children themselves.

The way in which risk anxiety contributes to the ongoing construction of childhood is especially clear in relation to sexualized risk. Just as children are constructed as a 'special' category of being, so sexuality is constructed as a 'special' aspect of social life, as uniquely pleasurable but also potentially dangerous, and is itself the focus of a great deal of risk anxiety. Both childhood and sexuality are emotive issues which serve as barometers of public sensitivities. Not only are childhood and sexuality each singled out as special, but they are understood as inimical to each other – in particular, sexuality is seen as antithetical to the state of 'innocence' which has emerged as a defining characteristic of the 'normal' child (Jackson, 1982). Sex is defined as an adult preserve – hence 'adult' entertainment is a euphemism for erotica, and one of the markers of entry into adulthood is the age of sexual consent. That the age of consent in many countries, including Britain, is later for homosexual men than for heterosexuals indicates the ways in which 'deviant' sexualities, are regarded as particularly risky for 'vulnerable' young people.

Anxieties about children and sex may be nothing new. Historically, once children came to be constructed as a special, protected category of being and childhood as a special state, the obverse of adulthood, children and childhood could be constructed as 'at risk' and in need of particular protection and vigilance. Nineteenth-century history offers many examples of public concern about children, often framed in sexual terms: the campaign to exclude children from underground work in the mines was fuelled by prurient depictions of semi-nudity and children's exposure to lewd conduct and language which was supposedly part of their working conditions (John, 1980); philanthropists concerned about the housing conditions of the poor dwelt on the spectre of incest thought likely to occur when whole families slept on one room (Wohl, 1978); the moral purity movement gained momentum from exposing 'child prostitution' which led to the raising of the age of consent to sixteen (Gorham, 1978; Weeks, 1990; Walkowitz, 1992).

Despite these historical continuities, it can be argued that particular forms of risk anxiety are specific to the conditions in which we find ourselves at the end of the twentieth century. Today we live in a climate of heightened risk awareness coupled with a nostalgia for an imagined past in which children played safely throughout a carefree innocent childhood. Recent social theory has conceptualized risk anxiety as a social state engendered by an increasing lack of trust in both the project of modernity and expert knowledges (Giddens, 1990, 1991; Beck,

1992). Whereas these writers have concentrated primarily on the social consequences of technological change, we are suggesting that the anxieties specific to childhood are part of a general sense that the social world itself is becoming less stable and predictable. Of course, such fears have always surfaced in periods of rapid social change, but in the past social disorder was more often thought of as located within particular classes and communities and therefore as potentially containable even when perceived as threatening to more 'respectable' groups and neighbourhoods. While some symptoms of social disorder continue to be associated with the rebarbative elements of an 'underclass' and the areas they inhabit, others are seen either as more ubiquitous or as less predictable, identifiable and locatable – as liable to disrupt social life at any time in any place. Threats to children's wellbeing are seen as coming from all-pervasive, global social 'ills' such as the 'pernicious' consequences of sex and violence in the media and also from the unforeseen (but constantly anticipated) danger from a specific 'monstrous' individual – the shadowy figure of the paedophile which haunts the popular imagination. The furore surrounding the release of the new film version of *Lolita* in 1998 has been fuelled by the convergence of both sets of fears: the film has been represented as symptomatic of a generalized moral depravity and as a potential incitement to individual paedophiles.[1]

As we write there has been a wave of near hysteria in Britain concerning known 'paedophiles' at large in the community. This has occurred in the context of increased public and professional anxiety about the sexual abuse of children, in which notions of sexual risk increasingly inform political debate, public policy and child-education campaigns around safety and danger. Hence the panic currently being whipped up by the possibility of a 'paedophile' moving into a given locality locks into the more generalized anxieties which parents feel in relation to the world and the safety of their children. Such risk anxiety is a constant and pervasive feature of everyday consciousness, managed through everyday practices; it might be fuelled by public discussions of risk, but individuals are left to find their own ways of coping with the uncertainty it engenders.

> The point . . . is not that day to day life is inherently more risky than was the case in prior eras. It is rather that, in conditions of modernity, for lay actors as well as for experts in specific fields, thinking in terms of risk and risk assessment is a more or less ever-present exercise. (Giddens, 1991: 123–4)

Individualization within modernity entails the almost constant reflexive monitoring of risk which pervades our sense of how to manage ourselves and the world. Risks may be produced by social conditions, but we are expected to assess and manage them as individuals. Beck associates individualization with the process of de-traditionalization, which has also produced a less predictable world in which we are faced with many options and no easy solutions.

Risk Society begins where tradition ends, when, in all spheres of life, we can no longer take traditional certainties for granted. The less we can rely on traditional securities, the more risks we have to negotiate. The more risks, the more decisions and choices we have to make. (Beck, 1998: 10)

Risk assessment becomes, then, part of a set of attempts to render the world more manageable or at least to indicate on what basis to make decisions. Risk anxiety is a prism through which we anticipate possibilities, imagine outcomes of present actions and thus attempt to control or colonize the future (Beck, 1992, 1998).

Issues relating to risk raised by theorists such as Beck and Giddens coalesce around the figure of the child. De-traditionalization engenders anxieties about the loss of stable families embedded within secure communities. The everyday world of childhood thus no longer seems so safe and predictable. At the same time, individualization renders each parent uniquely responsible for their children and encourages them to invest in their children's childhood as part of their own life project (Beck and Beck-Gernsheim, 1995; Beck-Gernsheim 1996). Having and caring for a child 'can in fact become the very core of one's private existence' (Beck and Beck-Gernsheim, 1995: 107). Taken together, these two processes – individualization and de-traditionalization – create a context in which greater parental investment in children occurs within what seems to be a less predictable and less safe world. In addition, colonization of the future has made space for specific anxieties in relation to children. Parents must not only guard against immediate threats to their children's wellbeing, but must also plan for any event which might disrupt their development towards physically and psychologically healthy adulthood. Hence the developmental paradigm, so central to modern constructions of childhood, may heighten risk anxiety. Childhood is thought of as a linear trajectory towards the future and children as themselves representing the future. Under conditions of individualization it is not the future of society as a whole which is the issue but the capacities of parents to live vicariously through their children, to treat them as carriers of their own hopes and dreams:

With the future lying ahead the child confronts its parents with their own biographies and ambitions, disappointments and fears, including old dreams of being a huge success and making it to the top. Anyone suggesting that 'my child should have it better than I did' is not just thinking of the child, but mostly of him/herself. (Beck and Beck-Gernsheim, 1995: 138)

Risk, children and childhood

It is these individualized parental hopes and fears for their children which are mobilized in wider, publicly aired concerns about children and childhood. Increasing anxiety about risk has been superimposed upon an older 'protective discourse' (Thomson and Scott, 1990) within which children are located as vulnerable innocents to be shielded from the dangers of the wider social (implicitly adult) world. The fusion of risk anxiety with protectiveness engenders a preoccupation with prevention (Scott and Freeman, 1995; Green, 1997), a need for constant vigilance in order to anticipate and guard against potential threats to children's wellbeing. To take just one example of this widespread preoccupation, in a recent edition of the magazine *Family Life*, produced by the British Broadcasting Corporation, and described as 'essential reading for families with children from four to fourteen', almost every article on child-rearing is couched in terms of risks to children and childhood. There is a 'home alone' piece advising on when it is safe to leave a child at home unsupervised and what precautions should be taken to ensure their safety; an article addressing parents' fears about young children's attraction to music and sports stars; a feature barked on the front cover by the question 'are our children growing up too soon?'. This last turns out to be about early puberty in girls: hence even the process of physical maturation is cast as a threat to childhood (*Family Life*, March 1998).

Existing empirical research on children and childhood, even where not addressed specifically to questions of risk and risk anxiety, also suggests that risk management might be central to an understanding of the social construction of childhood and the everyday experience of children. Ideas about children's competencies (or lack of them), their specific vulnerability and their (im)maturity, inform adult decisions about the degree of surveillance children require and the degree of autonomy they can be permitted. At a wider, cultural, level, risk anxiety may play a part in constituting the idea of childhood, in that concern for children's safety is of a different order from concerns about adult safety. Risks to children are represented as inherently more grave than risks to adults: it is almost beyond debate that we should 'protect' children, that any potential risk to children should be taken very seriously. As adults we can decide to take risks, or to balance risk against pleasure, in our pursuit of sexual gratification or a sun-tan. Where children are concerned, risk assessment entails weighing some risks against others, for example fears for their safety as against the concomitant dangers of overprotection. Moreover, these judgements are made from an adult perspective, by adults, on children's behalf.

Managing and balancing these risks gives rise to a number of key antinomies in relation to children and childhood: in particular contradictions between recognizing children's autonomy and the increasing emphasis on child protection; the paradoxical perception of children as both at risk and as a potential threat to other children and to social order. These contradictions may be expressed as tensions between two conceptualizations of children, as active, knowing, autonomous individuals on the one hand and as passive, innocent dependants on the other.

The social construction of childhood

In arguing that childhood is socially constructed rather than being intrinsic to the state of being a child, we suggest that the construction of childhood needs to be understood at a number of different levels: the structural, the discursive and the situated. Childhood is institutionalized through family, education and the state resulting in dependence on adults and exclusion from full participation in adult society. Indeed, it can be argued that many aspects of childhood today have been shaped through the structural and institutional changes of the last two hundred years (Qvortrup, 1997). At the level of discourse, childhood was constituted as an object of the scientific gaze primarily through psychology (Rose, 1989); subsequently social workers, educationalists and others have claimed expertise in monitoring, categorizing and managing childhood and children. These expert knowledges have shaped common-sense understandings of childhood as a natural state, so that we are all assumed to 'know' what a child is, to be able to comment on what constitutes a 'proper' childhood. The meaning of childhood is also negotiated through everyday situated interaction. Here, within the structural constraints of adult–child relations, generalized understandings of childhood may be modified; they may not, in concrete social settings, coincide precisely with adult views of children as such, and these views about children in general may differ again from parents' ideas about their own children.

In everyday life, abstract ideas of 'the child' come up against the actuality of children of different ages and genders, with a range of attributes and capacities (Backett, 1988). Children themselves enter into the picture here as active social agents. However, children's participation in constructing their own everyday world takes place within the constraints set by their subordinate location in relation to adults, where their own understanding of what it means to be a child has been shaped by their interaction with more powerful, adult, social actors with pre-existing, albeit re-negotiable, ideas about childhood and children. There is no free and autonomous realm of childhood outside the social relations in which childhood in general, and particular individual child-hoods, are forged. The social world of the child is bounded by adult surveillance (Brannen and O'Brien, 1995).

Traditionally, social scientists conceptualized childhood primarily within the socialization paradigm, in which children were seen as adults in waiting whose experiences were only worth investigating insofar as they shaped adult attributes or life-chances (Thorne, 1987). Recent sociological work has challenged such adult-centred approaches (Waskler, 1991; Leonard, 1990; Mayall, 1994; Thorne, 1987, 1993; James and Prout, 1990),[2] but developmental perspectives remain promi-nent in everyday thinking and professional and public discourse. It is still taken for granted that the process of maturing from child to adolescent to adult unfolds as a series of naturally occurring stages, that there is a 'right age' at which children should develop certain competen-cies and acquire particular freedoms and responsibilities. These assump-tions are so pervasive that it is difficult to think outside them, so widely accepted that they have become unquestioned 'truths'. As we will see, the developmental or socialization paradigm is at the heart of risk anxiety and risk management in relation to children.

Endangered and dangerous children

Children most often come under public scrutiny when they are per-ceived as in danger (as victims of adult abuse or neglect) or as a danger to others (as delinquents and vandals) (Thorne, 1987). Often such concerns can be seen to reflect risk anxiety as much as actual danger – for example, the recent heightened awareness of sexual and fatal risk from strangers in the UK, despite the lack of evidence that risk to children comes primarily from this quarter. While there has been an increase in *recorded* crimes of violence against children, three quarters of the perpetrators are parents and other relatives. The children most at risk of being murdered are infants under the age of one: hardly those most exposed to 'stranger danger'; children aged five to fifteen are, of all members of society, the least likely to be victims of homicide. It is not until children reach the age of fifteen or sixteen that danger from strangers becomes more significant than that from intimates (CSO, 1994, 1995). In the UK, up to February 1996 (prior to the killings in Dunblane) fewer than six children under fourteen had been killed by strangers each year since 1984. This can be contrasted with approximately 600 per year who die in accidents (CSO, 1994). Media coverage would suggest a reverse order of danger. The existence of this threat from strangers is taken for granted as beyond question and it is widely assumed to be a sexual threat. For example, in a discussion of children and gardening on *Women's Hour* (BBC Radio 4, 30 January 1998), gardening was promoted as a safe outdoor activity for children since 'you can't let them play out in the street any more – they may get molested'.

While it is well documented that sexual risk to children is most likely to be posed by intimates, it is 'stranger danger' which hits the headlines, captures the popular imagination and informs education campaigns. In Britain a Home Office campaign was launched in Leeds in 1988 warning children against strangers, since when 'stranger-danger' programmes carried out through police visits to primary schools have proliferated throughout the country. It is therefore hardly surprising that a recent British study found that fear of attack by strangers was seen as the single most significant risk to children when they ventured outside the home, and in the case of girls this was identified as a specifically sexual risk (Hood *et al.*, 1996). A recent quick and dirty poll, discussed on the television programmeme *Frontline Scotland* and reported in *The Scottish Daily Mail* on 20 January 1998, reported that parents vastly over-estimated risks to children and were over-protecting them as a result.

It is unwise to interpret this apparent gap between parental worries and statistical probabilities as indicative of ignorance or stupidity – the line taken by *The Scottish Daily Mail*. We cannot assume, in the absence of reliable research, that parents fail to assess risks 'realistically'. If parents do not take danger seriously, perhaps they risk being seen by others as uncaring or irresponsible. Parents may know the statistical probability of their child being sexually assaulted or murdered by a stranger to be slight, but the fact that it happens at all might be enough to make them fear for their own. It is a pessimistic version of the impetus which draws people to lotteries: the chances of the desired or feared outcome are small but, in the words of the UK national lottery slogan, 'it could be you'.

Risk anxiety has material effects. Parental fears can limit children's lives and experiences in a range of ways, thus increasing their dependence on adults. For example, whereas 80 per cent of seven and eight year olds in the UK went to school on their own in 1971, only 9 per cent were doing so in 1990 (Hillman, Adams and Whitlegg, 1990). While there are undoubtedly other factors which contribute to this trend, such as increased car ownership, this statistic is nevertheless indicative of

The demonization of child killers parallels the media representation of women such as Myra Hindley and Rosemary West; women and children who kill are deemed monstrous, doubly transgressive – in having murdered they have also acted against feminine or childlike 'nature'. Once a monster, always a monster. In May 1998, considerable controversy was generated in the UK by the publication of a book about Mary Bell who had killed two small children thirty years earlier when she was aged thirteen. Bell was retrospectively re-demonized as both a child who killed and a woman who is culpable and unforgivable in that she has profited from her crime by accepting payment for her story. Her depiction as monstrous is highly gendered:

Her extraordinarily pretty, heart-shaped face looked out beneath headlines, as it looks out again now: a beautiful icon of evil. (*The Observer*, 3 May 1998: 3)

Here our attention is drawn to the appearance of feminine, childish innocence and the 'truth' of the evil beneath the surface. We are reminded of the lack of remorse shown by Mary Bell at her trial (and by implication since) in contrast with her co-accused who was acquitted and was

. . . deemed to be a passive partner; a slow witted, fragile creature led astray by her quick, clever, devious partner. Her reactions seemed normal, she cried, stumbled in her speech, was uncomprehending and frightened. Her escorts hugged and comforted her. She was just a little girl. (*The Observer*, 3 May 1998: 3)

Mary Bell, however, was clearly not a proper 'little girl'. Throughout the trial she was 'tearless and defiant, bandying words with the prosecution.' (*The Observer*, 3 May 1998: 3). Her cleverness, her refusal to be cowed by the full weight of adult power, represented by the court, underline her exclusion from normal childhood and her status as a monstrosity.

Childhood in danger

Whether cast as demons or innocents, children are constructed as radically other, separating them off from the 'real world' of adults – who have the power to define. There is a strong cultural emphasis on marking the boundary between childhood and adulthood – on keeping children childlike (Jackson, 1982). For example, in a recent British television debate, those in favour of retaining or raising the age of consent continually emphasized the distinctiveness of adults and children and the necessity of preserving this distinction. One participant, Melanie Phillips, claimed that we have 'lost sight of the distinction between childhood and adulthood' and argued that society should start 'treating children as children and adults as adults' (*The Heart of the Matter*, BBC 1, 1 February 1998).

Both threats to the wellbeing of children and children who are themselves threatening seem to de-stabilize this boundary. This produces anxiety about childhood itself. It is, of course, the childhood of innocence which is seen to be threatened:

To have to stand and wait as the charm, malleability, innocence and curiosity of children are degraded and then transmogrified into the lesser features of pseudo-adulthood is painful and embarrassing and, above all, sad. (Postman, 1994: xiii)

Here Postman is expressing a widely aired concern that children are growing up too quickly without experiencing childhood to the full (an example of which we consider below). Precocity in a child is something to be guarded against – and the word precocious has acquired all manner of negative connotations. The precocious child is not only one who knows more than she or he ought, but is also a child who does not know her or his place, who speaks out of turn, who refuses to affect a properly childlike, cute and subservient demeanour. Childhood is seen as being at risk from pressures towards early maturity, conspicuous consumption and precocious sexuality (as well as any experience of pain, suffering or loss), highlighting a fundamental contradiction in discourses around children and childhood: childhood is regarded as a natural state and yet also as perpetually at risk. Constant vigilance is required in order to protect, preserve and manage childhood for the sake of the children.

There are two distinct but often conflated notions of nature and the natural which are mobilized in relation to childhood. The first of these can be designated 'scientific nativism' (cf. Connell and Dowsett (1992) on sexuality). Here childhood is understood as a series of biologically ordained developmental stages, as in the socialization paradigm. The second form of nativism draws on understandings of a natural order in which children have their proper place. These give rise to different forms of anxiety: on the one hand concerns about the consequences of perverting the normal course of development and on the other, fears of disrupting social order.

Children themselves seem to threaten the institution of childhood when they are 'out of control', when they are disruptive at school or turn to crime. Such children refuse to remain in the spaces allotted to them by adults or disrupt these spaces from within. These are children whose conduct directly contradicts the ideal of the innocent child. The figure of the child-criminal is one evoked by Postman (1994) as evidence of the disappearance of childhood and also features prominently in the press.

We hear about children who rob, steal and commit assault and about joyriders so young they can barely see over the steering wheel. We are often incited to moral outrage by the supposed newness of such events. Hence much of the coverage of the James Bulger story ignored previous child murderers (see Jenks, 1996). Anxiety about child crime, however, is not new. The history of the Victorian era is littered with public concern about the morals of the young and gangs of child criminals roaming the streets – children who are not fully children, who overstep the proper boundaries of childhood (Pearson, 1985; Davin, 1990). One way of dealing with the unruly child, with the spectre of the demonic child is to declare that child not a child – as in the case of Mary Bell.

Fears for children tend to be expressed through the idiom of children robbed of their childhood. Here there is general discomfort about loss of sexual innocence, pressures to be grown up, as well as more specific concerns about the hot-housing of child prodigies or children forced to take on adult responsibilities. Paradoxically, worries about children being denied a childhood are occurring in the context of social trends which appear to reinforce childhood dependency; for example the evidence we have cited on children's declining autonomy. Yet this too can be re-framed in the idiom of lost childhood, a loss of freedom expressed as nostalgia for the fictive childhood of *Swallows and Amazons* or the *The Famous Five*. It is interesting to note that childhood is the only form of social subordination equated with a state of freedom.

The two elements of the story of lost childhood, pressures to early maturity and restricted freedom, are interconnected: the former is assumed to lead to the latter. An example of this process can be found in media accounts of child beauty pageants in the USA. This issue was initially brought to the attention of the British public when, early in 1996, BBC2 screened a documentary following the progress of five-year-old beauty queens Brooke Breedwell and Asia Mansur.[3] On Boxing Day 1996 another star of the child-pageant circuit, six-year-old JonBenet Ramsey, was found murdered in Boulder, Colorado. Common themes emerged in media responses on both occasions. At first, children were represented as having been deprived of their childhood by over ambitious parents:

Childhood is forgotten in a whirl of singing lessons, modelling tutorials, photo-sessions and hairdressers' appointments. (Alison Graham on Brooke Breedwell, *Radio Times*, 27 January–2 February 1996)

Her face plastered in make-up, her hair dyed a perfect blonde like an animated Barbie doll, she was the very pattern of a child pushed forward and exploited by her mother, turned to adult ambitions and fantasies while still an infant. (*Glasgow Herald*, 13 January 1997 on the murder of JonBenet Ramsey)

Quite apart from mother blaming, this latter comment reveals what was often at the heart of the concerns expressed in the media. The *Glasgow Herald* compares JonBenet Ramsey's situation with that of young gymnasts and musicians, driven on by their parents, but comments that these at least do not 'carry a whiff of sexual exploitation and pornography'. It is the sexualization of these girls which is seen as particularly problematic – their make-up, their clothes, the routines they perform, their whole demeanour. Alison Graham describes Brooke Breedwell as 'pretending a sexuality she should know nothing about'.

The media concentrated on what marks the 'difference' between these girls and 'normal' children, summed up in the headline to Tim Cornwell's piece in *The Independent* (entitled 'Too much too young'), in which he describes JonBenet Ramsey as a 'precocious and pretty child' involved in a 'grotesque' enterprise. Yet the phenomenon of child beauty contests would not be possible without the institutionalized subordination of children, the almost absolute power which parents have over their children, the remarkable degree of control they exert over the child's body (Hood-Williams, 1990). Moreover, the sexualization of girlhood is not exceptional. Many a small girl has been taught that 'in order to be pleasing she must be pretty as a picture' and encouraged to gain attention through 'childish coquetry' (de Beauvoir, 1972: 306). Innocence itself is routinely sexualized (Kitzinger, 1988; Ennew, 1986) and this may indeed be part of the attraction of the pageant.

Children and sexuality

Both public and parental anxieties accrete around the issue of early sexual maturity, which is seen as a particular threat to cherished ideals of childhood. Panic about teenage pregnancy rates and negative views of sex education illustrate the common equation of childhood innocence with sexual ignorance. Early interest in sex is commonly construed as a danger sign – often as an indicator that the child has been abused – but also that the child might be a potential abuser of others. An article in the *Sydney Morning Herald* (19 November 1996) on abusive children advised parents to seek professional help if their child displayed 'sexual knowledge too great for (their) age' and commented that early detection and treatment was necessary for children who engaged in 'age inappropriate or coercive sexual behaviour'. This bracketing together of age inappropriate and coercive acts is particularly worrying implying as it does that they are one and the same. While we are sensitive to the possibility that children who display sexual knowledge may indeed have been abused, there are other reasons why children might be sexually knowledgeable. It is dangerous to assume that there is something inherently wrong in children knowing about sex.

Access to sexual knowledge is an important boundary marker between children and adults (Jackson, 1982). This is evident, for example, in public debates about the 'nine o'clock watershed' through which television programming in Britain is divided between 'family' and 'adult' entertainment. Television has become a locus of parental anxiety about children's exposure to sex and violence (Buckingham, 1994). Moreover, recent technological developments such as video and the Internet may mean that parents cannot effectively control the information their children are receiving. Indeed children can often directly access knowledge which their parents cannot. Technological literacy is profoundly gendered and mothers in particular may feel ill equipped to police their children's access to new sources of information. Even where new technologies are not involved, parents are capable of being surprised and shocked by the sexual information available to their children, as evinced by the recent public debate on the content of magazines read by girls in their early teens (Jackson, 1996).[4]

While there may be cause for feminist concern in relation to the reinforcement of a heterosexual ideal in these magazines, it is also important to point out their potential value. They may be the main, if not the only, source of useful and accessible information about sex for those girls who might otherwise lack the means through which to explore their understandings of sexuality. Public anxiety in relation to these magazines seemed to entail the assumption that preserving girls' ignorance was a means of preserving their purity. Not only is ignorance no protection, but it is crucial to point out that there is no real evidence that knowing more about sex increases sexual activity (Scott, Wight and Buston, 1997). Teenage girls are not as easily led as is often supposed, but are quite capable of reading magazines critically (Frazer, 1988). While adult assumptions about the impressionability of youth demean and devalue young people in general, it is girls who are considered to be particularly at risk. Nobody seems particularly anxious about sexual content of what boys are reading; in the case of boys, adult concerns centre on violence rather than sexuality – and on boys as potentially threatening to others rather than being 'at risk'.

Adults worry about access to sexual knowledge for children of all ages, particularly that they might learn too much too soon. Parents often appear willing to mandate teachers to undertake sex education on the assumption that they will be told the right things at the right time just as they will learn addition before multiplication (Scott, Wight and Buston, 1997). Yet when schools depart from these expectations once again we are faced with scares about innocence corrupted. Of course there is a real sense in which sex does pose a threat to children, not through their own knowledge but through the abusive actions of adults.

As we have already suggested, parental risk anxiety often crystallizes around the threat of sexual violence from strangers, but the sexual component of such risks is rarely made explicit to children. Adults project their sexual scripts and anxieties onto children in ways which are relatively inaccessible because they are bounded by what cannot be said. This makes it extremely difficult to communicate to children the precise nature of the danger they are being warned about. Hence children have to struggle to make sense of a jigsaw puzzle of knowledge from which many pieces are missing (Jackson, 1982; Thomson and Scott, 1990). Children are denied access to the 'full story' which informs adult understandings, because sex itself is often thought of as a risk to children (Jackson, 1982; Stainton-Rogers and Stainton-Rogers, 1992), and indeed to childhood itself.

Local and global contexts

The negotiation of risk entails both strategies for managing actual risks and dangers and also strategies for the rationalization of fear and anxiety. Adults may know that some imagined hazards are unlikely to befall their children, yet nonetheless feel anxious about them. Similarly children may know that some dangers are very real while others are part of fantasy worlds – but might still find the latter frightening.

The social world of children is divided into safe and dangerous places which has consequences for children's use of space, where they are allowed to go and the places they themselves feel safe in, frightened or excited by. Safety and danger depend upon the immediate locality in which children live their lives. Ideas about safe and dangerous places also have a temporal dimension. Both children's and parents' perceptions of safe and dangerous spaces in the city and the country might vary with context and time of day. For example, spaces regarded as safe for children in daylight hours can be considered dangerous after dark. Interestingly for our concern with sexualized risk, darkness seems to be associated in the minds of parents with fears of violent sexual assault (Hillman, Adams and Whitlegg, 1990). The lateness of the hour also focuses parental minds on the risk of consensual sex and is a major rationale for curfews on teenage girls in particular.

Both parental risk anxiety and children's consciousness of risk need to be set in the context of what children actually do, their journeys to and from school, their patterns of leisure. These are likely to differ in terms of class, ethnicity and gender and in varying local and national contexts. For example, rural and urban children may lead very different lives. However, given that the meanings of the 'urban' and the 'rural" are socially constructed (Savage and Warde, 1993), these meanings, and the specific fears associated with them, may differ from one country to another. For example, in the British popular imagination cities are dangerous spaces haunted by the spectres of crime and violence, whereas nostalgia for an imagined long-lost rural idyll serves to romanti- cize the countryside (Williams, 1973). The salience of these ideas was clear in the aftermath of the Dunblane tragedy: numerous commenta- tors have suggested that small towns ought to be safe, that the incident would make more sense had it happened in inner-city Glasgow.

There are also likely to be differences in children's images of urban and rural space depending on their own experience of them. What a city child finds terrifying may leave a rural child unmoved and vice-versa. The particularities of urban and rural settings suggest that whatever globalization of experience has occurred it is always mediated through the specificity of local practices and contexts. There are vast differences between the cosseted and indulged lives of children in wealthy (post) industrial nations and the harsh realities facing street children in, say, India or Brazil. The anxieties parents feel about the former have little relevance to the latter. Yet 'western' ideas about childhood profoundly affect the ways in which children in poorer countries are represented in the global media. They are almost universally depicted as helpless victims deserving of our sympathy – an image exploited in charity fund- raising campaigns in terms of children deprived of the childhood they should have had, a childhood entirely inappropriate to the contexts in which such children live. The autonomy and resilience of these children, their ability to look after themselves is rarely acknowledged or, where it is noted it is seen as either a tragedy or a threat.

Ideas about childhood and sexuality are also culturally specific. The examples we have used pertain primarily to Britain. The peculiar anxieties about childhood and sexuality prevalent in Britain and the USA are not, for example, so evident in Scandinavian and Nordic countries. Even among western societies, then, there are cultural differ- ences in anxieties about and responses to sexual risk to children. While child sexual abuse appears to be a global phenomenon, some of its manifestations are culturally specific. The exploitation of children in sex-tourism in Asia is produced within social relations which differ from those underpinning even organized abuse in wealthy nations. The gendered and generational power hierarchies may be similar in both contexts, but the poverty which drives children into sex work in the

Asian context is specific to their local situation within the global economy. Cultural meanings of both children's work in general and sex work in particular also vary.

We hope that we have made it clear that we are not discounting the real dangers facing children today in Britain and elsewhere. We do not share the libertarian agenda of Frank Furedi (1997) who suggests that all concerns about risk are imaginings produced by the 'culture of fear'. The goal of protecting children, however, is not best served by keeping them dependent and fearful. For example, British children who have been given generalized warnings against all strangers, without information about the threat they may pose, are unlikely to be able to differentiate between threatening and non-threatening situations. If children are schooled never to speak to strangers they may also be afraid of seeking help in an emergency.[6]

Moreover risk anxiety, engendered by the desire to keep children safe, frequently has negative consequences for children themselves, serving potentially to curtail children's activities in ways which may restrict their autonomy and their opportunities to develop the necessary skills to cope with the world. However, parents are likely to be seen as culpable if they allow their children greater independence and harm comes of it. Parental risk anxiety is heightened by particular discursive constructions of responsibility. Parents are not only responsible for the care of their children, they are also *held* responsible for their children's wellbeing and conduct and are thus accountable if their children are victimized or if they victimize others. Hence anticipating, averting or otherwise managing potential risks to children is part of self-conscious, reflexive parenting practices predicated on the assumption that children are what their parents make them.

A child can no longer be accepted as it is, with physical idiosyncrasies, perhaps even flaws. Rather, it becomes the target of a diversity of efforts. All possible flaws must be corrected . . . all possible talents must be stimulated . . . Countless guides to education and upbringing appear on the book and magazine market. As different as each one is, at bottom they all have a similar message: the success of the child is defined as the private duty and responsibility of the parents/the mother. And the duty reads the same everywhere: the parents must do everything to give the child 'the best start in life'. (Beck-Gernsheim, 1996: 143)

Central to the pressures which parents face is the issue of how to keep young children 'free' of the taint of sexuality and of how to manage the transition to sexual awareness when they are deemed to have reached the appropriate stage of development. The sexualization of risk reflects historically and culturally specific constructions of both childhood and sexuality. Both are thought of as precious but in need of careful nurturance and containment in order to promote happy, carefree child-hoods and healthy (adult) sexual fulfilment. Indeed the former is often seen as a precondition for the latter – a childhood free from the shadow of sexuality is thought necessary both to keep children safe and to secure their future sexual health and happiness.

Here risk anxiety focuses disproportionately on the relatively rare risk of stranger danger as opposed to the all-too-common dangers posed by abusive fathers and other male carers.[7] When children are sexually abused, this is frequently constructed as a despoilation of innocence rather than an abuse of power. The idea that sexuality *per se* is inimical to children's wellbeing and the concomitant withholding of sexual knowledge from them may not promote their safety – certainly insofar as they are kept ignorant of forms of adult behaviour which pose a threat.

Sexual risks to children, then, should be understood as integral to the social construction of childhood and sexuality, and as consequent upon the different levels at which that construction operates. Structurally, the sexual abuse and exploitation of children is made possible by hierarchies of gender and generation which render children powerless and which shape adult male sexuality. Discursively children are constituted as vulnerable and sexually 'innocent' and sexuality is represented as a powerful, adult, drive which men in particular may be unable to control. Within these discourses it is deemed acceptable for men to be attracted to youth, vulnerability and innocence provided the object of desire is not *too* young, too vulnerable and too innocent. The man who oversteps this boundary, who cannot limit his desires to appropriate objects, is deemed more monster than man. At the level of situated interaction, the boundaries between asexual childhood and sexual adulthood are con-stantly being tested by young people as they enter into consensual sexual relations. Here, too, the gendered meanings and power relations of sexuality are continually re-enacted and sometimes re-negotiated (Holland *et al.*, 1998). Interactional settings, however, also include those where sexually ignorant children encounter sexually predatory adults, where the latter hold a virtual monopoly on both knowledge and power.

NOTES

1 Actually, the film is so boring that the corruptible would need to struggle hard to stay awake long enough to be corrupted. One interesting feature of the film is that the 'real paedophile', Clare Quilty, whose evil is contrasted with the troubled confused protagonist Humbert Humbert, is literally a shadowy figure. Throughout the film his face remains in shadow, always half obscured, until the scene where Humbert shoots him where he is revealed and exposed (in full frontal nudity) as totally grotesque.

2 The current ESRC initiative, 'Children 5–16, growing into the twenty-first century' also prioritizes a research focus on children as social actors and will vastly increase our knowledge of the world from the point of view of children.

3 This programme was recently re-run, introduced with a passing reference to JonBenet Ramsey's murder and concluding with an update on the two protagonists' subsequent careers on the child-pageant circuit. In publicizing the repeat, *Radio Times* played up the public response to the original showing: 'It was fantastic television but it caused absolute uproar. People found it very disturbing to see these youngsters actually looking like barbie dolls rather than playing with them.' We were reminded that the girls' parents had been criticized for 'coaching their offspring to display a sexuality completely inappropriate to their age' (*Radio Times* 7–13 February 1998: 92).

4 These anxieties led to, and were given further publicity by, the introduction of a private members bill in February 1996 which aimed to make it mandatory to print minimum recommended ages on the covers of the magazines.

5 In the US, the rape and murder of a child by a man with a record of sex offences who lived across the street led to a successful campaign to change the law, so that the whereabouts of convicted sex offenders can be made public. In the UK public pressure has led to the establishment of a register of sex offenders.

6 A Lothian and Borders Police 'Stranger-Danger' talk to nine year olds in a primary school in 1997 identified police officers, shopkeepers and 'ladies with children' as 'safe strangers'.

7 We are aware that women can abuse children and occasionally sexually abuse them, but this is far rarer than male abuse – and it is the disjunction between perceptions of major risks and statistically more probable risk which concerns us here.

REFERENCES

Backett, K. (now Backett-Milburn) (1988) *Mothers and Fathers: a Study of the Development and Negotiation of Parental Behaviour.* London: Macmillan.

Beauvoir, S. de (1972) *The Second Sex.* Harmondsworth: Penguin.

Beck, U. (1992) *Risk Society: Towards a New Modernity.* London: Sage.

(1998) Politics of risk society. In Franklin, J. (ed), *The Politics of Risk Society* Cambridge: Polity Press.

Beck, U. and Beck-Gernsheim, E. (1995) *The Normal Chaos of Love.* Cambridge: Polity Press.

Beck-Gernsheim, E. (1996) Life as a planning project. In Lash, S., Szerszynski, B. and Wynne, B. (eds.), *Risk, Environment and Modernity: Towards a New Ecology* London: Sage.

Brannen, J. and O'Brien, M. (1995) Childhood and the sociological gaze: paradigms and paradoxes, *Sociology,* 29(4), 729–37.

Buckingham, D. (1994) Television and the definition of childhood. In Mayall, B. (ed.), *Children's Childhoods.* London: Falmer.

Connell, R. and Dowsett, G. (1992) 'The unclean motion of the generative parts': frameworks in western thought on sexuality. In Connell, R. and

Dowsett, G. (eds.), *Re-Thinking Sex*. Melbourne: University of Melbourne Press.

CSO (1994) *Social Focus on Children*. London: HMSO.

(1995) *Social Trends*, 25. London: HMSO.

Davin, A. (1990) When is a child not a child? In Corr, H. and Jamieson, L. (eds.), *The Politics of Everyday Life*. London: Macmillan.

Ennew, J. (1986) *The Sexual Exploitation of Children*. Cambridge: Polity Press.

Frazer, E. (1988) Teenage girls reading *Jackie*. *Media, Culture and Society*, 9(4), 407–25.

Furedi, F. (1997) *Culture of Fear: Risk-Taking and the Morality of Low Expectation*. London: Cassell.

Giddens, A. (1990) *The Consequences of Modernity*. Cambridge: Polity Press.

(1991) *Modernity and Self- Identity: Self and Society in the Late Modern Age*. Cambridge: Polity Press.

Gorham, D. (1978) 'The maiden tribute of modern Babylon' reconsidered: child prostitution and the idea of childhood in late Victorian England. *Victorian Studies*, 21, 357–78.

Green, J. (1997) *Risk and Misfortune: the Social Construction of Accidents*. University College London Press.

Hillman, M., Adams, J. and Whitlegg, J. (1990) *One False Move: A Study of Children's Independent Mobility*. London: Policy Studies Institute.

Holland, J., Ramazanoglu, C., Sharpe, S. and Thomson, R. (1998) *The Male in the Head: Young People, Heterosexuality and Power*. London: The Tufnell Press.

Hood-Williams, J. (1990) Patriarchy for children: on the stability of power relations in children's lives. In Chisholm, L., Büchner, P., Krüger, H-H. and Brown, P.(eds.), *Children, Youth and Social Change: a Comparative Perspective*. London: Falmer.

Jackson, S. (1982) *Childhood and Sexuality* Oxford: Blackwell.

(1990) Demons and innocents: western ideas on children's sexuality in historical perspective. In Money, J. and Musaph, H. (eds.), *Handbook of Sexology* vol VII. Amsterdam: Elsevier.

James, A. and Prout, A. (eds.) (1990) *Constructing and Reconstructing Childhood*. London: Falmer.

Jenks, C. (1996) *Childhood*. London: Routledge.

John, A. (1980) *By the Sweat of their Brow: Women Workers at Victorian Coalmines*. London: Croom Helm.

Kitzinger, J. (1988) Defending innocence: ideologies of childhood, *Feminist Review*, 28, 77–87.

Leonard, D. (1990) In their own right: children and sociology in the UK. In Chisholm, L., Büchner, P., Krüger, H-H. and Brown, P. (eds.), *Children, Youth and Social Change: A Comparative Perspective*. London: Falmer.

Mayall, B. (ed.) (1994) *Children's Childhoods: Observed and Experienced*. London: Falmer.

Pearson, G. (1985) *Hooligan*. London: Macmillan.

Postman, N. (1994) *The Disappearance of Childhood*. New York: Vintage Books.

Qvortrup, J. (1997) 'Childhood and societal macrostructures.' Paper presented to programme meeting, ESRC Children 5–16 Programme, Keele University.

Rogers, A. and Pilgrim, D. (1995) The risk of resistance: perspectives on the mass childhood immunization programme. In Gabe, J. (ed.), *Medicine, Health and Risk*. Oxford: Blackwell.

Rose, N. (1989) *Governing the Soul*. London: Routledge.

Savage, M. and Warde, A. (1993) *Urban Sociology, Capitalism and Modernity*. London: Macmillan.

Scott, S. and Freeman, R. (1995) Prevention as a problem of modernity: the example of HIV and AIDS. In Gabe, J. (ed.), *Medicine, Health and Risk*. Oxford: Blackwell.

Scott, S. and Watson-Brown, L. (1997) The beast, the family and the little children. *Trouble and Strife*, 36.

Scott, S., Wight, D. and Buston, K. (1997) Innocence and ignorance: professionals' and pupils' discourses of sex education. Paper presented at the Scottish Medical Sociology Conference, Kinloch, Rannoch.

Sibley, D. (1995) Families and domestic routines: constructing the boundaries of childhood. In Pile, S. and Thrift, N. (eds.), *Mapping the Subject: Geographies of Cultural Transformation*. London: Routledge.

Skolnick, A. (1990) Children's rights, children's development. In Empey, L. (ed.), *Children's Rights and Juvenile Justice*. Charlottesville, VA: University of Virginia Press.

Stainton Rogers, R. and Stainton Rogers, W. (1992) *Stories of Childhood: Shifting Agendas of Child Concern*. Hemel Hempstead: Harvester Wheatsheaf.

Thomson, R. and Scott, S. (1990) *Learning about Sex*. London: The Tufnell Press.

Thorne, B. (1987) Revisioning women and social change: where are the children? *Gender and Society*, 1(1), 85–109.

(1993) *Gender Play: Girls and Boys in School*. Buckingham: Open University Press.

Valentine, G. (1996) Angels and devils: moral landscapes of childhood, *Society and Space*, (14), 581–99.

Waksler, F. C. (ed.) (1991) *Studying the Social Worlds of Children*. London: Falmer.

Walkowitz, J. R. (1992) *City of Dreadful Delight*. London: Virago.

Weeks, J. (1990) *Sex, Politics and Society*. (Second edition). London: Longman.

Williams, R. (1973) *The City and the Country*. London: Paladin.

Wohl, A. S. (1978) Sex and the single room: incest among the Victorian working classes. In A. S. Wohl (ed.), *The Victorian Family*. London: Croom Helm.

5   Constructing an endangered nation: risk, race and rationality in Australia's native title debate[1]

Eva Mackey

A nation at risk?

As Mary Douglas has pointed out, debates about danger and risk are, more importantly, contests over politics and justice (1990: 3, 1994: 44–6, 22–37). Indeed, the debate about native title, perhaps the most important political and cultural debate in contemporary Australia, is laden with images of risk, danger, fear and threat. Since colonization, as I discuss in more detail later in the chapter, Australia has had a doctrine of *terra nullius*, in which the land was legally considered unoccupied prior to European settlement. Aboriginal land rights were therefore not recognized. The 'Mabo decision', passed in 1992 by the Australian High Court, overturned *terra nullius*, and recognized, in principle, Aboriginal people's prior occupation of the continent, and their common-law rights to land. The result has been the onset of intense political debate and conflict about history, justice, rights and nationhood within Australia. The debate has grown more volatile since the High Court's 'Wik decision' in 1996, which was seen by some to extend Aboriginal land rights even further than the Mabo decision.

Newspaper headlines have presented native title as an issue that has brought the nation to the brink of a dangerous abyss, to the point of destruction. *Sydney Morning Herald* (hereafter *SMH*) headlines warned of 'Wik Chaos' (5 September 1997), of a 'race crisis' (18 November 1997), and of the possibility of 'legal apartheid' (24 November 1997). Other headlines emphasized Prime Minister John Howard's 'threat' of a 'race election' and his 'threat to play race card' (*The Australian*, 8–9 November 1997; *SMH* 8 November and 2 December 1997). Images of war and battle were evident as 'Black Leaders' went 'global in war over Wik' (*SMH*, 6 November 1997), the Governor-General gave a 'heartfelt plea over Wik war' (*SMH*, 7 November 1997), and the Government accused the Opposition (the Labor Party) of 'putting freehold titles at risk' in the 'Wik battle over cities' (*SMH*, 28 November 1997). The 'war' later reached the countryside, as a 'farm family' fired the 'first shot' in the '"momentous" native title battle' (*SMH*, 10 April 1998).

Although it is tempting to imagine that the images of risk and danger are simply ploys by newspaper editors to attract readers with images of dramatic confrontations, 'risk discourses' play a role in the arguments made by all parties in the debate. Risk discourses are integral to political debate and the 'contest to muster support for one kind of action rather than another' (Douglas, 1990: 3). Whereas supporters of native title stress that justice, truth, history, morality, indigenous culture, human rights and Australia's international reputation are at risk if native title is *not* recognized, opponents of native title have tried to draw a circle of rationality and progress around their position. The Government, the National Farmers Federation and mining interests in Australia have attempted to represent native title – and most recently the Wik Bill – as a risk to the progress and prosperity of the Australian nation. The 'uncertainty' about land tenure engendered by native title, is presented as dangerous to mining and farming interests, and thus to the nation as a whole. Prime Minister Howard has tried to present it as an issue of 'land management' rather than one of history or justice. For Howard, native title should be 'fixed' as soon as possible so the nation can move forward, especially in the context of the risks and dangers of globalization. The Government has also appealed to fear and danger more directly and viscerally on several occasions, specifically when Howard, in an interview on national television, held up what I call the 'race map' of Australia (discussed in more detail below). It also made the spurious claim that native title could threaten freehold land, specifically urban backyards.

Such heated political debates about risk, danger and minority rights in Australia are part of a larger global 'backlash' to the gains made by minorities in western nation states over the past decades. This process is evident in the strong defensive reaction of some members of dominant ethnic groups within nations who argue that *they* are threatened by the demands made by minority groups (Hall, 1991a, 1991b, 1993). These people feel that their nation – or their particular vision of the nation – is at 'risk', and the perception of an endangered and threatened nation can be mobilized to bolster racial and cultural intolerance.

During my fieldwork on national identity and cultural pluralism in Canada – a nation that defines multiculturalism as an integral part of its national identity – descriptions of the nation 'at risk' and 'in crisis' because of constitutional uncertainty were constant. While the Government tried to pass constitutional amendments intended to solve national 'problems' that emerged from contests over power relations between different historically constituted groups, 'risk discourses' of nationhood increased. Meanwhile, at local levels, many white Canadians perceived multiculturalism and the rights of minority groups, including aboriginal people, as a risk to 'mainstream' national identity, and as a threat to the 'social cohesion' of Canadian society (Mackey, 1999). We might say that multiculturalism and indigenous rights were seen by some as a risk to the 'body politic' of the nation. The construction of minority rights as 'dangerous' to the nation was mobilized to bolster the cultural/political programme of the New Right.

Images of risk and danger to the nation, to national culture, and to national progress can, therefore, be mobilized to legitimate particular political, social and economic programmes. This is most obvious in the rhetoric of politicians representing the New Right, from the Conservatives of Margaret Thatcher's Britain in the 1980s, to the Progressive Conservatives of Canada in the 1980s and 1990s, and now John Howard's Liberal Government in Australia. Risk discourses are even more obvious in the rhetoric of more extreme New Right parties such as Canada's Reform Party and Pauline Hanson's One Nation Party in Australia. Hanson argues for the reduction of the rights of Aboriginal people, the abolition of multiculturalism and changes to immigration policy, on the basis that these programmes are a major risk to a harmonious, unified, and prosperous Australia.

Analysts of 'white backlash' often point to the anxiety and sense of 'crisis' that is used to rationalize it. Winant argues that white US racial identity is now contradictory, confused and anxiety-ridden as a result of post-war challenges to white supremacy such as the civil rights movement. The sense of crisis has resulted in a series of political projects aimed at wresting back the gains made by minorities, projects in which whites construct *themselves* as disadvantaged and endangered. Winant contends that 'imaginary white disadvantage – for which there is almost no evidence at the empirical level – has achieved popular credence, and provides the cultural and political "glue" that holds together a wide variety of reactionary racial politics' (1997: 42). In the Australian context, Johnson suggests that the white backlash, or 'revenge of the mainstream', 'involves a retrospective challenge to the attempted incorporation of marginalized groups into "mainstream" identity' (1997: 422). Hage (1994) contends that the 'discourse of decline' in Australia results from a previously powerful Anglo-Celtic group struggling to maintain/reclaim its legitimacy during the ascendancy of a new middle-class, urban, Anglo-Celtic elite defined by 'Cosmo-multiculturalism'. I argue that a key issue in Canada's backlash is not the embracing or rejection of cultural difference or cultural similarity *per se*. Rather, people are demanding *loyalty* to the progress-oriented modernist nation-building project as it has been historically defined. It has historically been the white majority's unquestioned right to define the nation – and their right to decide when and how minorities are allowed both their similarities *and* their differences. The language of white victimization defends that right to bestow or withdraw tolerance (Mackey, 1999). Stuart Hall (1992) argues that a retreat to a more fundamentalist majoritarian politics emerges from the insecurities and uncertainties that have increased with globalization. In all of these situations, images of risk and danger to the nation are key mobilizing factors.

Despite the prominence of such politicized metaphors of risk and danger tied to nationalism and minority rights, few analysts have drawn on sociocultural theories of risk to understand this unexpected resurgence of cultural and racial intolerance. Risk theory has most often focused on environmental and health risks, and on 'at risk' populations. Although others explore the characteristics of 'risk society' in the late twentieth century (Beck, 1992, 1998; Beck, Giddens and Lash, 1994; Franklin, 1998; Giddens, 1998), they often focus on the environmental risks of globalization and late modernity, not the social construction and mobilization of risk discourses concerning nationalism, citizenship, cultural diversity and intolerance.

This chapter analyses how the government of Australia uses metaphors of risk, danger and threat in the native title debate. I conceptualize risks and dangers as social constructions that people mobilize to support and defend political and moral positions and to define and maintain conceptual boundaries between self and other. Danger and risk are also discursive devices, used to construct some political and moral positions as natural, 'common-sense' and rational, and other opposing positions as irrational and disloyal. In exploring the mobilization of 'risk discourses' I take a broadly anthropological approach (cf. Shore and Wright, 1997). My goal is to problematize axiomatic assumptions that inform these debates, and to explore how these assumptions and frameworks link to co-existing discourses such as nationalist discourse and earlier racial ideology. This approach can also reveal how key axioms and concepts work as broader organizing principles of society (Shore and Wright, 1997).

Notions of risk and danger, I argue, implicitly construct an imagined 'normal' state of affairs that should be defended from the perceived danger – whether it be a 'normal' or 'healthy' body at risk from disease, or a 'healthy' and 'prosperous' nation endangered by insiders or outsiders. Notions of risk not only define inclusion and exclusion, they are also normative. They construct an ideal of 'normal' through defining abnormalities and dangers. In terms of nationalism, they draw on and reinforce axiomatic assumptions about the values taken to be central to the nation. As I discuss below, the government's construction of the 'risks' of native title indicate that the value it holds dearest is the economic health of the nation, defined in a specific way as the economic health of *certain portions* of the population. On the other hand, supporters of native title argue that the protection of justice, Aboriginal culture and forms of democracy are key to the health of the nation. Debates about danger, risk and native title, therefore, articulate deep-seated and long-contested conflicts about the history, present and future of the nation, and the kinds of normative values that the nation should hold. I propose that the Howard Government mobilizes 'risk discourses' to construct the rights of Aboriginal people as a dangerous inversion of the historically constructed spatial integrity of the nation, and as a risk to the progress of the nation. These discourses, I argue, are an attempt to make racial thinking rational in the native title debate, in order to promote their version of the Australian nation.

The endangered body of the nation

In an interview on national television in September 1997, John Howard held up a map of Australia with 78 per cent coloured brown. The area not painted brown was white – and mostly along the more populated edges of the nation. While holding up the map, he argued that the 'Labor Party and the Democrats are effectively saying that the Aboriginal people of Australia should have the potential right of veto over further development of 78 per cent of the landmass of Australia' (cited in Gordon, 1997). The map, showing the white landmass of Australia being consumed by an ever-expanding mass of brown (colour coded to represent Aboriginal people) was an overly simplistic ploy intended to persuade Australians of the necessity of Howard's proposed legislation. He admitted that his map was 'a very simple message' that the Australian people would understand. Such a 'simple message' misrepresented the actual workings of native title legislation, particularly the right of veto, which no matter how Wik is interpreted, would never grant Aboriginal people the right to veto, much less have *de facto* control over, such a large part of the landmass.

There is more going on here than numerical interpretations of the actual provisions of native title legislation. Maps, as Ryan (1996) points out, are not simply representations of reality, they serve ideological and political functions. Rather than see maps as 'real' in empiricist terms, it is 'more useful to see mapping as a semiotic practice temporally embedded and transformative of previous maps, rather than as an innocent inscription started afresh on blank paper' (103). Howard's map was an attempt to influence people by drawing on and inciting fear, and the map refers to former colonial times and earlier colonial cartography. It was, after all, not so long ago that maps of the world – British colonies all coloured the same shade of pink – were seen to represent the light of progress and 'civilization' spreading over the dark and 'savage' world.

Since early colonial times, Australia has consistently been constructed as a blank, a *tabula rasa*, a continent uninhabited and empty (Ryan, 1996). As the explorer Charles Sturt put it in the journal of his 1844–45 expedition,

Let any man lay the map of Australia before him, and regard the blank upon its surface, and then let me ask him if it would not be an honourable achievement to be the first to place foot in its centre. (Quoted in Ryan, 1996: 101)

The image of Australia with creeping brown swallowing white, invokes and makes manifest older, deep-seated, racialized fears that have been embodied in the practice of mapping. Further, the process of 'imperial inscription' on maps of the land as empty, soon becomes, as Ryan points out, 'all too material for the indigenes whose presence is erased' (104). Below, I consider the significance of Howard's map within the spatial imaginary of the nation, and argue that it draws on representations of the land itself as the symbol of the 'embodied settler nation'.

The nation, the body and the individual

As Howard's map illustrates, anxieties and fears about risk and danger are often directed towards already stigmatized and marginal groups. Mary Douglas' influential work in *Purity and Danger* (1966) outlines how 'the Other' can be the subject of fear and desire to control, especially if that Other threatens to penetrate our carefully constructed boundaries of self and the body. As Lupton (1999) points out, such anxieties 'tend to emerge from and cohere around the body, which itself is a highly potent symbolic object' (124). I have suggested that the notion of danger implies a normative non-endangered state, and that it is through ideas of 'normal' – and its opposite 'deviant' – that, as Douglas suggests, social order is maintained and institutionalized. If so, to explore the significance of Howard's map it is important to question what a 'normal' nation might look like in terms of its spatial imaginary. How do we visualize, in terms of space, an ideal and healthy nation? And what is 'normal' in Australia? I suggest, drawing on theorizations about bodies, risk and danger, that the way we imagine a healthy nation draws on the way we imagine a healthy individual and a healthy body within a western framework. Howard's map, I suggest, represents the land as the endangered body of the Australian nation.

Handler argues that nationalism, a modern social form,[2] is an ideology based on a notion of 'possessive individualism', an ideology 'concerned with boundedness, continuity and homogeneity' (1988: 6).[3] He compares the way we imagine nations and ethnic groups to the way we imagine the self and the individual in modern western culture. Characteristics of individualism are highly valued in most western societies, and most could recite that individualism entails the 'equality, freedom and uniqueness of each person; it also entails opportunity, talent, competition, achievement, just reward and so on' (Handler, 1991: 63). Further, the modern individual is expected to be 'a self-sufficient and self-contained monad. Each of us stands, or should stand, on his or her own two feet, as the cliché has it. Each of us is, or has the potential to become, a complete human being' (64). He draws on Louis Dumont's work to argue that in modern culture, nations are seen as 'collective individuals', each group or nation is 'imagined to be bounded and apart, and internally homogeneous' (66).

Handler uses the image of a modern map to illustrate his point. A map uses dark unbroken lines to represent the fixed boundaries between nations, and each bounded unit (nation) is filled with a different colour. He argues that 'cartographic conventions suggest, first, that each nation is unambiguously separated from its neighbours; second, that each nation, coloured differently from its neighbours, possesses a unique identity and culture; and third, that each nation, of one and only one colour, is internally homogeneous' (66).

This particular conception of an individual (or a social group or nation), as Handler suggests, is not universal, but rather specific and modern. He contrasts individualist notions of culture with cultures that value social hierarchy. Outlining notions of self in European Christianity during the Middle Ages, he points out that in such a culture it would have been

blasphemous to pretend that an individual was complete, *per se*, a monad. To the medieval mind . . . any human person, indeed, any tree, rock, flower, or angel was merely a tiny element in God's vast creation, each such element deriving its value from its place in the whole. Moreover, all such places were ranked relative to all others: hence no equality, but all elements of creation ordered, from the highest to the lowest, according to their distance from God. (Handler, 1991: 64)

Although such a world might sound alien to us, and perhaps unfair, he argues that, 'we must endeavour to see our own conception – that each separate individual is complete – as equally strange; as creatures who depend on both our physical and social environment, we are obviously not alone, apart, and complete' (64). Our sense of the ideal and healthy nation, therefore, draws on modern western notions of self and person-hood, notions that are neither universal nor inevitable.

Concepts of the body have also changed over time and in similar ways. Lupton (1999) draws on the work of Elias, Bakhtin, Ferguson, and Muchembled to trace these changes, arguing that during the Middle Ages, people had a concept of the 'open body' – perceived as uncontrolled, sensuous, volatile, communal and open to the world. Later, the 'closed body', seen ideally as autonomous, controlled, orderly, 'individuated and closed off from other bodies', became the ideal. The transformation from the open 'grotesque' body to the closed 'civilized' body was accompanied by increased networks of regulations on how to manage, control and self-discipline the body. In modern western cultures, bodies, like individuals and like nations, ideally have firm boundaries between inside and outside, are self-contained and self-regulating, are unified and whole in and of themselves, and do not allow uncontrolled penetration of body boundaries, either by other bodies or substances.

In 'civic' or western nationalism the land and territory become the embodiment of the idealized nation,[4] and are represented on maps as bounded and homogeneous entities.[5] The western individualist national body of civic nationalism must be developed, cared for and protected, both from penetration from without and disease from within, because in an individualist framework ideally the nation's body, like the body of the individual, should be autonomous, unified and contained. Nationalist discourse in Canada and Australia is replete with such developmental and defensive policies and images, especially concerning immigration. One of the first actions of the newly formed Australian Federal Government in 1901 was, after all, to institute the 'white Australia policy', restricting immigration to the nation on the basis of race. An 1888 cartoon from the Melbourne magazine *Punch* demonstrates how the idea of protecting Australia from the threat of 'Others' was expressed through gendered images of the nation as body. It shows Australia as a group of young white women holding up the banner of 'Federation' as they fend off the monstrous head of an Asian man with the title 'the Chinese fist' emblazoned on his evil looking forehead (reprinted in Lane, 1998). If Australia is represented as young women whose purity must be defended, Asian immigration is more than a policy to import workers, it offers the potential of defilement and rape of that (national) purity.

If the land and territory is the embodied nation, and a healthy nation is seen as an image on a world map (a bounded, single-coloured, unified whole), then Howard's two-tone, brown-and-white map takes on a number of complex meanings. It represents native title as a danger akin to the penetration of carefully maintained body boundaries. The brown invasion also disrupts the spatial integrity of the nation, which, according to the dominant national imaginary, should be a homogeneous and undifferentiated colour. Further, because the base colour of the map (the normal state of the nation) is white, being taken over and penetrated by brown, it is the brown that becomes foreign and deviant and an invasion (rape) of the 'normal' and 'healthy' nation. The map, as I discuss below, also speaks to longer standing fears about the spatial distribution of populations on the body of the Australian landmass.

The 'normal' nation in Australia: space, danger and control

Howard's so-called dangers to the nation arise because of a fundamental change in Australian law that throws into question over 200 years of history. In national history it was 'normal' to control and develop the 'body of the nation' – its space and land – through the erasure, control and containment of Aboriginal people. Until 1992, indigenous peoples' access to the land of Australia was controlled by the doctrine of *terra nullius*, the idea that the land was empty when the settlers arrived. Australia's indigenous peoples thereby had no inherent land rights as first peoples. The 'Mabo decision' of June 1992 overturned this legacy of land law based on race when the High Court declared that Australian common law recognized native title. It judged that indigenous people who demonstrated an ongoing connection with their traditional lands could, potentially, claim them back. Poynton says the Mabo decision 'overturned at a stroke 204 years of colonial mythology about an empty continent inhabited by inexplicable nomads' (1994: 41).

The actualities of implementing the legal changes and claiming title was and is extremely complex. Within the confines of the Mabo decision the possibilities of native title claims were also limited, as title could not be claimed on land that, during the course of the conquest, had been alienated into freehold or leasehold. The High Court's Wik decision of January 1996 again changed the terms of the debate when it judged that native title could exist over leasehold land, and therefore native title could co-exist with the rights of pastoralists on leasehold land. However – demonstrating how the decision also limits the 'rights' of Aboriginal people – in the case of conflict between leaseholders and native title holders, the rights of pastoralists would prevail (Attorney General's Legal Practice, 1997). The possibility of co-existence and negotiation imbued terror into the hearts of the (then) new Howard Government. It has engaged in an outright attack on the High Court, and has sought, without historical precedent, to go against it by attempting to change the law (Marcus, 1998). John Howard developed a ten-point plan to restrict the implications of Wik, and took this plan to Parliament and the Senate.

This doctrine of *terra nullius* – on which the normality, health and prosperity of the nation was based for over 200 years – emerged from and was justified by a range of historically changing forms of constructing indigenous people. In the early days of settlement they were often seen as less than human, as flora and fauna, and as noble savages (Pearson, 1994: 3–4). As settlement and dispossession increased, racial ideology developed, and legitimated dispossession through supposedly 'scientific' means.[6] These policies and ideologies were of course not uncontested, but were subject to debate and resistance over time (see Reynolds, 1998). Nevertheless, Aboriginal people were thus subject to a constantly changing series of colonial policies that sought to erase them, dispossess them, or assimilate them. These processes included outright massacre during the early years of conquest and settlement; the more subtle 'disciplinary' (*pace* Foucault, 1977) methods of containment on missions and control of movement (Nicoll, 1998: 177), and the masked 'cultural genocide' of the removal of Aboriginal children from their families and homes (Human Rights and Equal Opportunity Commission, 1997). Morris (1989) has shown, following Foucault, that Aboriginal people in Australia were subject to a series of disciplinary regimes intended to generate particular forms of subjectivities through techniques including surveillance and pastoral care. These programmes, despite the supposed 'good intentions' behind some of them (Edwards and Read, 1989), drew on changing forms of racial ideology that ultimately legitimated the foundation of Australian land law. As Frank Brennan argued, it has been the 'dispossession of [Aboriginal] Australians on which we have constructed the monolith of Australian society and its prosperity' (quoted in Poynton, 1994: 43). The erasure, control, containment and assimilation of Aboriginal people – especially their link to their lands – has therefore been foundational to the nation and national prosperity.

The Mabo decision may have upturned the legal basis of *terra nullius*, although not necessarily the implicit ideologies of race that informed it, a legacy that Aboriginal activist Noel Pearson argues still lingers 'in the baggage' of Australia's 'national inheritance' and infects its 'national psyche' (quoted in Pearson, 1994: 3). As Foucault (1977) has taught us, disciplinary power functions in part through the spatial distribution of individuals and deviant groups who are taught and coerced to 'know their place' within the body politic and the economy of space. Although Foucault focuses on the criminal and the deviant, and does not to a large extent, as Anna Laura Stoler (1995) points out, explore colonial power relations and colonial bodies, it is possible to draw on Foucault's insights to argue that the history of land and politics in Australia was an attempt to either make invisible or control the presence and spatial distribution of indigenous people in the body politic and economy of space in the nation. They, as indigenous people with potential rights to land, are seen as dangerous and risky to the nation and progress. Indeed, the discourses that justified all the processes of erasure and control – from the discourse of 'savagery' which justified the massacres in the 1800s to the discourses of aid and assistance which underpinned the practice of the removal of Aboriginal children from their homes – were laced with images of danger, risk and fear. In order to have the ideal spatial image of a homogeneous and bounded nation – of a single colour (white) – Aboriginal people's presence needed to be controlled, contained or obliterated from the body politic. Therefore, to have them reappear as on Howard's map, penetrating the carefully defended nation, challenges those centuries of history; it inverts the historically constructed economy of space and embodiment of the settler nation. Howard's map presents the national body as a victim of invasion by disease from within – a black cancer that threatens the sacred history and homogeneity of the (white) nation. The map presents a body part that, after years of training and coercion to 'know its place', does not know and refuses to 'know its place' – a deviant and uncontrollable danger to the nation.

Nicoll, along similar lines, examines what she calls the 'hysterical rhetoric' of the anti-Aboriginal backlash (1998: 180), one example of which is the claim made by Pauline Hanson in January 1997 that 'this whole Mabo, native title issue has got out of control and the inmates are running the asylum' (cited in Nicoll, 1998: 177). Nicoll argues that the original and ongoing system of managing Aboriginal people in Australia is that of a 'carceral regime' (*pace* Foucault, 1977) in which indigenous people were first dispossessed, and then faced with increasing 'govermentalization', including confinement, enforced labour, restrictions on movement and activities, and the 'exercise of state sanctioned punitive force' (176-7). She demonstrates that in the months after the Wik decision, opponents of co-existence increasingly represented *themselves* as 'objects of an Aboriginal regime of punishment'. Examples such as

Hanson's 'spectre of punitive Aboriginality' in which the 'inmates are now running the asylum', signify, for the anti-native title lobby, a 'dystopian order of things whereby the existing relationship between Aborigines and the State is inverted'. From this neo-colonial perspective, Nicoll argues, a 'state of affairs in which Aborigines are controlling the state apparatus is, by definition, "out of control"' (1998: 178). Similarly, the map which shows the (white) 'normal' nation being invaded and taken over by the (black) 'abnormal', represents a nation out of control, a nation in which the old masters feel like victims, a body in which a long-repressed and controlled disease threatens to take over from within.

Risk to national interest and progress

Lupton (1999: 148) argues that 'the emphasis in contemporary western societies on the avoidance of risk is strongly associated with the ideal of the "civilized" body, an increasing desire to take control of one's life, to rationalize and regulate the self and the body, to avoid the vicissitudes of fate'. Further, notions of the self, even the very category of 'the self', are not universal (see Rose, 1990). As Beck-Gernsheim (1996) points out, the concept of the 'individualization' of subjects, which developed in the shift from pre-industrial to industrial society, means we tend to think of our lives, and our bodies, as planning projects. Life is 'no longer . . . a wonderful gift of God, but the property of an individual, which must be permanently defended. More than that, it becomes a task to be carried out, an individual project' (Kohli, quoted in Beck-Gernsheim, 1996: 141). Also, the project is inculcated with the 'religion of progress' (Schmitt, quoted in Beck-Gernsheim, 1996: 148). The body, the soul, the person, must develop, improve and progress throughout a lifetime. In the native title debate, the collective individual – the nation – is also perceived in modernist terms, ideally as an entity that should progress, be controlled, be made rational, be regulated, and that should not be victimized by 'uncertainty'.

Indeed, one of the most recurring themes in the native title debate is the way in which the government constructs native title as a danger and risk to 'the national interest', particularly the risk to competitiveness, opportunities and progress. The entire anti native title lobby have all stated, in particular, that the *uncertainty* over native title is dangerous for investment and economic competitiveness. It is assumed that economic competitiveness is the defining feature of a healthy nation. Yet the discourse of 'the national interest' – defined as it is in such a specific and limited way – becomes, I argue, a means to exclude Aboriginal people and their human rights from 'the national interest' because it is they who endanger it.

In an interview with *Sydney Morning Herald* journalist Margot King-ston, Special Minister of State and architect of the Wik ten-point plan, Nick Minchin, argued that one of Labor's 'problems was that it was seen to be beholden to a whole range of vested interest groups . . . not doing things in the national interest'. Minchin made it clear, says Kingston, that for the Howard Government, 'Aborigines are just another special interest group which once captured the Labor Government, and whose rights under the conservatives will be subsumed to their view of the "national interest"' (Kingston, 1998). Here, Aboriginal people are set up in opposition to the national interest, and their rights, as I will discuss in more detail below, become secondary to a particular version of national progress.

What is the national interest? Minchin suggests that the public want the Wik situation 'fixed', they want it 'out of the way':

[T]heir sympathy overwhelmingly lies with Australian farmers. They don't want to see Aborigines maltreated, but they fundamentally believe . . . that Australian farmers should be able to get on with doing what they've always done, producing the nation's wealth, without interference from native title holders. (Quoted in Kingston, 1998)

Here the farmers do not simply farm, they 'produce the *nation's wealth*'. They are therefore constructed major contributors to the national interest and national progress, whereas native title holders 'interfere with', and endanger national progress. According to Minchin the Australian people want this disturbance to the progress of the nation removed. These constructions of national interest that include and embrace farmers and exclude and demonize Aboriginal people, assume a particular modern liberal version of nationhood and progress.

In doing so they draw on a long history of ideas about nationalism – itself a form of social life that is modern and liberal. Concepts of unity and progress are essential to most common-sense ideas of national health. A nation is often ideally conceived as a collection of individuals who, although they may be divided by all kinds of differences, are unified in their desire to see the nation prosper and move forward. Nationalism is based on notions of temporal continuity: a nation should have a shared past (often glorified in nationalist mythology) moving on a continuum to the present, and then onwards to an improved future. Nation-building, as Talal Asad argues, is a western project in that, no matter what form it takes, it entails the 'continuous physical and moral improvement of entire governable populations through flexible strategies' (Asad, 1993: 12). A central part of the project is the notion of improvement, of progress.

Axiomatic assumptions about national progress, in the Australian context, were mobilized to exclude some citizens from national belonging. For Nick Minchin, progress, economic rationalism and notions of communal versus individual interest come together to reveal his version of national progress. He argues that one of the major problems with native title is that it 'is inalienable, it's common law, it's communal', and on the value of communal land ownership he says:

[I]t's hard to think of something more important to the sustainability of higher living standards in western society than certainty in property . . . communal common-law systems went out the door 200 years ago, and when they did there was a huge increase in personally generated wealth. That's why this [native title] issue is so fundamentally important; it can't be driven by some sense of guilt or emotion. (Quoted in Kingston, 1998)

This very complex statement enacts a number of important moves. First, the highest value for Minchin is to sustain western living standards. This 'fundamentally important' value is dependent on *private*, not communal, land ownership. Private ownership is a concept that, according to Minchin, kicked progress and civilization off in the first place. Progress is seen as an advancement in 'personally generated wealth'. This highly valued progress – both forward looking and wealth producing – is opposed to communal (Aboriginal) land practices. He thereby constructs Aboriginal people as backward savages who are still mired in the outdated practice of communal-land-ownership systems, which, according to Minchin, 'went out the door 200 years ago'. It is noteworthy that 200 years ago is approximately when white settlers engaged in the mass slaughter of Aboriginal people so that they could take over the land and 'generate personal wealth'. Communal land ownership did not simply, as Minchin implies, go 'out the door' by some natural process of evolution. It was pushed, shoved and shot into submission in the name of progress.

Minchin's fears for progress resonate with earlier arguments in the native title debate. In placing Aboriginal people and particular land systems way in the past, as he does, he invokes an older pseudo-scientific hierarchical racial ideology based on evolutionary notions of progress (Stocking, 1968; Banton, 1987). He also draws on what Reynolds calls 'developmentalism', or the belief – central to the 'perception of settler Australia'– that the need to develop the country is the *raison d'être* of the nation. Reynolds argues that each generation may have 'a different way of expressing this [developmentalism]', but the central idea has 'run on like a river through settler Australia'. He argues that developmentalism is 'linked to racism in the sense that it is related to ideas about Aboriginal culture – that it is not interested in development, that it is static – which go back, even beyond racism, to the idea of stages of human development' (1997: 32).

In early colonial days, the way that Aboriginal people related to their land was used to justify the doctrine of *terra nullius*. As Nicoll points out, *terra nullius* was a 'self-serving interpretation' of Aboriginal mobility. Rather than acknowledge that the mobility of Aboriginal people was 'confined to specific territories, of which different clans enjoyed ownership, the British took the mobility of the Aborigines as evidence that nobody owned the land' (1998: 176). Further, in an 1842 speech, Sydney barrister Richard Windeyer used the nomadic practices of indigenous people as the basis of what Reynolds calls 'perhaps the most sustained and intellectually powerful attack on Aboriginal rights ever mounted in early colonial Australia' (20). He argued that the tribes of Australia did not inhabit the land, rather they ranged over it, never tilling the soil, nor clearing the land, enclosing it or planting it. Therefore they did not own it and their occupation did not 'by the law of nature establish any title to the substance of the soil' (Quoted in Reynolds, 1998: 20–1).

While Minchin's argument invokes such colonial ideologies, it also plays on hysterical and unfounded fears that native title might endanger progress by throwing Australia back to precolonial times. A similar, although less subtle, version of this argument was made during the debates about the impact of Mabo during 1993. When warnings of financial analysts in the United States and Britain that the uncertainty about native title might 'stall the flow of capital' into Australia, it inspired one mining analyst from the investment banking house, Lehman Brothers, to say that the Mabo decision must be reversed if Australia was to be a modern economy. He said that if 'this decision stands, Australia could go back to being a stone age culture of 200,000 people living on witchetty grubs' (quoted in Lagan and Davies, 1993).

Minchin's opposition to communal land ownership also reflects a broader opposition to group rights which is integral to liberal nationalism. The refrain that 'all Australians should be equal' and none should have 'special rights' has been used by the Howard Government as well as Pauline Hanson's One Nation Party to counter claims by Aboriginal people on the basis that they are special groups because of their particular history. Minchin defines this individualist 'egalitarianism' as an integral feature of Australian identity. He suggests that many Australians share the core philosophy driving the Government's Wik response, that of formal equality based on *European values*. The difficulty, he argues,

is that Australia has a profound sense of egalitarianism, and we were all taught that the thing wrong in the past was rights based on race . . . That is . . . why, as an immigrant society, it's worked so well. That's where the indigenous issue is quite difficult, because for some Australians it does offend that deep sense of egalitarianism . . . in the sense that they are being told that these people must be treated differently because their origins pre-date Europeans. (quoted in Kingston, 1998)

Here Minchin draws on critiques of Australia's history as racist (often used to promote native title), and uses those critiques to promote racialized policies now. He implicitly constructs the racial policies utilized to bolster the dominance of an already dominant group in the past, as structurally similar to policies designed to correct historically created inequalities in the present. He thereby uses the notion of 'equality' to promote and bolster inequality. As Reynolds suggests, this version of inequality is 'profoundly assimilationist while seeming not to be . . . it also allows people to attack indigenous causes while proclaiming profoundly that they are not in any way racist – they just believe in equality' (1997: 33). These examples support Goldberg's claim that the 'irony of modernity, the liberal paradox comes down to this: As modernity commits itself progressively to idealized principles of liberty, equality, and fraternity . . . there is a multiplication of . . . the sets of exclusions they prompt and rationalize, enable and sustain' (1993: 6).

According to Minchin's view of land ownership and 'egalitarian' national interest, in which progress based on the accumulation of wealth through private ownership is paramount, the Government is forward looking and good for the national interest, while Aboriginal people are backward looking and opposed to the national interest. Minchin implies that the issue of native title is so important because it threatens the entire progress-oriented nature of western civilization. The issue should therefore not be driven by some sense of emotion or guilt (such as that of the backward and emotional supporters of native title), but by the 'common-sense' rationalism of his own capital accumulation version of national interest, bolstered by supposedly universal western values.

Risk, race and rationality

Prime Minister John Howard, like One Nation Party leader Pauline Hanson, often invokes the image of the 'ordinary Australian' and the 'Australian people'. At a 9 April 1998 press conference, he defended the possibility of calling an election on native title because, as he argued, it would be 'democratic', it would allow *the people* of Australia to decide' on the issue. The Australian people, he said, should be 'trusted to make a calm, *rational, dispassionate* judgement' on the native title issue. At the same time he did not want to risk being perceived by the Australian people or the international community as 'racist', because in the same press conference he stressed that, as far as the Government was concerned, 'it will not be a race election. I will not seek to exploit issues of race. I will not seek to use racist language. I will not seek to drag issues of race into the election campaign . . .' He continued by arguing that the 'issue of whether or not something is fought on the issue of race depends upon the attitude taken, the words uttered, and the use made of political differences in terms of race' (cited in Tingle and Kingston, 1998), implying that the issue of native title is only about race or 'racist' if people *say* overtly racist or discriminatory *words* about Aboriginal people. This assertion depends upon a specific definition of racism – defined as the words people use and as rhetoric and attitude. Here Howard draws on popular understandings of racism that see it as irrational or ignorant hostility to people of other races based on erroneous generalizations and stereotypes. This definition allows people, as it allows Howard and his proposed native title legislation, to uphold, defend, and even promote processes that create racial disadvantage, while at the same time allowing them to believe they are not racist if they do not express direct racial hostility. Cowlishaw argues that 'the existence of racism does not depend on expressed hostility but on the consequences of actions and beliefs'. It is part of a 'series of processes whereby racial inequality is structured into the whole social matrix' (1988: 6). As we know, 'racism' is not static, but transforms and changes through time, and new forms of 'cultural racism' do not depend on overt references to biological inferiority to do their work (Barker, 1981; Gilroy, 1987).

In opposition to Howard's ten-point plan and his declaration of innocence about racism, supporters of native title, such as Kimberly Land Council Chair Peter Yu, offer a different interpretation of race and native title. Yu argues that the government:

would like to see us assimilated, little black bodies and white minds, for that is what this current native title debate is about . . . They can't rip babies out of their mothers' arms any more but they can change the law and appropriate our distinctiveness as a people and they can try to assimilate us . . . There is no doubt that the current native title debate is about racism. (Peter Yu, 11 November 1997)

While Howard's limited definition of racism vacates it of historically structured processes of racial thinking and policy, Yu's statement encompasses history and culture. Howard's assertions are an attempt to strip the native title debate of dangerous implications that it is racialized. Yet a major sticking point in negotiations over the ten-point plan was that the Government refused to have the Native Title Act subject to the

Racial Discrimination Act. Also, it is likely that the ten-point plan contravenes the International Convention on all Forms of Racial Discrimination (CERD), and that it entails *de facto* extinguishment of native title. Howard attempts to present his ten-point plan as a rational response to land management issues, so that the people will make, as he sees it, a 'calm, rational, dispassionate judgement' on Wik. His job, and the job of others in support of his ten-point plan will be to continue in this vein – to sell racial thinking to the Australian people as 'rational' and 'dispassionate'.

One method that he and his followers have used to try to make racism rational is to construct a sense of a nation at risk. They construct native title as a risk and danger to the body politic of the nation and to the progress oriented nation-building project. Aboriginal people and their outmoded forms of land ownership become an impediment to the progress of the nation, and they are constructed as a backward-looking and interfering 'special interest group'. These frameworks, as well as Howard's constant invocations of the 'ordinary people' and 'the ordinary Australians', are characteristic of a broader, so-called 'populist' neo-liberal discourse on the rise in many nation states (Johnson, 1997; Brodie, 1995). These frameworks, used to discount the claims of minorities and to re-define citizenship, naturalize the exclusion of some citizens from national belonging, and try to do so without direct reference to culture, race, sexual preference and gender (Mackey, 1997).

In a *SMH* article entitled, 'A Wik plan to serve the nation', Minchin extends the supposedly rational argument about national progress and the dangers of 'special interest groups' such as Aboriginal people. He argues that the government's main goal with native title is to 'ensure workable land management'. The current act, he argues, is deficient because its 'long and complex processes are delaying and impeding economic development'. Minchin outlines the Government's opposition to having the Native Title Act subject to the Racial Discrimination Act (RDA), arguing that to do so would be

a recipe for *legal chaos* and endless litigation. It means anything done in line with the Native Title Act could be legally challenged at any time on the grounds that somehow it was not consistent with the RDA. Investors, miners and farmers would face *'double jeopardy'* and *impossible land management uncertainty* . . . While the government's firm view is that the current bill is not racially discriminatory, this proposal [is] unacceptable. (Minchin, 1998, emphasis added)

Here, the human rights of Aboriginal people – and the protection of those rights in law through the Racial Discrimination Act – become dispensable if they threaten nation-building and progress. Human rights are sacrificed to the version of 'national interest'– as defined by the current government. If protecting people from racism is inefficient, if it will create 'chaos and uncertainty' that might risk the supposedly rational progress of the nation, human rights will be subsumed to 'the national interest'.

It is important to remember that the rationality of progress, especially when combined with a sense of threat and danger to self-interest, has a longer history, and can have serious repercussions. Bauman has argued that the holocaust was enabled by modern rationality – that it was a result of processes of western modern civilization, in particular bureaucratic processes of social engineering and instrumental rationality with the goal of improvement and progress. He argues that 'the civilizing process' is, amongst other things, a process of 'emancipating the desiderata of rationality from interference of ethical norms and moral inhibitions' (Bauman, 1989: 28). He outlines the complex construction of 'the Jew' as object of threat, danger and chaos in Germany. Finally he suggests that one lesson of the holocaust is that when people such as the Germans, en masse and as individuals, were put into situations of believing they were threatened and endangered, they were able to 'argue themselves away from the issue of moral duty . . . adopting instead the precepts of rational interest and self-preservation' (206).

What does it mean, then, to make a 'rational' decision on Wik, as Howard proposes? Does it mean allocating history, justice, human rights and morality (a term that seems strangely archaic in these times), to the morass of the irrational, as Minchin proposes? Indeed, in December 1998 John Howard admitted that he believed there was 'no moral choice involved in the Wik issue' (quoted in Kingston, 1997). Further, he suggested that the 'constant indication of morality' about native title is 'an attempt to use moral intimidation against the government in the belief that it will change its position' (quoted in Kingston, 1997). The absurdity of proposing that citizens should not use 'moral intimidation' against their government only belies the Government's attempt at what I call the 'rationalist intimidation' of indigenous people and other Australians in pursuit of their goals.

Conclusion

This chapter has mapped out the ways in which the Howard Government has mobilized metaphors of risk, danger and fear in the native title debate. I have discussed how these discourses construct the rights of Aboriginal people as a dangerous inversion of the historically constructed spatial integrity of the nation, and as a risk and threat to the progress of the nation. These discourses are an attempt to make racial thinking rational. They are part of a scenario in which rational economic 'progress' is the ultimate value that must be defended at all costs and to which human rights can be sacrificed. The discourses draw on earlier forms of constructing Aboriginal people as dangerous to the nation, in order to justify current attempts to re-inscribe racial inequality in Australia through land law. In Canada, as my research showed, the rights of minorities were considered by some as 'risky' to the nation and the nation-building project. The risk discourses used by the Australian government, not only construct Aboriginal people as disloyal, dangerous and trapped in the past because of their desire to counter the historical and racial essence of Australian land law, their politicized presence is seen as dangerous because it upturns and questions the history, policies and spatial imaginary that have made and developed the nation and its myths. The blatant racialization of these risk discourses leads me to conclude that, despite mythology to the contrary about Australia being a 'postcolonial' nation, not only has colonialism not ended (Heiss, 1998; Marcus, 1998), it is constantly being re-created and defended, in part through discourses that construct the nation and the nation-building project as 'at risk' and 'endangered' by Aboriginal people.

NOTES

1 I am grateful to Julie Marcus, Mary Millen and Deborah Lupton for their comments on earlier versions of this chapter.

2 Theorists of nationalism generally agree that it emerged with European modernity (Anderson, 1991; Greenfeld, 1996; Chatterjee, 1986), specifically in the shift from agricultural to industrial society. Gellner (1983) suggests that the idea of nationalism emerged with the notion of a singular culture at its core, a singular culture and language which promoted the flexibility of workers, a necessity for industrial capitalism. Despite their novelty, nations have become the most universally legitimate, and seemingly natural, political units of our time. In modernity the nation state 'has been granted universal recognition and validity as the authorised marker of the particular' (Ang and Stratton, 1996: 26).

3 As the idea of the nation developed over the course of the eighteenth and nineteenth centuries it was thought of – in its ideal form – as containing a single culture and language and of being bounded and sovereign. Nevertheless, very few if any nations can be seen to in reality contain a single culture, and any cultural homogeneity or national consciousness that does exist is a result of mass communication systems and government programmes such as education. These programmes create citizens and subjects who will take on the idea that the nation should be a loyalty that supercedes all other less 'fundamental' identities such as region, ethnicity, race, gender and sexual preference (see Hall, 1992: 292–95). In Canada and Australia, for example,

immigrants after World War Two were regularly trained in 'the Australian way of life' or the 'Canadian way of life'. Similarly, the removal of Aboriginal children from their homes was an attempt to assimilate them into 'mainstream' society.

4 Smith distinguishes between 'civic' and 'ethnic' nationalisms by pointing out that 'non-western' or 'ethnic' nationalism emphasizes 'common descent' and common ancestry, whereas the western or 'civic' model is primarily territorial or spatial: nations must possess territories, and people and territory belong to each other (1991: 10–11).

5 The relationship between maps and bodies has a longer history. In the thirteenth century, the Ebstorf map of the world places the body of Christ in the centre (see Ryan, 1996: 104). In Australia in 1997, several months after Howard held up the 'race map', a cartoon by Nicholson entitled 'Native Title Claims', appeared in *The Australian* (25 November 1998). It showed an outline of John Howard's body flat on the ground – his body itself becoming a map – with some areas painted brown. The caption said 'The brown areas on this map are subject to a veto by the National Party [the party forming Howard's Coalition Government with the Liberal Party]'. Howard's 'race map' was now imprinted on his own body.

6 For a detailed history of law and dispossession in Australia see Reynolds (1987).

REFERENCES

Anderson, B. (1991) *Imagined Communities: Reflections on the Origin and Spread of Nationalism*. London: Verso.

Ang, I. and Stratton, J. (1996) Asianing Australia: notes toward a critical transnationalism in cultural studies. *Cultural Studies*, 10(1), 16–36.

Asad, T. (1993) *Genealogies of Religion: Discipline and Reasons of Power in Christianity and Islam*. Baltimore, MD: Johns Hopkins University Press.

Attorney-General's Legal Practice. (1997) Legal implications of the High Court Decision in *The Wik Peoples* v. *Queensland*, Current Advice. Department of the Prime Minister and Cabinet, Office of Indigenous Affairs.

Banton, M. (1987) *Racial Theories*. Cambridge University Press.

Barker, M. (1981) *The New Racism*. London: Junction Books.

Bauman, Z. (1989) *Modernity and the Holocaust*. Cambridge: Polity Press and Basil Blackwell.

Beck, U. (1992) From industrial society to risk society: questions of survival, social structure and ecological enlightenment. *Theory, Culture and Society*, 9, 97–123.

(1998). Politics of risk society. In Franklin, J. (ed.), *The Politics of Risk Society*. Cambridge: Polity Press.

Beck, U., Giddens A. and Lash, S. (1994) *Reflexive Modernization: Politics, Tradition and Aesthetics in the Modern Social Order*. Cambridge: Polity Press.

Beck-Gernsheim, E. (1996) Life as a planning project. In Lash, S., Szerszynski, B. and Wynne, B. (eds.), *Risk, Environment and Modernity: Towards a New Ecology*. London: Sage.

Brodie, J. (1995) *Politics on the Margins*, Halifax, Nova Scotia: Fernwood Publishing.

Chatterjee, P. (1986) *National Thought and the Colonial World: a Derivative Discourse?*. London: Zed Press.

Cowlishaw, G. (1988) *Black, White or Brindle: Race in Rural Australia*. Cambridge University Press.

Douglas, M. (1966) *Purity and Danger: an Analysis of Concepts of Pollution and Taboo*. London: Routledge & Kegan Paul.

(1990) Risk as forensic resource. *Daedalus*, 119(4), 1–16.

(1994) *Risk and Blame: Essays in Cultural Theory*. London: Routledge.

Edwards, C. and Read, P. (1989) *The Lost Children*. Moorebank, New South Wales: Doubleday.

Foucault, M. (1977) *Discipline and Punish: the Birth of the Prison*. New York: Pantheon Books.

Franklin, J. (ed.) (1998) *The Politics of Risk Society*. Cambridge: Polity Press.

Gellner, E. (1983) *Nations and Nationalism*. Oxford: Blackwell Publishers.

Giddens, A. (1998) Risk society: the context of British politics. In Franklin, J. (ed.), *The Politics of Risk Society*. Cambridge: Polity Press.

Gilroy, P. (1987) *There Ain't No Black in the Union Jack*. London: Routledge.

Goldberg, D. T. (1993) *Racist Culture: Philosophy and the Politics of Meaning*. Oxford and Cambridge: Blackwell.

Gordon, M. (1997) Lighting the Wik. *The Weekend Australian*, 22–3 November 1997.

Greenfeld, L. (1996) Nationalism and Modernity. *Social Research*, 63(1), 3–40.

Hage, G. (1994) Anglo-Celtics today: cosmo-multiculturalism and the phase of the fading phallus. *Communal/Plural*, 4, 41–7.

Hall, S. (1991a) Old and new identities, old and new ethnicities. In King, A. D. (ed.), *Culture, Globalization and the World System*. London: Macmillan.

(1991b) The local and the global: globalization and ethnicity. In King, A. D. (ed.), *Culture, Globalization and the World* System. London: Macmillan.

(1992) The question of cultural identity. In Hall, S., Held, D. and McGrew, T. (eds.), *Modernity and its Futures*. Cambridge: Polity Press in Association with Open University.

(1993) Culture, community, nation. *Cultural Studies*, 7(3), 349–63.

Handler, R. (1988) *Nationalism and the Politics of Culture in Quebec*. Madison, WI: University of Wisconsin Press.

(1991) Who owns the past?: History, cultural property, and the logic of possessive individualism. In Williams, B. (ed.), *The Politics of Culture*. Washington, DC: Smithsonian University Press.

Heiss, A. (1998) Reconciliation, native title and Aboriginal authors. Paper presented at Charles Sturt University, Bathurst.

Human Rights and Equal Opportunity Commission (1997) *Bringing Them Home: Report of the National Inquiry into the Separation of Aboriginal and Torres Strait Islander Children from Their Families*. Sydney: HREOC.

Johnson, C. (1997) John Howard and the revenge of the mainstream: some implications for concepts of identity. *Australasian Political Studies 1997: Proceedings of the 1997 APSA Conference*, 409–31.

Kingston, M. (1997) Wik not moral issue, says PM. *Sydney Morning Herald*, 9 December 1997.

(1998) Selling Howard's way on Wik. *Sydney Morning Herald*, 6 March 1998.

Lagan, B. and Davies, A. (1993) PM mobilises Labor on Mabo. *Sydney Morning Herald*, 14 June 1993.

Lane, B. (1998) Race power play. *The Weekend Australian*, 4–5 April 1998.

Lupton, D. (1999) *Risk*. London: Routledge.

Mackey, E. (1997) The cultural politics of populism: celebrating Canadian national identity. In Shore, C. and Wright, S. (eds.), *Anthropology of Policy*. London: Routledge.

(1999) *The House of Difference: Cultural Politics and National Identity in Canada*. London: Routledge.

Marcus, J. (1998) The shadow of race: form and function in heritage institutions. Unpublished manuscript.

Morris, B. (1989) *Domesticating Resistance: the Dhan Gadi Aborigines and the Australian State*. London: Berg.

Nicoll, F. (1998) Backlash: reconciliation after Wik. *Meanjin*, 57(1), 167–83.

Pearson, N. (1994) A troubling inheritance. *Race and Class*, 35(4), 1–9.

Poynton, P. (1994) Mabo: now you see it, now you don't. *Race and Class*, 35(4), 41–56.

Reynolds, H. (1987) *The Law of the Land*. Ringwood: Penguin.

(1997) Racism and other national discourses. In Gray, G. and Winter, C. (eds.), *The Resurgence of Racism: Howard, Hanson and the Race Debate*. Clayton: Monash Publications in History.

(1998) *This Whispering in Our Hearts*. St. Leonards: Allen and Unwin.

Rose, N. (1990) *Governing the Soul: the Shaping of the Private Self*. London: Routledge.

Ryan, S. (1996) *The Cartographic Eye: how Explorers Saw Australia*. Cambridge University Press.

Shore, C. and Wright, S. (1997) Policy: a new field of anthropology. In Shore, C. and Wright, S. (eds.), *Anthropology of Policy*, London: Routledge.

Smith, A. D. (1991) *National Identity*, London: Penguin.

Stocking, G. W. Jr. (1968) *Race, Culture, and Evolution: Essays in the History of Anthropology*. New York: The Free Press.

Stoler, A. L. (1995) *Race and the Education of Desire*. Durham, NC: Duke University Press.

Tingle, L. and Kingston, M. (1998) Howard's pledge to voters: 'It won't be a race election'. *Sydney Morning Herald*, 10 April 1998.

Winant, H. (1997) Behind blue eyes: whiteness and contemporary US racial politics. In Fine M., Weiss, L., Powell, L. C., Mun Wong, L. (eds.), *Off White: Readings on Race, Power and Society*. New York and London: Routledge.

6   Risk, calculable and incalculable

Mitchell Dean

> Nothing is a risk in itself; there is no risk in reality. But on the other hand, anything *can* be a risk; it all depends on how one analyses the danger, considers the event.
>
> (Ewald, 1991: 199)

Introduction

There is no such thing as risk in reality. Risk is a way – or rather, a set of different ways – of ordering reality, of rendering it into a calculable form. It is a way of representing events so they might be made governable in particular ways, with particular techniques, and for particular goals. It is a component of diverse forms of calculative rationality for governing the conduct of individuals, collectivities and populations. It is thus not possible to speak of incalculable risks, or of risks that escape our modes of calculation, and even less to speak of a social order in which risk is largely calculable and contrast it with one in which risk has become largely incalculable.

A second proposition follows: the significance of risk does not lie with risk *itself* but with what risk gets attached to. Risk, to put it in Kantian terms, is a category of our understanding rather than intuition or sensibility (cf. Ewald, 1991: 199). If the task of critique – after the work of Michel Foucault – is to investigate the historical conditions of true knowledge, then the critique of risk will investigate the different modes of calculation of risk and the moral and political technologies within which such calculations are to be found. Most importantly, it will investigate what I would call the 'regimes of government' in which risk is imbricated and the political programmes and social imaginaries that deploy risk and its techniques and draw their inspiration from it. What is important about risk is not risk itself, but the forms of knowledge that make it thinkable from statistics, sociology and epidemiology to management and accounting, the techniques that discover it from the calculus of probabilities to the interview, the social technologies that seek to govern it from risk screening, case-management and social insurance to situational crime prevention, and the political rationalities and pro-grammes that deploy it, from those that dreamt of a welfare state to those that imagine an advanced liberal society of prudential individuals and communities.

This leads us to a third point that clarifies the title of this chapter. If what is significant about risk is its connection with all these things, then our analysis of risk must rid itself of the opposition between the calculable and the incalculable in order to understand those practices, techniques and rationalities that seek to make the incalculable calcul-able, and the different ways they do so. This is the central point of the chapter. It will be made by comparing two forms of analysis of risk, a contemporary sociological one derived from the influential writings of Ulrich Beck, and one drawing its general orientation from Foucault's lectures, now commonly identified as the 'governmentality literature'. In the first, risk is viewed within a general schema and narrative of phases of modernity and as a feature of the ontological condition of humans within current social forms. In the second, risk is analysed as a com-ponent of assemblages of practices, techniques and rationalities con-cerned with how we govern. In the sociological account, risk forms an axial principle that characterizes types of society and the processes they are undergoing. In the 'governmental' account, risk is a calculative rationality that is tethered to assorted techniques for the regulation, management, and shaping of human conduct in the service of specific ends and with definite, but to some extent unforeseen, effects. In the sociological account, we can talk of a 'risk society' in a realist sense, that is, as an actually existing global entity – or at least a global entity nascent within processes of modernization. In the governmental account, notions of risk are made intelligible as specific representations that render reality in such a form as to make it amenable to types of action and intervention. Indeed, from the standpoint of the governmental account it is possible that the proliferation of rationalities of risk has become linked to the end of 'society' as a way of thinking about the field of political action and governmental interventions (Dean, 1997). This has led one practitioner of the governmental approach to raise the question of 'the death of the social' (Rose, 1996).

The concept of governmentality is perhaps not as well known in Germany or even France as it is in Anglophone countries. In the latter, there is now a substantial body of applied research that employs Foucault's notion of government in quite disparate ways.[1] This litera-ture takes from Foucault's broad definition of government as 'the conduct of conduct' the injunction to examine the different practices in which various social, communal and political agencies and authorities attempt to direct the actions of individuals and populations in the name of ethical ideals, political ends, economic necessity and social goals. Foucault's notion of government displaces a concern for 'the state' onto the plurality of governing bodies and the practices, techniques and rationalities through which governing is accomplished and authority exercised. This literature thus seeks to rescue an older sense of the word 'government' which can encompass the government of families, religious communities, or even of souls, as well as the government of populations, economies and states. The shifting boundaries of public and private, and the divisions between what is within and outside the state, emerge as the field of effects of such practices rather than act as a principle of explanation. Of crucial importance in this literature are the technologies through which governing is made practicable and the forms of rationality – understood in a substantive rather than normative sense – that render domains and problems of government thinkable and analysable. A shorthand for these rationalities, or *'mentalités'*, of government, is 'governmentality'. This term also makes particular reference to those mentalities of rule, such as *Polizeiwissenschaft*, cameralism, *raison d'état*, mercantilism, liberalism and social welfarism, that have arisen in Europe since the early modern period. Foucault's own account discusses the 'governmentalization of the state' as the process whereby the exercise of sovereignty over subjects within a given territory comes to be linked to forms of knowledge and techniques concerned to govern for the welfare of 'each and all' (1991: 102–4). The formation of 'the economy', 'the population' and 'society' as domains of knowledge and fields of governmental intervention and the emergence of the human, social and behavioural sciences are of key import to this governmentalization of the state. Rather than proceed with a general discussion of this literature, however, we shall here examine certain of its concrete analyses pertaining to risk.

Risk, government, society. These are the central themes of this chapter. I will argue that the 'privatization of risk' or 'individualization of risk' is a key index of a retraction of the socialized risk-management techniques associated with the welfare state and the emergence of new forms of governing in contemporary liberal–democratic states. The technical form of social insurance was crucial to the establishment of a certain form of social rights and social citizenship in the nineteenth century, and to the notion of a government of society. The individualization of risk brings into question the very notion of social rights and is linked to a form of governing that seeks to govern not through society but through the responsible and prudential choices and actions of individuals on behalf of themselves and those for whom they feel an emotional bond or affinity. Social citizenship makes way for an economic citizenship in which the risk-taking and risk-managing attributes associated with a type of economic activity are to be generalized to all aspects of personal, moral and collective conduct. Risk today is associated, as Colin Gordon might say (1991: 44), with the injunction to make one's life into an enterprise and for the individual to become an entrepreneur of him or herself.

It is my contention that the sociological account of risk society and the governmental account of risk as calculative rationality have something to offer our understanding of the fate of the social and that both have something to learn from the other. Beck's sociology can learn from the emphasis on the analysis of the particular practices, techniques and rationalities through which risk becomes constructed as a governable entity. Yet the governmental account also has certain limitations. To emphasize the specificity of particular practices and rationalities of risk would seem to deny the possibility of offering any general understanding of the processes of the transformation of contemporary governmental practices. In this respect, Beck's riposte to 'post-ism' (i.e. the view that we are living in an age that can only be characterized by what it displaces) provides us with a 'thought-figure' that might be usefully adapted to governmental concerns. Following and adapting Ashenden (1996), I shall thus introduce into the governmental lexicon the notion of 'reflexive government'. Reflexive government – or the governmentalization of government – does not mean the 'death of the social' but the shifting of the liberal problematic of security from the security of social and economic processes to the security of governmental mechanisms. The hypothesis of 'reflexive government', however, does not imply that government has ceased to try to change society. Quite the contrary.

This chapter thus covers: (i) some critical notes on Beck's themes of risk society and reflexive modernization; (ii) an introduction to the governmental account of risk starting from Ewald's work on insurance; (iii) a characterization of the contemporary processes of transformation of rule; and (iv) an elaboration of the concept of 'reflexive government' as a way of making intelligible present forms of rule.

Risk and reflexive modernization

Firstly, however, let us briefly recall certain aspects of Beck's well-known account of risk and its presuppositions and some of the more general features of the literature on governmentality. The sociological account of risk is concerned to displace what might be called 'post-ism', post-modernity, post-industrialism, *post-histoire*, and so forth (Beck,

1988: 86; 1992b: 9). It attempts to provide a positive account of the present (the present is specified by what it is rather than what it is not) and to situate that account in relation to previous accounts of modernization and modernity. However, the sociological account shares with modernization theory the view that it is indeed possible to give a general characterization of that present, failing only to grasp the extent to which the legitimation of progress in industrial capitalism was secured by an instrumental rationality that claimed to control the risks it produced.

For Beck, unlike earlier theories, the contemporary stage of modernization faces not a world of traditional mores, beliefs and hierarchies but industrial society itself, its science and technology, and its politics and culture. Modernity now exists in an agonistic relation to an earlier modernity, industrial society. Hence this stage of modernization is 'reflexive modernization', a modernization of modernization. Beck discusses reflexive modernization as a 'creative (self-)destruction' of the epoch of industrial society, a radicalization of modernity' without revolution or even necessarily with the mandatory crisis and systems failures, and an undercutting of the features of that epoch (1994: 2–3). What is appealing about this notion of reflexive modernization is not simply its bypassing of now sterile debates or its theoretical elegance; it is that it begins to identify a line of emergence that is unintended but involves contests over the status of knowledge. These contestations make the future an open horizon. Reflexivity is hence sharply distinguished from reflection. To speak of reflexivity is thus not to say that society has become more reflective or thoughtful or necessarily better informed about decision making. Rather, it is to say that modernity finds itself in a state of 'self-confrontation with the effects of risk society that cannot be assimilated in the system of industrial society' (5). Beck enjoins us to participate in a reflection on reflexive modernization, but is clear that reflexivity can proceed with or without reflection.

Beck's methodological approach to risk rests upon three major presuppositions. The first is the *totalizing* assumption that risk should be approached within a narrative of the modernization process that brings about a 'risk society'. Following from this is the assumption of *uniformity* of risk so that it is possible to make a general and abstract characterization of risk in a given type of society, i.e. that risk has fundamentally the same characteristics in all spheres. Despite his dissent from the assumption of the untroubled efficacy of scientific knowledge, and emphasis on truth contestation and fragmentation, Beck follows the Weber–Frankfurt School view to the extent that all kinds of reason compose a hegemonic form of instrumental rationality (*Zweckrationalität*) – with often demonic effects.[2] Finally, there is the *realist* assumption that the reason why risk is a feature of quotidian existence in this risk society, and a component of individual and collective experience and identities, is that real riskiness has increased so much that it has outrun the mechanisms of its calculation and control.[3] By this I mean not that Beck fails to recognize the socially produced nature of risk but that he wants to treat risk ontologically. Thus we can talk of the reality of industrial risk society because it has produced massive, physical, incalculable and illimitable hazards for which it can no longer provide precaution.

The point here is not that these assumptions are mistaken but that they are relatively unhelpful for the analysis of risk. However, it is relatively easy to displace all three and to reveal an alternative perspective on the question of risk. Instead of a totalizing approach of risk, it is easy to show the virtue of focusing on the concrete and empirical and to analyse specific types of risk rationalities and practices. Instead of assuming that the empirical varieties of risk are but instances of one type of instrumental rationality, it is possible to demonstrate that risk rationalities are not only multiple but heterogeneous and that practices for the government of risk are assembled from diverse elements and put together in different ways. There is a complex relation between Weber and critical theory (from Adorno to Habermas) and the Foucauldian analysis of rationality.[4] For present purposes one could contrast the two approaches on several points. Critical theory involves a search for the normative content of reason, the tendency towards a dialectical unification of processes of rationalization, and the privileging of the abstract. The Foucauldian analysis adopts a resolutely substantive analysis of the dispersed forms of reason, which are grasped in their practical and technical form and found in multiple and intersecting genealogies. Finally, against the assumption of realism, is it easy to show the virtue of adopting a more nominalist position, i.e. one that analyses forms of risk as among the ways in which we are required to know and to act upon ourselves and others today in a range of moral and political programmes and social technologies.[5] All three assumptions are sustained, however, by a simple dichotomy, the identification of which allows us to specify a more fruitful way ahead.

Drawing on the work of a contributor to the 'governmentality' literature, François Ewald, on the emergence of social insurance, Beck argues that private and public insurance practices were essential to the legitimation of technical and economic development of industrial society and to the achievement of a consensus on progress (1992a: 100). Industrial society finds ways of calculating risks and a technology for creating present security in the face of the future hazards that are the result of that society. 'Modernity', Beck claims (original emphasis), 'which brings uncertainty to every niche of existence, finds its counter-principle in a *social compact against industrially produced hazards and damages*, stitched together out of public and private insurance agreements'. By contrast, a risk society becomes an uninsured society. It cannot insure against the 'worst imaginable accident' or mega-hazards of say nuclear power or the chemical industries because they abolish the 'four pillars of the calculus of risks' – compensation, limitation, security and calculation (102). According to Beck, risks are now global in the sense that it is no longer possible to localize them spatially and temporally. The scenario of the 'worst imaginable accident', such as the Chernobyl meltdown, or the hazards attendant upon the destruction of the ozone layer, means that the 'accident becomes an event with a beginning and no end; an "open-ended festival" of creeping, galloping and overlapping waves of destruction' (102). Such events are not amenable to monetary compensation because damage can no longer be limited. There can be no security against risks because it is impossible to plan against the effects of the fatal hazards of the worst imaginable accident. Finally, there can be no standards of normality or measuring procedures against risk. Calculation, for Beck, becomes obfuscation.

We can note several things about this account. First, risk, which was once calculable, has become incalculable and it is this becoming incalculable that is at the heart of the transformation of society. Contrary to Beck's express intention to produce a positive account of the present that avoids 'post-ism', his risk society is perhaps more adequately characterized as a post-risk-calculation society. Second, this dichotomy rests on a double confusion. The first part of the confusion is the identification of risk with insurer's risks so that the possibility of events that can no longer be insured indicates the existence of incalculable risks. The other part of the confusion follows from this: risk is identified with quantitative forms of calculation. I shall address both these aspects of confusion in the course of discussing the diversity of risk rationalities today. For now, I want to turn to François Ewald's account to exemplify an alternative, and in some ways, more satisfactory approach.

Insurance and government

In light of these comments, first consider Ewald's (1991) account of insurance and the emergence of social insurance. What is crucial is that he locates notions of risk in insurance with those of chance, probability and randomness rather than with notions of danger and peril (199). If we make a distinction between modes of calculating and objective conditions, Beck's risk society is more properly conceived as one in which there is an increase in the condition of danger arising from the development of technological forces. For Ewald, by contrast, risk is a form of rationality, a way of thinking about and representing events. To say that risk is calculable is to say that it is a form of reasoning that allows us to make events calculable is a specific way. It is thus not possible to contrast calculable risks and incalculable risks. For insurance rationality, everything can be treated as a risk and the task of insurers has been both to 'produce' risks and to find ways of insuring what has previously been thought to be uninsurable. In insurance, risk is a form of calculation based on a statistical table that establishes the regularity of events and a calculus of probabilities in order to evaluate the chances of that event actually occurring (202). This account thus first contrasts with that of Beck in its preparedness to examine the particular form of *calculative rationality* in which notions of risk are found. Thus risk can give rise to or be a component in multiple forms of calculative rationality and should not be assigned to the calculable–incalculable dichotomy.

Insurance might be approached as an attempt to make the incalculable calculable. Ewald (204–5) argues that what is insured is not the actually lived and suffered injury itself but risk as a capital against whose loss the insurer offers a guarantee. The effects of the loss of a limb, or of a parent, are indeed incalculable. Nevertheless, viewed from the perspective of insurance, it is possible to compensate for such losses by assigning them a price based on the calculus of probabilities of such an event and the contractually agreed upon contribution of the insured. That this compensation can never truly compensate for the suffering is clear from the history of conflicts between insurers and the insured. Insurance risk does not mark the limited historical moment between premodern hazards and contemporary incalculable risk. Rather, it is an effort to render what is felt to be incalculable, what is understood to have no price, amenable to calculation and monetary compensation. The suffering of the injury can never be limited, only the indemnity for a loss of a specific form of capital.

Such forms of the rationality of risk do not exist in an ideal form. This leads us to the second departure from Beck's approach – the requirement that we investigate *the technical and practical dimension aspect of the governing risk*. In Ewald's account risk is indissociable from the practices of insurance and from the techniques that allow us to intervene in a world rendered amenable to risk calculations. Indeed one might wish to say that the rationality of risk is bound up with a host of technical means for intervening in reality for the achievement of specific ends. Thus we have just noted that insurance risk depends upon particular calculative techniques such as the statistical table and the calculus of probabilities.

Moreover, insurance itself can be regarded as technical in several different ways (206–8). First, it is an economic and financial technique to create remuneration for risk. Second, it is a moral technology in that it is a means by which an individual can conduct his or her life in a way that maintains responsibility in the face of the ill fortunes of life. Third, it is a technique for the indemnification and reparation of damages. In this regard it is a mode of administering justice '. . . under which the damage suffered by one is borne by all, and individual responsibility is borne by all' (207). All of this makes insurance, finally, a political technology in that it is a way of combining and using social forces in a specific fashion, one in which the possibility of the optimization of individual responsibility is combined with a maximization of social solidarity. Insurance is thus a 'form of association which combines a maximum of socialization with a maximum of individualization' (204).

Ewald's account exemplifies a third dimension of the analytic of government – the way in which practices for the government of risk rely upon, presuppose, and help fabricate, particular *forms of identity, agency and expertise* (201–2; emphasis added). Insurance practices displace the abstract, invariant norm of a responsible juridical subject with an individuality relative to other members of an insured population, an 'average sociological individuality'. In legal judgements concerning damages, the victim and the author of an accident are singularized and isolated and placed into an opposition. It is a matter of finding where, if any where, fault lies. In insurance, risk is a characteristic of the population, a form of regularity that no one can escape but which each individual bears differently. Individuals are thus both members of the population and distinguished by the probability of risk that is their share. Insurance associations give rise to a kind of mutuality between members by which they benefit from association but which leave each individual free. The movement then is from a notion of fault based on legal subjectivity to one of the socialization of risk.

Insurance risk is always collective. It implies a social rule of justice rather than a natural one. In legal judgements, the judge must apportion blame or responsibility for an accident to a particular party and fix damages according to a table which sets the rate for certain kinds of loss, e.g. of a hand, a leg, a life, etc. The accident itself is to be regarded as a unique event that disturbs an otherwise harmonious order. Law seeks the restoration of that order by means of restitution to the victim. Insurance, in contrast, indemnifies the individual according to a contractually agreed tariff worked out in relation to the calculus of risk. The judge's position is taken over by the actuary who calculates tables or scales of compensation.

One can readily appreciate, then, why such a political technology would come to be taken up in nineteenth-century social legislation. In issues of worker's compensation for industrial accidents, insurance renders the relation between the employer and employee not as a class struggle between worker and boss, or as a matter of individual responsibility, but as a technical, calculable matter in which insurance experts assign a person an insurable identity and compensate accordingly. The struggle then becomes one of the worker seeking to receive as much as possible from the insuring association. Social insurance emerges and is deployed as a technology of solidarity that renders accidents, illness, unemployment and other ills associated with social life as insurable risks that are collectively borne and individually indemnified.

This rationality of risk, bound to a technology for creating solidarity out of individual contribution, is thus at the heart of the emergence of a form of social government, with its related notions of social justice. Several further points should be made about this insurance rationality of risk. Firstly, insurance risk is a means of creating social right and social citizenship. Civil and political rights and liberties accrue to citizens as individuals, e.g. the right to enter into contracts, freedom of speech, religion and assembly, and the right to vote or participate in politics. Under social insurance, individuals are entitled to social provision in a quite different fashion – as a member of a collectivity defined by occupation or profession. The political imaginary is of a contractual form of justice no longer established by a natural order of rights but by the conventions of society, and of an ideal of a society in which each member's burdens and shares are fixed by a social contract which is no longer a political myth but something made real by technical means. Risk and insurance technology become a social solution to the problems of capitalist industry, particularly of poverty and working-class insecurity. If the emergence of social citizenship, according to Procacci (1993, 1998), concerns the problem of inequality in a society of equals, then insurance surely is the most perfect technical realization of social rights. Each individual is a member of an association by which all agree to accept responsibility for each other's burdens. Yet because risk is distributed unequally the proportional share that each will receive varies according to the insurance calculus. This is why, at the end of the nineteenth century, particularly in the Third Republic in France, social insurance emerged as the principal political technology of establishing social rights and providing solutions to the problems of poverty and inequality. The socialization of risk does not seek to undermine capitalist inequality, precisely the opposite. It is a means of treating the effects of that inequality.

The success of social insurance as a political technology, however, was neither a feature of its efficiency, its 'de-dramatization of social conflicts', nor a matter of the teleology of citizenship. The success in France was only made possible by a process which Defert calls the 'demutualization of the workers' movement' a dual process during the nineteenth century by which employers sought to take over the mutual benefit societies of the workers, which often doubled as a source of strike funds, and by which insurance companies started offering indemnification against risks in competition with employers' benevolent funds. The strategy of insurance rests upon a dissociation and reconstitution of the fabric of working-class association (Defert, 1991: 213). It is for this reason that workers' organizations only gradually accepted the law on industrial accident compensation and embraced it only after it had been passed without its support (211). Risk techniques are taken up under given historical conditions, in the service of particular political rationalities and by various social forces and agents in the course of historical struggles.

There is a last and important feature on the landscape of this genealogy of insurance risk that I can only mention here. The socialization of risk is welded onto general and abstract forms of political and social rationality that provide disciplines such as sociology and the 'new social economy' with an image of society and politicians and jurists with a doctrine of state (Donzelot, 1988, 1991). It is in this sense that notions of 'society' can be viewed as much as an artefact of risk as *vice versa*. The Third Republic in France, which implements a programme of social insurance, is also the period of the invention of a notion of society as a reality *sui generis*. At a midway point between Emile Durkheim's notion of the shift from mechanical to organic solidarity and the calculative rationality of insurance risk lies the progressive republican doctrine of state, Léon Bourgeois' *solidarisme*. The privileged technical form of intervention in the Third Republic is social insurance. Given their close historical proximity and their common linkage in the notion of solidarity, it is tempting to read the implementation of social insurance in Durkheimian terms. To do so, one would view social insurance as a technology of solidarity for all individuals in a society that renders accidents, illness, unemployment and other ills the result of the collective reality of the new division of labour. Social insurance thus expresses a form of organic solidarity and social legislation can be justified by this means. On the other hand, individuals receive entitlements not as individuals but as members of different collective bodies defined by profession, occupation or age. Thus social insurance also recognizes and reinforces the bonds between members of the same institutions and groups – their mechanical solidarity. Social insurance as a political technology can thus produce and reconcile two diverse images of society and forms of solidarity.

Insurance risk, as we shall see, is not the only type of risk. However, the above sketch might suggest why it is important to analyse the specific form of risk rationalities rather than immersing that analysis in a global narrative of risk society. It is important to analyse four dimensions of the government of risk. First, how we come to know about and act upon different conceptions of risk, i.e. the specific forms of risk rationality. Second, how such conceptions are linked to particular practices and technologies. Third, how such practices and technologies give rise to new forms of social and political identity. Fourth, how such rationalities, technologies and identities become latched onto different political programmes and social imaginaries that invest them with a specific ethos. I shall now try to describe some different forms of risk and suggest ways in which the prudential understanding of risk today is a function of a transformation in modalities of governing.

Risk and contemporary government[6]

Despite having concentrated on insurance risk in the preceding section of the chapter, I have already suggested that it is mistaken to identify risk rationality with any one of its forms and to identify risk with the quantitative calculation of probabilities of insurance risk. The existing governmentality literature has already investigated a number of different forms of risk rationality. This is not to suggest that this literature enables us to constitute an exhaustive typology of risk. Rather, by identifying its different forms, we might begin to understand the diversity of under-standings of risk, how risk can be linked to quite different programmes and technologies, and the way the vocabulary of risk can cross and bind together quite distinct sets of practices. We can also begin to delineate some of the moral, political and social significance of contemporary practices of risk.

The first, as we have just seen, might be called *insurance risk*. One can contrast this kind of risk with another long-standing and pervasive form of risk rationality, *epidemiological risk*. Epidemiological risk is concerned with the rates of morbidity and mortality among popula-tions. It is similar to insurance risk in that the calculus of risk is undertaken on the basis of a range of abstract factors and their correlation within populations and, indeed, can be linked to insurance risk in public and private practices of health insurance. However, it has its own distinctive rationality and set of techniques and interventions. It is not the losses of capital but the health outcomes of populations that are subject to risk calculation. Its technical means are public health interventions such as sanitation, quarantine measures, inspection of food supply, inoculation programmes, and so on. More recently, as Castel (1991) suggests, it has become linked to the 'screening' of populations as procedures for monitoring populations in order to engage in a 'systematic pre-detection' that eliminates or minimizes future pathologies through interventions on 'modifiable risk factors'. Epidemiological risk therefore has a preventive, rather than restitutive ethos, as insurance risk does.

In contrast to these two quantitative forms of risk rationality, it is possible to identify another form that is principally qualitative. I shall call this, for want of a better term, *case-management risk*. This kind of risk again has a long history. It is linked to a clinical practice in which certain symptoms lead to the imputation of dangerousness, e.g. of the likelihood of a mentally ill person committing a violent act (Castel, 1991). Here risk concerns the qualitative assessment of individuals and groups, especially families, as falling within 'at risk' categories. Risk techniques are closely allied to the use of case management in social security, social work, policing and the sphere of criminal justice. Those judged 'at risk' of being a danger to the wider community are subject to a range of therapeutic (e.g. counselling, self-help groups, support groups), sovereign (prisons, detention centres) and disciplinary (training and re-training) practices in an effort either to eliminate them completely from communal spaces (e.g. by various forms of confinement) or to lower the dangers posed by their risk of alcoholism, drug dependency, sexual diseases, criminal behaviour, long-term unemployment and welfare dependency. Rather than being replaced by newer risk technologies, we have witnessed something of a proliferation of case-management approaches beyond the older delineation of social work and clinical medicine, e.g. as a response to structural unemployment in Australia and other OECD countries (Dean, 1995).

Case-management risk draws upon the techniques of the interview, the exercise of bureaucratic or clinical judgement, the case note and the file. These techniques might be supplemented by other, less observational modes that might employ techniques that are derived from quantitative analysis. In the case of the unemployed in Australia bureaucratic judgement about being at 'high risk of long-term unemployment' is aided by the development of such instruments as the Jobseeker Classification Index, based on questions about factors that increase risk of long-term unemployment, including age, education, access to labour markets, disability, country of birth, language abilities, Aboriginal status, duration of unemployment, work experience and stability of residence (Dean, 1998a).

In its combination of the use of bureaucratic judgement and instruments to assess the existence of risk factors, case-management risk may perhaps be regarded as a variation on what Weir has recently called *clinical risk* (1996). Clinical risk relies on epidemiological calculus of risk but combines techniques of risk screening with both diagnostics and therapeutics. Its procedures are those of the 'circumscription of individual pathology'. Mobilizing risk-screening techniques, and combining them with more traditional modes of face-to-face diagnosis, clinical risk seeks to attach risk to the bodies of individuals so they might become objects of more intensive surveillance and treatment. The Ontario Antenatal Record analysed by Weir is used as a case record that summarizes clinical observation and test results and presents qualitative categories of risk for maternal and foetal health (380). What is interesting about clinical risk is that it involves both quantitative analysis of the calculus of probabilities across a population to distinguish risk factors and qualitative judgements based on clinical judgement of doctors and midwives.

Of course even those already mentioned do not exhaust the forms of risk rationality. Pearce and Tombs (1996), for example, have examined changing forms of risk management in the United States' chemical industry. Such a case that would appear to strongly resemble those envisaged by Beck's scenario of a festival of destruction. The hazards of that industry constitute an 'actuarial nightmare', 'involving mass victims, multiple injuries, fuzzy loss, multicollinearity (complex causal chains) and latency' (438). Indeed, liability under tort law, the unwillingness of insurance companies to provide comprehensive general liability without significant exemptions, disasters such as Bhopal, pressure from citizens' groups, and so on, suggest that risk has indeed become incalculable. However, it is clear that even here Beck's case is overstated. Rejecting techniques of risk assessment to deal with low probability/high consequence events, the chemical companies have turned to comprehensive risk-management strategies that recognize worst-case scenarios. Such strategies encompass attention to training, managerial and organization systems, emergency procedures such as evacuation plans, risk education and other contingency measures. Crucially, strategies of risk management include the participation of those previously excluded by a scientific–technological rationality of risk assessment, such as workers and local communities. The point to be made here is that comprehensive risk-management techniques may fail – just as case-management techniques cannot prevent long-term unemployment – but that does not mean that we should regard them as merely obfuscating. One feature of governmental rationalities is that they might be regarded as 'congenitally failing' (Miller and Rose, 1990). Failure (itself judged through a particular epistemological framework) does not mean the abandonment of the attempt to construct coherent programmes of government. Rather, its discovery is an incitement to the problematization, reformation and replacement of such programmes.[7]

It is clear that the genealogy of risk is much more complex than the theory of risk society allows. Risk and its techniques are plural and heterogeneous and its significance cannot be exhausted by a narrative of a shift from a quantitative calculation of risk to the globalization of incalculable risks. Having made such a statement, however, will the analysis of these rationalities of risk permit of any generalization? A fundamental tenet of the governmentality literature, though not always remembered, is that calculative rationalities such as those of risk have a certain political polyvalence, i.e. they can be invested with different sets of purposes depending on the political programmes and rationalities they come to be latched onto (O'Malley, 1996). A central significance of the rationalities of risk today is that they have been attached to a set of political programmes and formulae of rule that represent a major retraction of social rights and the ideal of a welfare state that drove social provision for much of the now receding century. At the end of the nineteenth century in France the socialization of risk was linked to the invention of social forms of government. In the twilight of the twentieth century, we might say that the individualization of risk is linked to new forms of liberal government.

The crossing of risk rationalities and technologies with contemporary liberal political programmes and formulae of rule might be approached in a number of ways. The first might be described, with O'Malley (1992), as the 'new prudentialism'. Here, we witness an emphasis on individuals, families, households and communities taking responsibility for their own risks – physical and mental ill-health, unemployment, poverty in old age, poor educational performance, becoming victims of crime. Competition between public schools, private health insurance and superannuation schemes, community policing and 'neighbourhood watch' schemes, and so on, are all so many instances of contriving governmental practices in which the responsibilities for risk minimization become a feature of the choices that are made by individuals, households and communities, as consumers and users of services.

Among the preferred models of the 'neo-liberal' prudential subject is the rational choice actor who calculates the benefits and costs or risks of acting in a certain way and then acts (O'Malley, 1996: 197-8). As

O'Malley points out, the prudential subject of neo-liberal programmes faced with health and crime risks overlays the responsible and the rational, the moral and the calculating (200–1). The rational subject, located within a governmentally contrived set of arrangements (e.g. the rules governing private and public health insurance) calculates the best means of providing security against risks. The responsible subject seeks to optimize his or her independence from others and from the state, e.g. by employing epidemiological data of health risks, and undertaking diet, lifestyle and exercise regimes recommended by private health and fitness professionals or publicly funded health promotion. As O'Malley has pointed out, it is not only unhealthy but, some would suggest, 'immoral' to engage in risky behaviour such as smoking or lack of exercise and for 'high income earners' to depend even on indexed public health insurance.

The new prudentialism differs from older, nineteenth-century forms of prudentialism in a number of ways. It first multiplies the domains to be monitored and prudently managed. Early nineteenth-century Malthusianism added procreative prudence and independence from poor relief to earlier injunctions to industry, frugality in domestic economy and sobriety (Dean, 1991). A hundred years later, Brentano will recommend that the worker contract six types of insurance; life, aged pension; funeral; sickness; infirmity; and unemployment (Ewald, 1991: 207–8). Today active citizens must add the monitoring of their risks of physical and mental ill-health, of sexual disease, of dependency (on drugs, alcohol, nicotine, welfare or in personal relationships), of being a victim of crime, of their own and their children's education, of low self-esteem and so on. Further, what is calculated is not the dangerousness of certain activities (e.g. gambling, drinking, poor hygiene), places (the alehouse, ghettoes) and populations (the dangerous classes) but the risks that traverse each and every member of the population and which it is their individual and collective duty to control. Dangerousness is a qualitative judgement based on observable symptoms or empirical occurrences. Risk is both qualitative and quantitative; it is indicated by observable symptoms or by invisible abstract correlation of factors. It does not divide populations by a single division (the dangerous classes versus the labouring classes), so much as follow the warp and weft of risk within a population. There are only 'at risk' groups, high and low risk groups. Some spaces and neighbourhoods, times of day and night, are inherently risky. Some are more risky than others. Risk is a continuum rather than a break. Risk, in this sense, never completely evaporates or disappears. It can be minimized, localized and avoided, but never dissipated. There are, it is true, subpopulations to be targeted, but the entire population remains the primary locus of risk.[8]

One might want to talk about a division – that exists along with and, to some extent, re-inscribes older divisions of class and disadvantage – between *active citizens* (capable of managing their own risk) and *targeted populations* (the 'at risk', the high risk) who require intervention in the management of risks. The crucial thing, however, is to realize that these are liminal categories marking a fluid threshold rather than a strict divide. One of the consequences of the language of risk is that the entire population can be the locus of a vulnerability that can also single out specific populations, in a way that the language of danger, class or disadvantage cannot. Moreover, the new prudentialism suggests, if not a new, at least an additional role for professions as calculators, managers and tutors of risk, taking on educative, estimative and preventive functions. The calculations of risk are intertwined with two different types of governmental technology. One is invoked from below. The other, as it were, deployed from above.

We might first of all consider the several broad types of technologies concerned in the first instance with deploying the agency and capacities of individuals and populations. These might be called *technologies of agency*. As charted by Yeatman (1998), the extra-juridical and quasi-juridical use of 'contract' can be regarded as a pervasive technology of government used today in the 'contracting out' of formerly public services to private and community agencies, the agreements made by the unemployed, the 'learning contracts' of the schoolroom, performance contracts between ministers and senior public servants, enterprise agreements, and so forth. These technologies of agency also comprise what Cruikshank (1994, 1996) has called 'technologies of citizenship'. These are the multiple techniques of self-esteem, empowerment, consultation and negotiation used in community action and development programmes, social and environmental impact studies, health promotion, community policing, and the combating of various kinds of dependency. Technologies of agency also include the instruments of 'voice' and 'representation' by which the claims of 'consumers' can enter into the negotiation over needs (Yeatman, 1994: 110). These technologies of citizenship engage us as active and free citizens, as consumers of services, as members of self-managing communities and organizations, as actors in democratizing social movements, and as agents capable of taking control of our own risks. This is not to cancel out agency but to seek to show how it is produced, how it is inserted in a system of purposes, and how it might overrun the limits established for it by a particular programme or even the strategic purposes of a regime of government.

Two points can be made here. First, these technologies of agency often come into play when certain individuals, groups and communities become what I have called targeted populations, i.e. when, through the prism of specific forms of knowledge, judgement and evaluation, they become populations that manifest high risk, or are composed of individuals deemed at risk. Victims of crime, smokers, abused children, gay men, intravenous drug users, the unemployed, indigenous people and so on, are all isolated in this way and hence subject to these technologies of agency, the object being to transform their status, to make them active citizens capable, as individuals and communities, of managing their own risk and purchasing those services that fit their needs.

Second, the two types of technologies of agency can be combined, e.g. in the government of the unemployed (Dean, 1995). The long-term unemployed enter into agreements to subject themselves to technologies of citizenship (e.g. counselling to improve self-esteem, training to increase labour-market skills, etc.). The advantage of this particular assemblage over earlier techniques of empowerment is that the contract (often underwritten with sanctions, e.g. the cutting-off of allowances) acts as a kind of obligatory point through which individuals are required to agree to a range of normalizing, therapeutic and training measures designed to empower them, enhance their self-esteem, optimize their skills and entrepreneurship, and so on. Technologies of agency are concerned to foster the agency of individuals and groups. As far as risk is concerned, these technologies disperse risk onto all types of locales (families, schools, university departments, neighbourhoods) and devolve it onto professionals, specialists, service providers and consumers.

These technologies of agency are complemented, however, by a host of technologies concerned to monitor, compare and evaluate the performance of those whose agency is thereby activated. Thus we could talk about *technologies of performance* such as the setting of performance indicators, the establishment of benchmarks, the contrivance of markets in expertise and service provision, the 'corporatization' and 'privatization' of formerly public services, the devolution of financial responsibility to 'budget units' or 'cost centres', the operation of 'quality audits' and the extensive contracting-out of services, are all means for linking the moral and political requirements of the shaping of conduct into the optimization of performance. These plural technologies may be said to penetrate the enclosures of expertise fostered under the welfare state and to subsume the substantive domains of expertise (of the doctor, the nurse, the social worker, the school principal, the professor) to new formal calculative regimes (Rose and Miller, 1992). These technologies of performance then, are utilized from above, as indirect means of regulating agencies, of transforming professionals into 'calculating individuals' within 'calculable spaces', subject to particular 'calculative regimes', to use Miller's language (1992). These technologies of performance present themselves as techniques of restoring trust (i.e. accountability, transparency and democratic control) in the activities of firms, service providers, public services and professionals. As such, they presuppose a culture of mistrust in professions and institutions that they themselves contribute to, produce and intensify.

Power (1994), in his analysis of what he calls 'the audit society', argues that the explosion of audit represents an effort of the 'remanagerialization' of those risks which threaten to escape from their representations in insurance. Technologies of performance might be understood as attempts to reconcile two competing imperatives of 'neo-liberal' programmes of public management (302). The first is that of the 'enterprisation of the state', i.e. the devolution of the delivery of formerly public services in health, education and wealth, onto community sector, private and newly autonomized but still formally public bodies. The second is the 'governmentalization of enterprise': the re-regulation of these autonomized public, private-for-profit and community sites by the indirect measures discussed above. If the former suggests a dispersion of risk across the multiple agencies of contemporary rule, the latter represents the attempt to restore trust in agencies that have been rendered autonomous and constituted as loci of risk.

Risk has been to some extent de-socialized, privatized and individualized. One might want to argue that a new terrain for politics is associated with this process. This politics invokes a plurality of the different forms of association from the household to the neighbourhood to the region. I have called this politics, a 'pluralism of aggregations' (Dean, 1997). Looked at from 'top–down', those identified as 'at risk' or at 'high risk' are to be empowered or entered into partnership with professionals, bureaucrats, activists and service providers. With the help of markets – often artificially contrived – in services and expertise, these targeted populations are enjoined to recognize the seemingly natural bonds of affinity and identity that link them with others and to engage in their own self-management and political mobilization. These bonds of affinity and identity might be forged around the household, neighbourhood, workplace or region, through symbolic, virtual, cultural or lifestyle identities, or through political identifications and social movement associations. From below, these aggregations appear as consumer organizations, citizens' initiatives, social movements, cultures and subcultures, and communities, resisting and opposing the decisions of authorities, contesting the claims of expert knowledge, demanding consultation over planning and services tailored to their needs.

If this is something like the subpolitics of Beck's risk society it is important to recognize that these aggregations do not simply form around the risks engendered by techno-economic systems but in a complex reciprocity with diverse forms of authority deploying the rationalities and technologies of government described above. For Beck, subpolitics emerges in the space between what has conventionally been understood as political and what has been understood as non-political in a growing awareness of the risks generated by a techno-economic domain previously defined as non-political. This may well be the case. But surely this is only one manifestation of a politics that deploys the local solidarity of diverse aggregations rather than the attributes of the socially identified citizen, i.e. the individual whose principal identification is with a national society (cf. Rose, 1996)? It is important to realise that this politics is not simply about the growing appreciation of risks among certain populations but also how groups of various kinds have come to understand themselves, their future and their needs, in terms of risks with the assistance of a range of specialists and tutors in the identification and management of risk.

It may be that this proliferation of risk rationalities and reliance on the prudential individual means that authorities of all sorts – including national governments – have found a way of governing without governing society. Yet we must realise that there are limits to the 'solutions' that have been generated out of the diverse problematizations of the welfare state. If the development of social citizenship, the emergence of social government, and the socialization of risk correspond to the solution of an enduring problem of liberal–capitalist societies, i.e. the existence of inequality and poverty in a society of equals, then such a problem cannot be simply wished away by those who would retract the welfare state, individualize responsibility for the ills of the social system and disperse risks onto the multiple communities and bodies who are to be made to bear them. From a Durkheimian perspective, the problem of organic solidarity, of the interdependence of all these 'differents', has been left unresolved. One does not have to appeal to foundational normative morality to assert the necessity of *the social*.

Reflexive government

This emergent regime of government is, at least in part, the result of a more general process. While some have posed the question of the 'death of the social' to interrogate the transformation of contemporary government (Rose, 1996), this seems to me inadequate in at least two ways. First, the genealogy of the social shows the necessity of a sphere of practices and rationalities that address such questions of poverty, inequality and need within a liberal political community of equal and autonomous individuals. Second, to talk of a transition to a new form of governing in which citizens are regarded and enjoined to regard themselves as members of multiple and heterogeneous aggregations is to miss the sense in which these new forms of governing seek both to provide solutions to social problems and to effect a social and cultural reformation. Rather than 'death of the social' it is more appropriate to discuss its 'metamorphoses' (Castel, 1995).

Foucault suggested that liberal and social forms of government be understood as features on the trajectory of the 'governmentalization of the state'. One way of giving coherence and intelligibility to the new regime of government in advanced liberal democracies is to locate it on a different trajectory, the 'governmentalization of government'. The hypothesis is that the governmentalization of the state – by which the state came to take on the function of the care of populations and individuals – is today meeting, being partially displaced by, re-inscribed and re-coded within another trajectory whereby the mechanisms of government themselves are subject to problematization, scrutiny and reformation. This turning of the government of the state upon itself can be described as the governmentalization of government. What results might be called 'reflexive government'.

Classical liberal and social forms of government were the outcome of the governmentalization of the state. This is to say that the government of the state was conceived as acting on processes that are external to the state and independent of its existence. These included industrial, economic, social, biological and psychological processes. In order to govern on behalf of the welfare of the governed populations and individuals that make up the citizenry found within the limits of the sovereign state, it became necessary to rely on new forms of knowledge of such processes and techniques of intervention. Sociology (and other social sciences) and social insurance could be viewed as important instances of this. The first analyses the hazards produced by industrial societies and their social and economic processes. The latter provides security against such hazards by relying on a knowledge of processes immanent to the population – of numbers of accidents, of birth and death rates, of cyclical and structural unemployment, etc. The question of security is central here. Social and liberal forms of government are correlates of a liberal problematic of security in which the welfare of each citizen and the population as a whole is dependent on the security of social and economic processes.

Much of what has been under discussion concerning new ways of governing suggests that this problematic of security is itself undergoing a process of transformation. What is at issue is no longer the security of processes considered external to the formal apparatuses of government but the security of governmental mechanisms themselves. One could begin to elucidate this transformation by examining the shift in the government of national economies and the governmental perception that we have entered into a new type of economic globalization (Hindess, 1998). As Hindess has argued, the notion of 'the economy' as a self-regulating system and a part of system of national economies engaging in mutually advantageous international trade has been largely displaced by the less benign governmental perception of a global economic system that distributes countries and regions into winners and losers in a new 'zero-sum' competitive game. The task of national government is no longer to engage in the prudential management of self-regulating national economies so as to secure benefits to 'society' conceived as the totality of the members of a national population. Rather, the task is to reform those kinds of individual and institutional conduct that are considered likely to affect economic performance compared to that of the members of other national and even regional populations. A corollary of this view is that this is often best achieved by contriving and constructing market systems of allocation in domains where they had not previously been in operation. One of the conditions of such a transformation, Hindess argues, is that the technology of national accounting has led government and corporations to be more, rather than less, informed about the relative performance of their own and others' national economies.

There are several effects of this transformation. In the absence of a theoretically mandated set of technical means for conducting 'macro-economic' policy, national governments can only hope to improve their performance relative to other countries. Levels of public and private indebtedness, the condition of national and state budgets, and a raft of policies that go under the heading of 'micro-economic reform' – from reforming uncompetitive public sectors, 'corporatizing' and 'privatizing' public utilities, breaking union monopolies and 'de-regulating' labour markets – become the stuff of national economic governance. Rather than seeking to pull macro-economic levers, national economic governance is increasingly concerned to reform the conduct of individuals and institutions in all sectors to make them more competitive and efficient. In this sphere, at least, a government of economic processes is being displaced by a government of governmental mechanisms. Economic security is now less a matter of the security of economic processes and more the security of tax-raising measures, of national budgets, of systems and styles of public management, of privatization plans and of the implementation of micro-economic reform. Indeed, national and state governments who fail to secure these governmental mechanisms can themselves be subject to forms of direct and indirect government by private corporations (credit rating downgrades, capital flights), international non-government agencies such as the World Bank and IMF (as in contemporary Indonesia) and international associations (conditions of entry into the EU). In the economic sphere at least, the presence of a reflexive government is clear.

Reflexive government is not limited to the economic sphere. Ashenden (1996) has shown that public inquiries could be regarded as forms of 'reflexive government' in that they seek to arbitrate between different and competing forms of government, such as legal versus human science knowledge in the case of child protection. One could also argue that managerial doctrines, such as total quality management or customer-focused service provision, concern themselves with the forms of self-government of companies and other organizations. More significantly, there is a kind of elective affinity between reflexive government and the types of technology discussed in our earlier analysis. Cost or management accounting, the devolution of financial responsibility onto budget units or cost centres, the establishment of quasi-markets or the various uses of auditing are all forms of indirect regulation of other regimes of regulation, whether these be those of the school, the hospital, the university, the delivery of home care or child care services, as well as the corporation. What I have called 'technologies of performance' thus clearly indicate a contemporary form of reflexive government that is concerned to govern the risks to taxpayers, shareholders and governments of the activities of public servants, state professionals, community organizations and their workers, state-owned enterprises, and private companies and their management.

What may not be so clear is how what I have called 'technologies of agency' also indicates the governmentalization of government. The pervasiveness of the notion of consultation indicates a form of government that can only govern through existing or potential 'indigenous' mechanisms of government, whether these be of communities, cultural groups, neighbourhoods, and so on (O'Malley, 1998). More generally technologies of citizenship that foster the capacities for active participation might be viewed as constructing the conditions of reflexive government by establishing local sites of self-government that can be indirectly managed by the new technologies of performance. If classical liberal forms of economic government sought to foster economic liberty, this is because the security of economic processes is linked to the natural freedom of economic actors to pursue their own interests. Today the appeal to freedom is made because security depends on the constitution of individuals, professionals, communities, organizations and institutions as so many sites of the exercise of a 'responsible autonomy' that can be indirectly regulated by the technologies of performance. In this sense one might say that freedom, agency and choice become artefacts of particular governmental practices, including those that seek to elicit the enterprise of individuals and populations within contrived markets regimes, e.g. the reconstitution of the unemployed as an active job-seeker and customer within a market in 'employment placement services' (Dean, 1998a).

The pervasiveness and diversity of risk rationality and technique appears to be linked to this governing of government. Thus we have seen that risk management strategies are forms of evaluation of the internal government of chemical companies and nuclear power plants and that risk screening can be mobilized as a way of regulating the doctor–patient relation and so ultimately increase the efficiency of the use of clinical techniques. The explosion of audit now means that auditing is not only concerned with management of financial risks of companies to shareholders but with the risks that all types of governmental institutions – whether public, newly privatized or contractualized – pose to both taxpayers and customers.

My final hypothesis is then about this idea of the 'death of the social'. I would suggest that social government is not so much dispensed with as a victim or its own success. On the one hand, the welfarist regime is first subject to crises of governability – encapsulated by the almost endless identification of crisis from the 1970s (crisis of capitalism, crisis of the state, fiscal crisis, crisis of democracy, legitimation crisis) – and then enclosed in new regulatory regimes and knowledge and calculative practices. On the other, it is the success of liberal and social forms of governing in forming populations with the capacities of responsibility and autonomy that today makes it possible to govern through the aspirations and choice of individuals and groups.[9] Hence, there is some validity in the proposition that reflexive government no longer seeks to govern through society. This does not mean, however, that reflexive government no longer seeks to transform society. Societal transformation is at the heart of reflexive government. However it seeks to achieve this transformation no longer though the government of processes but through the government of the mechanisms, techniques and agencies of government themselves. The liberal problematic of security, in which security depends on the processes of economy and society, is displaced by a new problematic of security which concerns the securing of the mechanisms of government. Society itself can be changed, according to this view, but no longer through conscious design based on the rational knowledge of social processes but through the transformation of the mechanisms through which it had previously been governed.

Society perhaps is as much an artefact of risk as the other way around. The proliferation and individualization of risk today is not so much a component of the death of the social as a transformation of the liberal and social problematic of security. The many kinds of risk rationality are central to the forms of calculative rationality that seek to secure governmental mechanisms. They are components of what I have termed 'reflexive government'. Today it is possible to change society – perhaps even revolutionize it – by acting upon the mechanisms through which it is governed. If the discovery of risk was a component of the governmentalization of the state, a knowledge of social and economic processes and the emergence of a social form of citizenship, its contemporary diversification and proliferation is linked to the governmentalization of government, a knowledge and indirect regulation of the conduct of individuals and institutions and new forms of economic citizenship from the customer to the enterprise.

This chapter commenced by considering two ways of approaching the question of risk in the contemporary human science literature: the sociological approach of Ulrich Beck and the 'governmentality' account based on Michel Foucault's theses. I have argued that Beck's approach to risk can be characterized as totalizing, realist and relying on a uniform conception of risk. Moreover, his narrative of the emergence of risk society founders on the untenable binary, calculable/incalculable. Using François Ewald on social insurance, I have argued that risk is better approached as specific forms of calculative rationality, as ways of rendering the incalculable calculable. The strength of the governmental account is its capacity to analyse specific forms of risk rationality and technology, the different types of agency and identity involved in practices of risk, and the political and social imaginaries to which these practices are linked. Thus, using the governmentality literature, I have delineated various types of risk rationality (insurance risk, epidemiological risk, clinical or case-management risk, and comprehensive risk management) and placed their proliferation within a framework for the analysis of current forms of governing. The governmental account, however, encounters difficulties in moving beyond the analysis of particular risk rationalities to provide an account of transformation of the contemporary rationalities and technologies of rule. In this respect, I suggest that it could learn from Beck's argument concerning reflexivity. I have hence argued that one of the conditions of these new forms of government is the trajectory of the 'governmentalization of government'. Rather than current problematizations of the welfare state being viewed as 'the death of the social', it is better to understand them as features of the emergence of a 'reflexive government'.

NOTES

This chapter was originally published in *Soziale Welt: Zeitschrift für sozialwissenschaftliche Forschung und Praxis* 49: 25-42. Earlier versions of this chapter have been presented at the 'Risk and Sociocultural Theory' Conference, Charles Sturt University, Australia, 4 April 1997, 'Rethinking the Social' Conference, Griffith University, 11 July 1997, and at a seminar in the Department of Political Science at Roskilde University, Denmark, 10 February 1998. I should like to acknowledge the organizers and participants at those presentations, particularly Anne Aungles, Eduardo de la Fuente, Anni Greve and Bob Jessop, and to make particular mention of the editor of the present volume, whose suggestion stimulated me to write the chapter.

1 For a good range of this literature, see: Burchell, Gordon and Miller (1991); Barry, Osborne and Rose (1996); and Dean and Hindess (1998). See also my book, *Governmentality: Power and Rule in Modern Society* (1999a).

2 Thus, in a discussion of genetic engineering, Beck notes the over-generality of Horkheimer and Adorno's account of Nazism, but still insists that genetic engineering 'must be understood to issue from the Enlightenment as applied to technology' (1995: 29). The consequence is that the choice/consumerist aspect of current genetic engineering is viewed as largely illusory and that screening for hereditary disease is 'objectively eugenics'. Among other things, this approach begs the question of why the new genetics is liberal and pro-choice rather than authoritarian.

3 See Wynne (1996) for a related and much more extensive criticism.

4 I have made some attempt at beginning this task in *Critical and Effective Histories* (1994) and in an article on Habermas and Foucault on law, liberalism and democracy (1999b).

5 On Foucault's nominalism see Dean (1998b).

6 Parts of this section draw upon passages in Dean (1997).

7 Conversely, 'success' does not mean the continuation of a programme. See Barbara Cruikshank's (1994) analysis of the success of empowerment strategies in anti-poverty programmes in the US in the 1960s as a reason for their winding back.

8 I do not mean to suggest that categories of risk are exclusive of those of danger or other divisions of the population. In fact, one might suggest that the divisions of risk track the pathways already established in the identification of danger, and that the categories of 'high risk' are often conflated with divisions of social class. In this respect, the vocabulary of risk might better be

thought of as re-inscribing and re-coding earlier languages of stratification, disadvantage and marginalization. However, the consequences that follow from the vocabulary of risk are rather different from earlier ones: strategies of harm minimization in relation to drug use are distinct from sovereign interventions to proscribe dangerous drugs.

9 A point made by Hindess (1996). Beck similarly argues that a new modernity is a result of the successes as much as the failures of the old (1995: 74).

REFERENCES

Ashenden, S. (1996) Reflexive governance and child sexual abuse: liberal welfare rationality and the Cleveland Inquiry. *Economy and Society*, 25(1), 64–88.

Barry, A., Osborne, T. and Rose, N. (eds.) (1996) *Foucault and Political Reason: Liberalism, Neo-Liberalism and Rationalities of Government.* Chicago: University of Chicago Press.

Beck, U. (1988) On the way to the industrial risk society? Outline of an argument. *Thesis Eleven*, 23, 86–103.

— (1992a) From industrial society to risk society: questions of survival, social structure and ecological environment. *Theory, Culture and Society*, 9, 97–123.

— (1992b) *Risk Society: Towards a New Modernity.* London: Sage.

— (1994) The reinvention of politics; towards a theory of reflexive modernization. In Beck, U., Giddens, A. and Lash, S. *Reflexive Modernization: Politics, Tradition and Aesthetics in the Modern Social Order.* Cambridge: Polity Press.

— (1995) *Ecological Politics in the Age of Risk.* Cambridge: Polity Press.

Burchell, G., Gordon, C. and Miller, P. (eds.) (1991) *The Foucault Effect: Studies in Governmentality.* Hemel Hempstead: Harvester Wheatsheaf.

Castel, R. (1991) From dangerousness to risk. In Burchell, G., Gordon, C., and Miller, P. (eds.), *The Foucault Effect. Studies in Governmentality.* Hemel Hempstead: Harvester Wheatsheaf.

— (1995) *Les Métamorphoses de la Question Sociale.* Paris: Fayard.

Cruikshank, B. (1994). The will to empower: technologies of citizenship and the war on poverty. *Socialist Review*, 23(4), 29–55.

— (1996) Revolutions within: self-government and self-esteem. In Barry, A., Osborne, T. and Rose, N. (eds.), *Foucault and Political Reason: Liberalism, Neo-Liberalism and Rationalities of Government.* University College of London Press.

Dean, M. (1991) *The Constitution of Poverty: Toward a Genealogy of Liberal Governance.* London: Routledge.

— (1994) *Critical and Effective Histories. Foucault's Methods and Historical Sociology.* London: Routledge.

— (1995) Governing the unemployed self in an active society. *Economy and Society*, 24(4), 559–83.

— (1997) Sociology after society. In Owen, D. (ed.), *Sociology After Postmodernism.* London: Sage.

— (1998a) Administering asceticism: re-working the ethical life of the unemployed citizen. In Dean, M. and Hindess, B. (eds.), *Governing Australia: Studies in Contemporary Rationalities of Government.* Cambridge University Press.

(1998b) Questions of method. In Williams, R. and Velody, I. (eds.), *The Politics of Constructionism*, London: Sage.

(1999a) *Governmentality: Power and Rule in Modern Society*. London: Sage.

(1999b) Normalizing democracy: Foucault and Habermas on law, liberalism and democracy. In Ashenden, S. and Owen, D. (eds.), *Foucault contra Habermas*. London: Sage.

Dean, M. and Hindess, B. (eds.) (1998) *Governing Australia: Studies in Contemporary Rationalities of Government*. Cambridge University Press.

Defert, D. (1991) 'Popular life' and insurantial technology. In Burchell, G., Gordon, C. and Miller, P. (eds.), *The Foucault Effect: Studies in Governmentality*. Hemel Hempstead: Harvester Wheatsheaf.

Donzelot, J. (1988) The promotion of the social. *Economy and Society*, 17(3), 395–426.

(1991) The mobilization of society. In Burchell, G., Gordon, C. and Miller, P. (eds.), *The Foucault Effect: Studies in Governmentality*. Hemel Hempstead: Harvester Wheatsheaf.

Ewald, F. (1991) Insurance and risk. In Burchell, G., Gordon, C. and Miller, P. (eds.), *The Foucault Effect: Studies in Governmentality*. Hemel Hempstead: Harvester Wheatsheaf.

Foucault, M. (1991) Governmentality. In Burchell, G., Gordon, C. and Miller, P. (eds.), *The Foucault Effect: Studies in Governmentality*. Hemel Hempstead: Harvester Wheatsheaf.

Gordon, C. (1991) Governmental rationality: an introduction. In Burchell, G., Gordon, C. and Miller, P. (eds.), *The Foucault Effect: Studies in Governmentality*. Hemel Hempstead: Harvester Wheatsheaf.

Hindess, B. (1996) Liberalism, socialism and democracy: variations on a governmental theme. In Barry, A., Osborne, T. and Rose, N. (eds.), *Foucault and Political Reason: Liberalism, Neo-Liberalism and Rationalities of Government*. University College of London Press.

(1998) Neoliberalism and the national economy. In Dean, M. and Hindess, B. (eds.), *Governing Australia: Studies in Contemporary Rationalities of Government*. Cambridge University Press.

Miller, P. (1992) Accounting and objectivity: the invention of calculating selves and calculable spaces. *Annals of Scholarship*, 9, 61–86.

Miller, P. and Rose, N. (1990) Governing economic life. *Economy and Society*, 19(1), 1–31.

O'Malley, P. (1992) Risk, power and crime prevention. *Economy and Society*, 21(3), 252–75.

(1996) Risk and responsibility. In Barry, A., Osborne, T. and Rose, N. (eds.), *Foucault and Political Reason: Liberalism, Neo-Liberalism and Rationalities of Government*. University College of London Press.

(1998) Indigenous governance. In Dean, M. and Hindess, B. (eds.), *Governing Australia: Studies in Contemporary Rationalities of Government*. Cambridge University Press.

Pearce, F. and Tombs, S. (1996) Hegemony, risk and governance: 'social regulation' and the American chemical industry. *Economy and Society*, 25(3), 428–54.

Power, M. (1994) The audit society. In Hopwood, A. and Miller, P. (eds.), *Accounting as Social and Institutional Practice*. Cambridge University Press.

Procacci, G. (1993) On the social status of poverty in liberal democracies. Unpublished manuscript.

(1998) Poor citizens: social citizenship and the crisis of welfare state. In Hänninen, S. (ed.), *The Displacement of Social Policies*. Jväskylä, Finland: SoPhi.

Rose, N. (1996) The death of the social? Re-figuring the territory of government. *Economy and Society*, 25(3), 327–56.

Rose, N. and Miller, P. (1992) Problematics of government; political power beyond the state. *British Journal of Sociology*, 43(2), 173–205.

Weir, L. (1996) Recent developments in the government of pregnancy. *Economy and Society*, 25(3), 372–92.

Wynne, B. (1996) May the sheep safely graze? A reflexive view of the expert–lay knowledge divide. In Lash, S., Szerszynski, B. and Wynne, B. (eds.), *Risk Environment and Modernity: Towards a New Ecology*. London: Sage.

Yeatman, A. (1994) *Postmodern Revisionings of the Political*. New York: Routledge.

(1998) Interpreting contemporary contractualism. In Dean, M. and Hindess, B. (eds.), *Governing Australia: Studies in Contemporary Rationalities of Government*. Cambridge University Press.

7   Ordering risks

Stephen Crook

Introduction

Risk phenomena and sociocultural theory have developed a close reciprocal relationship during the past two decades. The defining text of the first defining form of the relationship is Douglas and Wildavsky's (1982) essay interpreting the expanding risk anxieties of the contemporary United States from the perspective of cultural anthropology. That of a second form is Beck's (1992) 'sociological diagnosis of the times' (Lash, 1994: 118) which placed risk phenomena at the heart of a transformed and radicalized modernity. To oversimplify to the point of injustice, the first form offers a 'sociocultural' account of risk processes while the second advances a 'risk' account of sociocultural processes. It will be argued that this distinction can only be analytic, that risk phenomena do structure, or 'order', sociocultural relations but under conditions in which broader sociocultural patterns, or 'orderings', have already structured risk phenomena.

The argument draws on two other related literatures that have contributed to recent discussions of risk and order. The first is the analysis of 'governmentality-government' and 'regulation' in work deriving from Foucault (1991) (see Burchell, Gordon and Miller, 1991 and Barry, Osborne and Rose, 1996a). The second is Law's (1994) discussion of the sociological problem of 'order' with its injunction that we must abandon 'the idea that there is a single order . . . the dream or the nightmare of modernity' (2). For Law, as for other 'actor network' analysts, 'perhaps there is ordering, but there is certainly no order' (1) (see also Latour, 1993). That the Foucauldian and actor network traditions have some convergences is well established (see Malpas and Wickham, 1995; Miller and Rose, 1990). Foucauldian models of 'regulation' have already been applied to risk definition and risk management (see Castel, 1991; O'Malley, 1996; Petersen, 1996).

The argument about risk and sociocultural order developed below attempts a simultaneous enrolment of these traditions of analysis. It

links them to a narrative in which, in advanced societies at the close of
the twentieth century, a previously hegemonic dream of a modern order
associated with the institutional arrangements of 'organized capitalism'
has lost its predominance (see Lash and Urry, 1987). It now competes
with two other dreams: of an order generated by the hyper-reflexive
programmes of global networks and the 'disembedded' human subject
(see Giddens, 1991) and of an order arising from an immediate and
intense 'neo-tribal' or 'neo-traditional' solidarity (see Maffesoli, 1996).
This narrative connects with risk phenomena in three ways. First, the
orderings associated with the three dreams of order incorporate distinct
regimes of risk identification, assessment and management ('organized',
'neo-liberal' and 'ritualized'). Second, widespread and intense risk
anxieties of the kind Beck takes as his starting point can be explained, in
part and in an inversion of his own argument, as effects of the relative
decline of modern ordering and organized risk management. Third,
where no regime of risk management is predominant, none is easily
stabilized and in consequence risk anxieties are incipiently 'disordering'
of broader sociocultural patterns.

These issues are considered in sequence in the three sections that
follow. The first expands on the concept of 'ordering' and its three major
contemporary instances. The next section relates these orderings to
regimes of risk management while a final section considers more closely
the decline of organized risk management, outlines the contemporary
problem of stabilizing risk management and explores its implications for
sociocultural ordering more generally.

Ordering

Order stands to ordering as governmentality stands to government in
the Foucauldian literature. As Miller and Rose put it, '"governmentality" is eternally optimistic, "government" is a congenitally failing
operation' (1990: 10). And later (14): 'programmes of government are
idealised schema for the ordering of social and economic life . . . a space
within which the objectives of government are elaborated, and where
plans to implement them are dreamed up'. By analogy, order is the
imaginary, the dream with reference to which myriad programmes for
the ordering of social (and cultural, political, economic) life take their
bearings. Of course, the practice can never complete the dream. Just as
failure is an unavoidable correlate of 'the necessary incompleteness of
government' (Malpas and Wickham, 1995: 39), so it is of the 'necessary
incompleteness of ordering'.

The Foucauldian insight that ordering is always failing and

incomplete gains a sharper methodological edge in actor network (AN) analysis. Law's insistence that there may be 'ordering' but no 'order' (above) is generalized as a call for a 'sociology of verbs, not nouns' (1994: 15). Three other well-known AN themes are also important here. First, if ordering is opposed to a unitary order it is also opposed to an homogenous order. The field of operations of ordering, 'the social', is not a single substance or a Durkheimian 'reality', but 'materially heterodox' (2). Orderings operate on and by heterogeneous materials, including: natural phenomena (for example, human genetics and disease phenomena, weather patterns), texts and devices for their inscriptions, production technologies, legal and organizational forms, material and immaterial cultural objects.

Second, programmes of ordering operate through the construction of 'sociotechnical networks' from such heterogeneous materials. Chains of 'translation' are established, linking one (human or non-human) actant to another in two dimensions: a syntagmatic 'association' (forming chains of actants) and a paradigmatic 'substitution' (of one order of actant for another) (see Latour, 1991). Third, translation chains do not simply follow a principle of expansion into a vacuum. Programs encounter the anti-programmes of actants, strategies meet resistance. This process is not a marginal irritant, but central to the dynamics of programmes: their direction and scope is shaped by the extent to which anti-programmes can be enrolled. Note that 'what is programme and what is anti-programme is relative to the chosen observer' (Akrich and Latour, 1992: 261). As Malpas and Wickham (1995: 43) put it, 'resistance is not merely the counterstroke to power, it is also that which directs and shapes power'. This point is consequential for the account of the relations between the three regimes of contemporary risk management developed below. Programmes are 'congenitally failing' here because in principle no chain of association can ever be complete, no 'stabilization' of a network can ever be other than regional and temporary.

Although AN and Foucauldian approaches to ordering converge on the themes of heterogeneity, contingency and incompleteness, there are differences of emphasis between them. Notably, strict AN principles confine analysis to the empirically given materials. 'There is no need to go searching for mysterious or global causes outside networks. If something is missing it is because the description is not complete' (Latour, 1991: 130). In contrast, Foucauldian analysis deploys an array of general concepts to designate types of network, such as the famous triad of 'sovereignty', 'discipline' and 'governmentality' (from Foucault, 1991). Foucauldian analyses are pulled back from the edge of a totalizing and idealized historicism through repeated injunctions against that temptation and equally repeated assertions of their own modesty (see Barry, Osborne and Rose, 1996b: 3–4 and Dean, 1996: 210–13). The effect, in both cases, is a suspicion of those standard sociological narratives of modernization that are so central to the Beck–Giddens analysis of risk phenomena. On the principle that my enemy's enemy is my friend, that suspicion suggests at least a partial further convergence between Foucauldians, AN theorists and Douglas' (1992) studies of the relations between risk and order which question clear-cut distinctions between the traditional and the modern.

Some of these complexities will be explored later, but in summary, the analysis to be developed here will suggest that new programmes and strategies do not, as it were, have to re-invent the basic format of a strategy or programme anew on each occasion. Models, dreams and imaginaries of order have a sociocultural currency that becomes a resource, a point of reference, for programmes of ordering. Equally, while historical change follows no ineluctable laws, neither is sociocultural analysis confined to an eternal present. Regional typifications of middle-range historical sequences are entirely possible and proper. They cannot be discredited with a passing reference to the folly of totalization. At the same time, Latour's principle can be maintained: models, dreams and imaginaries only have any effectivity in Latour's sense within networks and their historical dynamics are carried in the contingent play of programme and anti-programme. The immediate significance of such a compromise position here is that it permits both the typification and the sequencing of programmes of ordering.

On that basis, 'orderings' can be conceived as general frames or matrices within which models of order are projected and contested: an ordering projects both typical patterns of solidarity and typical patterns of conflict, or fragmentation, it enables both 'programme' and 'anti-programme' to be articulated as programmatic and anti-programmatic. The ordering practices collected under and oriented to orderings share with modes of 'regulation' and techniques of 'government' the characteristic that the 'orders' they project are never finally achieved. Ordering is always and everywhere in process. The focus of attention is squarely on ordering practices rather than achieved orders – on verbs rather than nouns.

It has already been signalled that three orderings are operative in contemporary advanced societies. The typology of the three orderings is not intended to be exhaustive in either of two ways. First, and perhaps obviously, it is not a logically derived typology of all the orderings that could, in principle, exist. Second, neither is it an historical sequence of all the orderings that there have, in fact, been in the history of advanced western societies. It is offered, tentatively, as a catalogue of the major orderings at work in advanced western societies at the close of the twentieth century. While it is no doubt incomplete, its pragmatic warrant is that, to a degree, it works: each ordering resonates with defining themes in varieties of contemporary sociocultural analysis, and the distinctions between them seem to match empirically observable tensions and divisions in many advanced societies. The three orderings are as follows.

Modern ordering operates at the level of national societies through differentiated, rationalized and organized institutions and through the technologies of mass production and mass communication. The exemplary institutions of state and market are the competing foci of different variants of modern ordering and each generates both solidarity and conflict around the distribution of rights and resources.

Hyper-reflexive ordering is global in scope and operates through networks rather than institutions and through computerized communications and production technologies. It is associated with radical individualization and the reflexive monitoring of self. Individuals are disembedded and linked by the simulations of global culture or shifting coalitions of interest. Conflicts cluster around matters such as rights to self-expression, exposure to risks and access to information.

Neo-traditional ordering is operative at sites of intense and 'mechanical' group solidarity such as that associated with shared ethnicity, shared taste or shared beliefs. The intensity of the solidarity engendered is matched by the intensity of the antagonism directed at other ethnicities, other tastes or other beliefs. The prefix 'neo' signals first, the element of choice in an individual's alignment with the group and second, the role of advanced communications technologies in the formation and maintenance of many groups.

If the cultural, political and social dynamics of the advanced societies appear disordered or confusing, as they do to so many commentators, it is largely because the three distinct orderings operate in the same space. It is not simply that no single 'postmodern' principle of ordering has definitively displaced the modern. Modern ordering, after all, accommodates as programme and anti-programme the tension between market and state that forms the major line of fault in the politics of the advanced societies from the late nineteenth to the late twentieth centuries. Marketized (or 'liberal') and statist (or 'social democratic') variants of modern ordering are usefully seen as variants, rather than as radically distinct orderings, because of their historically conditioned convergences: on the national state, society and economy; on the technologies of mass production and consumption, on the politics of distribution and on what Hindess (1996: 73) has termed the 'figure of the community of autonomous persons'. If the advanced societies were simply experiencing another swing of the pendulum, this time away from 'statist' and towards 'marketized' ordering, that change would be of considerable political and historical interest but would pose no fundamental challenge to modern dreams of order.

The simultaneous operations of modern, hyper-reflexive and neo-traditional orderings do pose such a challenge, however. Hyper-reflexive programmes can borrow the vocabulary of liberalism, but their networks enrol actants – from the transnational corporation to the genetically modified organism to the Internet – that escape the frame of a liberal market society. The neo-traditional programmes of ethnic groups, religious sects or social movements may appeal to modern conceptions of nation, justice and democracy, but they also project relationships and practices which erode the institutional arrangements and discursive conventions that give those conceptions their accepted modern meanings. In the present intersection between a fading, but once hegemonic, 'statist' variant of modern ordering and emergent hyper-reflexive and neo-traditional orderings, there is no longer a single and well-understood line of fault. Competing dreams of order do not spontaneously arrange themselves into self-evident clusters of 'programme' and 'anti-programme'. The ways in which risk management and risk anxieties are bound up in this syndrome is the theme of the remainder of the chapter.

Regimes of risk identification, assessment and management

In an influential sociological literature, 'risk' is definitively modern. Giddens (1991: 109–11) differentiates the future orientation of a modernity in which hazards become risks from traditionalist conceptions of fate and destiny, and traces the trajectory from one to the other. Luhmann (1993: 8–14) covers similar sociohistorical ground, while Beck's account of 'risk society' rather curiously has less to say about the emergence of risk. However, risk is defined as 'a systematic way of dealing with hazards and insecurities induced and introduced by modernity itself' (Beck, 1992: 21).

There is also an anthropological literature on danger, risk and pollution in non-modern societies in which Mary Douglas' work is canonical. When Douglas (1982) considers contemporary anxieties about environmental risk as variants of anthropologically widespread pollution anxieties, she brackets any stark and defining contrast between 'traditional' societies which unreflexively accept dangers as fate and 'modern' societies which reflexively process risks. All societies develop reflexive mechanisms for the processing of perceived hazards, although the mechanisms vary widely. In the selection and prioritizing of dangers 'there is not much difference between modern times and ages past' (Douglas and Wildavsky, 1982: 30).

An example that graphically illustrates both this fundamental point and its limitations is furnished by Clendinnen's (1991) *Aztecs*. She portrays the Mexica world as structured around the reflexive management of appalling dangers: that the sun would not rise, that the maize would not grow, that the fifth creation itself would end at one of the fifty-two yearly 'new fire festivals'. Catastrophe was averted by attention to a wearisome cycle of observances, many of which involved the ritual killing of up to 20,000 persons at a time. An entire imperial 'tribute economy' was built around these requirements. The Conquistadors noted the paradox of life in Tenochtitlan: grave and polite citizens of a sophisticated metropolis leading orderly lives, yet bound to horrifying ritual blood letting. But, of course, this did not appear as paradox to the Mexica themselves. The ritual order and the order of daily life were inseparable and accounted for in terms of the dangers threatening both.

The case is a vivid illustration of Douglas and Wildavsky's claim that risk selection and social organization are intertwined, so that 'to alter risk selection and risk perception . . . would depend upon changing the social organization' (1982: 9). A curiously similar claim is made in Luhmann's more abstrusely systems–theoretic account of risk. For Luhmann, the primary function of a system is the reduction of environmental complexity. However, systems can only operate within an environment to the extent that they can 'observe' it, and social systems observe only through communication (1989: 29). But anything communicable is, as it were, part of the system. Social systems can process 'external' risks only to the extent that they 'internalize' them (hence, for Luhmann, the difficulties advanced societies experience in communicating about and processing ecological risks). Thus, the dangers threatening the Mexica, and the observances necessary to manage them, were woven into the fabric of all Mexica institutions from warfare to trade to family life.

The Mexica, or at least Clendinnen's account of the Mexica, can also exemplify one element of Douglas' main contribution to the cultural theory of risk: her 'grid–group' model. This model is put to work in later sections and warrants a brief exposition here. The link between risk selection and sociocultural organization is mediated, for Douglas, through 'processes of blame-pinning or exonerating from blame' (1992: 60). Different types of political regime will handle this process in different ways in an effort, first to explain disasters, second to justify allegiances and third to stabilize the workings of the regime. Douglas identifies three broad patterns of response and therefore three main types of regime. The distribution of these responses and regimes is indifferent to conventional distinctions between the modern and the premodern or 'the West and the rest'.

The first two types of response and regime, labelled 'hierarchy' and 'market' by Douglas (73) are widely distributed and recognized. The former subordinates the individual to the group and interprets disasters as a punishment of the group (or tribe, organization or society) for a loss of commitment. This interpretation tends, of course, to strengthen group control. The latter type of regime is based on exchange and competition. Disasters are interpreted as a failure of the 'fetish power' or charisma of the current leader and therefore tend to intensify competition for leadership. Douglas (73) cites Olson's model of collective action to support a claim that market and hierarchical regimes can secure commitment because both are able to either distribute 'selective benefits' to members or coerce them. However, Douglas argues that the market–hierarchy dichotomy misses a third type of regime, noted in the anthropological literature, in which selective benefits are not available and coercive powers are weak. Here, disasters are interpreted as the result of a 'cosmic plot', a conspiracy of outsiders. Dissidents within the group can be painted as traitors, agents of the cosmic plot. Douglas labels this type of regime 'voluntary group' and notes that its exemplars, such as contemporary religious sects and communes, 'are most keenly attuned to low probability, high consequence danger' (1992: 77. See also 1986: chapter 9).

The 'grid–group' model itself constructs a matrix from 'grid', a vertical axis representing the degree to which social relations are structured (+) or unstructured (−) and 'group' a horizontal axis representing degrees of collectivism (+) or individualism (−). The two axes yield a square as follows (see Douglas, 1992: 106, 1992: 201, 1992: 264).

B	Grid +	Grid +	C
	Group −	Group +	
A	Grid −	Grid −	D
	Group −	Group +	

The three regimes discussed above can be distributed to three corners of the square. 'Market', with its unstructured individualism belongs at 'A'. 'Hierarchy', with its firmly structured collectivism belongs at 'C'. 'Voluntary group' with its unstructured collectivism belongs at 'D'. Corner 'B' represents a limit case of structural constraint with no group ties – the position of the isolate rather than the individualist (Douglas, 1992: 106).

Clendinnen's Mexica clearly meet Douglas' (78) criteria for hierarchy, position C in the 'grid–group' matrix. The threat of disaster supports group control and amounts to a threat of punishment for a loss of commitment to ritual observances and tribute. The subversive relativizing force of Douglas' analysis lies in the way it breaches cultural and historical boundaries. The Mexica can be shown to share a pattern of response to disaster, or the threat of disaster, with organizations and political regimes in the twentieth century. On that basis, the Beck–Giddens distinction between a non-reflexive premodernity beset by dangers and a risk-processing reflexive modernity is clearly in trouble: Mexica priests and the agents of a modern insurance company are both in the risk-management business. But there are also important differences in the way they go about that business: the anthropological relativization of risk does not efface questions about distinct and perhaps specifically modern regimes of risk management. The broadest answers to those questions must lie in general sociological accounts of modernizing processes. Modern regimes of risk management will have been shaped by processes of differentiation, rationalization, commodification and organization just like other sociocultural phenomena (see Crook, Pakulski and Waters, 1992: chapter 1). These general analytic issues will not be recapitulated here. A more narrowly focused narrative can carry the argument.

One critical difference between Mexica priests and the agents of the insurance company is that they employ different modes of calculation (not that insurance agents calculate while the Mexica did not: their forms of calculation were complex and sophisticated according to Clendinnen). Bernstein's recent (1996) popular treatment charts the trajectory of modern risk-calculation and links its stages to developments in the mathematics of chance, probability and uncertainty. For example, large-scale modern risk insurance was not an attractive business proposition until the mathematics of normal distribution and statistical sampling could be systematically applied. A similar point clearly applies to the epidemiological studies that are so central to the 'neo-liberal' regulation of health-cum-lifestyle risks (see Petersen, 1996). Following AN principles, one might map networks in which the institutional forms of the insurance business, mathematical formulae, legal and political forms, optimizing economic agents, disease processes, prevalent causes of injury and medical techniques become linked in the stabilized chains of association of life insurance.

If one critical principle here is that there can be no identification, assessment or management of risk without forms of calculation, another must be that there can be no regime for the identification, assessment or management of risk that comprises *only* a 'pure' form of calculation. This point may seem obvious to anthropologists or sociologists, but it is presented as daringly radical in the more technical discourses of risk assessment and management, particularly in the United States. Once again, this is an area in which Douglas has made a major contribution. Urging that risk perception is an unavoidably cultural and moral phenomenon, Douglas (1986: 3) laments the emphasis on individual cognition and choice in professional studies of risk perception because 'it is hard to maintain seriously that the perception of risk is private'. As she puts the point later, 'individuals do not try to make independent choices, especially about big political issues . . . they come already primed with cultural assumptions and weightings . . . the big issues reach them in the form of questions whether to reinforce authority or to subvert it' (Douglas, 1992: 58). An insight into just how limited the impact of these arguments has been in professional risk analysis, despite the renown of Douglas's work with Wildavsky, is provided by a recent collection of papers (Kunreuther and Slovic, 1996).

In a paper that epitomizes the tone of the collection, Viscusi and Zeckhauser discuss the difficulty of conveying 'risk information' to publics in a way that will promote 'appropriate risk perceptions'. A major source of the difficulty is that 'people often cannot process and act on quantitative risk information in a reliable manner' (1996: 111). As a result, risks must be conveyed in imprecise terms that produce over- or underestimates of risk. They argue in a separate chapter that media coverage encourages overestimation of 'lurking risks . . . of particularly catastrophic consequences that we have never experienced but fear greatly' (147). To illustrate the point, they assert that during the 1960s 'much of the US public believed that the chance of a nuclear war within a decade was about 1:3, whereas many experts estimated the annual risk to be from 10^{-3} to 10^{-5}' (147). To labour the point no further, Zechauser and Viscusi allow that 'culture' impacts on risk assessment and management, but only as an obstacle to correct and objective procedures. They conclude that 'Government policy should not mirror citizens' irrationalities but . . . should make the decisions people would make if they understood risks correctly' (14).

Other and more nuanced discussions note the proliferation of political demands for 'risk based' rather than 'public opinion based' risk management in the United States (see Freudenburg, 1996: 45; Pollack, 1996: 26), but warn that such schemes cannot break the cycle of

de-legitimation and declining trust in public risk management (Freudenberg, 1996: 53; Pollack, 1996: 33). Freudenberg (1996: 51) is
concerned that the credibility of scientific risk assessment is threatened
when government and industry use it for 'cover' in controversial cases.
Pollack (1996: 34) insists that even erroneous public risk perceptions
must be taken into account in democratic policy-making. However,
neither Freudenberg nor Pollack challenges the basic dream of an
objective calculation of real risks performed by experts. So Pollack
(1996: 29–30) cites and defends Douglas' account of risk perceptions,
but clearly excludes expert risk assessment itself from the scope of that
account. For Douglas herself (1986: 18), 'the wrong way to think of the
social factors that influence risk perception is to treat them as smudges
which blur a telescope lens and distort the true image'.

A step towards the right way to think about the social dimensions of
risk can be taken through the idea of 'regimes' of identification, assessment and management ('management' in shorthand). Regimes are very
broad, historically contingent and heterogeneous networks for the
ordering of risk. As with the list of more general orderings outlined
above, no claim is made that the three regimes identified here exhaust
all logical or historical possibilities. The main characteristics of the three
regimes can be outlined without further ado, and their relations in the
contemporary advanced societies will be explored in the next section.

Organized risk management is centred on the state. Generally as part of
a broader drive for modernization, states take on the task of regulating
and, if possible, eradicating risks. The welfare, social or what Beck
(1996) has termed 'provident' states of the mid twentieth century seek
to control or abate risk phenomena as diverse as unemployment,
infectious disease and industrial pollution. State intervention in these
areas is broadly supported by corporate labour and capital as elements
in a 'social armistice' (see Crook, Pakulski and Waters, 1992: chapter 3).
Organized risk management is a network of many classes of actant: the
production technologies of mid twentieth century industry, scientific
and technical experts, material and administrative instruments for
measurement of risk phenomena, vaccines and other medical technologies, the electoral programmes of mass political parties and many others
besides.

In historical perspective, however, the more obviously statist elements
of the network stand out: the batteries of regulation issued by all levels
of government and the armies of inspectors enforcing them in areas such
as child health, food hygiene, workplace safety, industrial emissions and
the rest. In all stabilized regimes of risk management, the identification
and selection of risks for attention is in large part a function of the

apparatuses in place for assessment and management. That much is implied in Douglas' account of structured 'selection' and Luhmann's concept of 'communication' in relation to risk. In an organized regime the activities of scientific and technical experts, inspectorates and enforcement agencies, legislators and concerned citizens do not simply process risks that appear 'externally' over the horizon of the regime in an *ad hoc* way. The apparatuses of surveillance and discipline, as the Foucauldians would have it, routinely produce the risks they assess and manage. The important corollary of this point is that only those risks are produced which are in principle 'manageable'.

Neo-liberal regimes are distinctive in their emphasis on 'the self-regulating capacities of individuals' (Miller and Rose 1990: 24), an emphasis apparently related to what Burchell (1991: 145) has described as 'a "return" to liberal themes in the politics of both the right and the left'. The critical point is not that the apparatuses of organized risk management simply disappear, leaving the bare individual to face a hostile world alone. These apparatuses may well be downsized, but more significantly their relationship to individuals changes. If organized regimes typically operate through surveillance and discipline, neo-liberal regimes typically operate through the provision of information and expert advice which responsible individuals will take into account in making 'lifestyle' choices. O'Malley (1996: 199) coins the apt terms 'privatized actuarialism' or 'prudentialism' for this pattern.

The proliferation of such advice in relation to health risks, for example, is central to the pervasive 'ideologies' of 'healthism and lifestyleism' (Lupton, 1994: 336). As Petersen puts it (1996: 48–9), 'neo-liberalism calls upon the individual to enter into the process of their own self-governance through processes of endless self-examination, self-care and self-improvement'. Here, the Foucauldian literature converges with the theme of 'reflexive modernization' in Beck and Giddens as well as Douglas' distinction between 'hierarchy' and 'market'. For Beck (1994: 14), 'individualization' is 'a compulsion for the manufacture, self-design and self-staging of not just one's own biography but also its commitments and networks'. For Beck, this process still takes place under the aegis of a welfare state. For the Foucauldian analysts of 'neo-liberalism', the recent mutation of state as well as self is consequential.

Neo-liberal risk management also attempts to stabilize extensive and heterogeneous networks of expertise, instruments, medical techniques, political programmes and the rest. However, neo-liberalism does not aim for the centralized abatement or control of risk. Individual agents must become risk monitors and risk calculators. It is important to note that neo-liberal regimes 'produce' more risks, and therefore more public awareness of risk, than organized regimes, for obvious reasons. Neo-liberalism requires a greater emphasis on publicity about risk if individuals are to perform their risk calculations, the provision of information becomes the major accountable role of the state in risk management, and there is little incentive to limit the production of risks when the main risk-producing agencies do not bear direct responsibility for control or abatement. As O'Malley (1996: 202) puts it 'the prudent subject of risk must be responsible, knowledgeable and rational. To rely on the State to deal with the harmful effects of known, calculable and individually manageable risks appears feckless and culpable.'

Ritualized risk management may not warrant the dignity of the label 'regime' in the same way as organized and neo-liberal risk management. It is less easy to identify states or major corporate actors that overtly follow a programme of ritualized risk management. However, there is an heuristic value in elevating a widespread but loosely connected and rarely stabilized syndrome to the status of a regime of risk management.

Douglas and Wildavsky (1982: 30) identify 'two backward steps towards premodernism' in the most technically proficient and 'modern' discourses about risk: a claim to 'a privileged and uncontested view on the nature of reality' and a denial that the prioritization of risk 'means choosing between political and moral consequences'. To re-connect with the issue of calculation discussed at the beginning of the section, the impossible dream of a purely calculative regime of risk management would be as 'premodern' in its drive for certainty as it was 'hyper-modern' in its techniques. Alexander and Smith (1996) push beyond Douglas and Wildavsky in their demand for a consistently culture-theoretic account of risk. They argue that discourses of technology and risk are 'fuelled by an underlying logic of utopic and dystopic narrative forms' (261). Anthropology and culture theory overlap here with the claims of Baudrillard (1983), Latour (1993) and most notoriously Maffesoli (1996) that 'we have never been modern', that sociological and technocratic meta-discourses of the modern mis-recognize the continuing and subterranean springs of human sociality. As Baudrillard (1983: 68) puts it, 'ultimately, things have never functioned socially but symbolically, magically, irrationally, etc.'

These arguments may need to be treated with some caution, but they provide a warrant for the model of a ritualized regime of risk management operating on at least two levels. First, the stabilization of any regime requires a capacity to engender confidence that risk phenomena are 'under control'. This might be seen as the most obvious effect of practices from Mexica ritual killings to fire-drills and disaster planning exercises. The imperative becomes directly political when risk phenomena – health risks or environmental risks, say – find a prominent place on political agenda. There are in-built pressures tending towards commitments to the maintenance of public safety and expressions of confidence in existing arrangements that exceed what experts in risk assessment might consider warranted. Thus, Zeckhauser and Viscusi (1996: 152) bemoan what they see as counterproductive 'ceremonial commitments to public safety'. A number of papers in the same collection (Fischoff, 1996; Freudenberg, 1996; Jamieson, 1996; Kasperson and Kasperson, 1996) emphasize the need for risk assessment and management to resonate with public 'values' and to engender 'trust'.

Risk management by corporate and government agencies in its public relations aspect can easily take on a ritualized quality. Public consultations are conducted, the 'best' expert advice is sought, environmental impact statements are published and informed decisions are taken. If, as Giddens would have it (1994: 64–5), ritual is the enactment of 'formulaic truth', much risk management strives for the status of ritual. If it so often fails, because the formulaic truths of risk assessment can be challenged and therefore rarely attain truly formulaic, traditional status, it is because of processes taking place at the second level of ritualized risk management.

Social movements, citizens' initiatives, community activism and the NIMBY (not in my backyard) syndrome have an important role in many accounts of risk phenomena. In Beck's model, groups protesting against dominant forms of risk management are the historical agents of new forms of 'societal self-criticism' (Beck, 1996: 33) that define the radical potential of risk society. This dimension of his work has led critics to see Beck as the prophet of a 'hyper-enlightenment' (Szerszynski, Lash and Wynne, 1996: 6). Alternative views see the group and movement phenomena involved in disputes about risk as the embodiments of a more direct, less cognitive, form of social solidarity. At one end of a broad spectrum, Lash (1994: 161) outlines the defining features of 'reflexive communities' while at the other Maffesoli (1996: 86) suggests that neo-tribes manifest an 'elective sociality', the contemporary expressions of the Dionysian *puissance* that is the basis of all social life.

Lash and Maffesoli come close in some ways to Turner's classic (1995) account of ritual. For Turner, ritual is a way cultures handle 'liminality'. 'Liminal entities are neither here nor there, they are betwixt and between the positions assigned and arrayed by law, custom, convention and ceremonial' (95). Liminal phenomena, such as rites of passage, are of interest to Turner (96) for their blend of 'lowliness and sacredness, of homogeneity and comradeship'. Liminality challenges hierarchical sociopolitical structures and distinctions or rank: it 'implies that the high could not be high unless the low existed, and that he who is high must experience what it is like to be low' (97). Rites of passage and other instances of liminality put into play, in opposition to structure and hierarchy, 'unstructured or rudimentarily structured and relatively undifferentiated *communitas*' (96).

Turner's distinction between 'structure' and '*communitas*' overlaps with Douglas' distinction between 'hierarchy' and 'voluntary group' (positions C and D in the 'grid–group' matrix above). However, two features of Turner's version of the distinction stand out. First, the link between *communitas* and liminality points to the marginal status, the potential dangerousness from the perspective of structure/hierarchy, of the individuals and groups concerned. Turner (1995: 110) notes the literary and mythic role of the despised and the outlawed as bearers of universal human qualities, and (perhaps unhelpfully) anticipates Maffesoli by linking liminality and *communitas* to the *élan vital*, 'instinctual energies' and 'biologically inherited drives' (128). Second, Turner (107) notes that in the advanced societies of the mid-to-late twentieth century, liminal *communitas*, 'a set of transitional qualities "betwixt and between" defined states of culture and society has become itself an institutionalized state'. In youth subcultures, new social movements and new age cults, *communitas* has found a permanent, if anxiety-provoking, place in advanced societies.

Whichever term is preferred – 'reflexive community', 'neo-tribe', 'voluntary group' or 'liminal *communitas*' – it is clear that the designated groupings have a rather particular relationship to risk perception and risk management. As Douglas suggests, they are especially drawn to a concern with low-probability, high-consequence risks understood as the outcome of 'cosmic plots'. As Turner argues, both the groups and the individuals who are drawn to them will be seen as marginal and dangerous by the denizens of the established 'structure'. In that sense, ritualized risk management is itself a risky and marginal enterprise. However, the activities of, say, environmental movements is never wholly disconnected from the ritualism of dominant forms of risk assessment and management. Environmental groups will often develop alternative expert risk assessments, for example. But they also frequently operate in the registers of symbolism and mythic narrative in the senses that Alexander and Smith (1996) use the terms: images of unspoiled wilderness, narratives of despoliation and redemption and the rest. The subterranean convergence between 'liminal' and 'official' ritualizations of risk management lies in a common recognition of the potency of mythic representations, or ritualized enactments, of danger and safety, risk and reassurance. The public relations stance of many corporate and governmental risk managers is that established assessment and management procedures ensure that the world is, and will continue to be safe. The oppositional stance of many risk-affected groups is that the world is far from safe because of cosmic plots, but should and can be made so.

To posit a distinct regime of ritualized risk management is to draw attention to a tendency for networks to develop around demands for reassurance and certainty in the face of risk. As in other networks, heterogeneous resources are enrolled: expert knowledges, mainstream and 'alternative' technologies, processes of group formation, symbols and narrative forms, natural phenomena. The ritualized character of such emergent regimes lies first in their repetition of practices that enact the promise of certainty, from weekly kerbside recycling and the mantra of 'reduce, re-use, re-cycle', through the regular monitoring of (say) beach pollution to the public enactment of 'accountable' planning procedures. Their ritual dimension resides, second, in multiple links to a dangerous liminality: to the boundaries between 'nature' and 'culture', to social outsiders and to an anti-hierarchical *communitas*.

Risk and (dis)order

Processes of risk identification, assessment and management are understood here as a special case of ordering practices. The three regimes discussed in the previous section are each aligned with a more general ordering as sketched in the second section; organized risk management with the statist variant of a modern ordering, neo-liberal risk management with a hyper-reflexive ordering and ritualized risk management with neo-traditional ordering. These alignments suggest virtuous cycles of reinforcement. Regimes of risk management order risks (and after all, the very idea of 'risk' cries for ordering) in ways that draw on more wide-ranging orderings. Successfully ordered risks, in turn, feed back into and amplify the efficacy and legitimacy of orderings. However, matters may not be, or may no longer be, that simple or benign. This final section considers the ordering–risk relation within a narrative that links the rise of the two pairs hyper-reflexive/neo-liberal and neo-traditional/ritualized to the decline of the pair modern/organized, and in which the problem of stabilizing any regime of risk management can appear to have become insoluble.

A useful point of entry into these issues is provided by the widespread puzzlement on the part of sociologists and risk experts that public concern about risk phenomena has increased so much over recent years. Giddens (1991: 115–7), for example, catalogues the developments over the past seventy years that have yielded improvements in 'basic life security' which outweigh any incidental 'new risks', at least in the advanced societies. Kunreuther and Slovic (1996: 117) note the irony that 'as our society has expended time and money to make life healthier and safer, many in the public have become more, rather than less, concerned about risk'.

Explanations of this curiosity fall into two main types that might be labelled 'realist' and 'culturalist'. Beck is the best-known realist. In his account, risk anxieties have increased because risks have become more prevalent. The once invisible risks of industrialization have reached the end of their period of 'latency' and now show themselves in acid rain, toxic accidents and the rest (Beck, 1992: 55). These risk phenomena 'increasingly tend to escape the institutions for monitoring and protection in industrial society' (Beck, 1994: 5), challenging the instrumental rationality of the modern state and releasing a 'sub-politics' that will produce a 'metamorphosis' of the state and a 'self-organising' society (38–9).

Beck's realism has been widely criticized (see Szerszynski, Lash and Wynne, 1996: 7 and Alexander and Smith, 1996: 254). The problem is that his diagnosis of sociocultural risk phenomena can appear to depend on gratuitous judgements about the 'natural' causes of the phenomenon in question, as in a claim that tornadoes in Florida have been caused by the Greenhouse Effect (Beck, 1996: 43n). However, and as Alexander and Smith (1996: 255) elegantly show, this realism appears in direct contradiction to Beck's equally frequent claims that contemporary risks are ubiquitous yet 'invisible'. Giddens is a less florid realist for whom increased risk consciousness comes from the low probability but high consequence and incalculable risks associated with our increasing dependence on the 'expert systems' that deliver us 'relative security' most of the time (Giddens, 1991: 133, 136). These risks are part of the 'sombre side' of modernization that promotes a 'risk climate' in which 'risk assessment' becomes a constant preoccupation (122–4).

Culturalist alternatives, exemplified by Douglas and Wildavsky (1982) or Alexander and Smith (1996), have considerable virtues as critiques of realism. They can show that the (cultural) work of selection and interpretation is an irreducible moment in the 'visibility' of risk, so that appeals to the latter must fail as explanations of the former. However, culturalism flirts with two major and related defects. First, there is a tendency to dissolve the work of risk identification, assessment and management back into generic human practice. The salutary lesson that there are fewer differences between we moderns and those non-moderns than we may imagine loses its bite if it becomes the claim that everything is always and everywhere the same. Douglas and Wildavsky avoid this pitfall because they can use the 'grid–group' model to show how different risk responses are entwined with different patterns of social organization. It is just this feature of the Douglas and Wildavsky approach that Alexander and Smith (1996: 256), as more thoroughgoing culturalists, most dislike. Alexander and Smith themselves come perilously close to an ahistoricism of universal narrative forms and symbolic representations (1996: *passim*).

If the first defect of culturalist accounts is their complicity in a myth of the unity of culture, the second is complicity in a myth of the purity, or homogeneity, of culture. Latour (1993: 10–11) gives the orthodoxies of structural anthropology a twist in portraying the radical distinction between non-human nature and human culture as the result of the modern work of 'purification'. As he puts it later, 'Cultures – different or universal – do not exist any more than Nature does. There are only nature-cultures' (104). In the end, appeals to a pure and unitary human 'culture' are no more able to engage with complex networks of risk identification, assessment and management than are appeals to the real 'nature' of the risks themselves.

The apparatus of 'orderings' and 'regimes of risk management' developed above can be mobilized in an account that gives, in a very simplified and sweeping way, some sense of the complex dynamics of contemporary risk phenomena. What have been labelled 'modern ordering' (in its statist variant) and 'organized risk management' achieved hegemonic status in the era of 'Organized Capitalism' or 'Fordism' that experienced its golden age in the immediate post-war period. In that period, welfare-state provisions in most advanced societies promised, and appeared to deliver, a measure of control over a wide range of risks and hazards in measures from health care to unemployment pay. Historically, these developments follow on the heels of attempts to abate gross environmental hazards in measures dealing with sanitation, public housing, airborne pollution and industrial health and safety. Even educational and social policies of various kinds can be understood as attempts better to equip citizens to manage routine life-risks. High wage economies fostered a mass-market consumerism in which availability of goods and limited choice could seem attractive but not too risky.

In short, during the post-war boom, citizens of advanced societies were offered the benefits of a modernity with few risks. Risks were eradicated (infectious diseases, pollution), limited and enjoyed as freedoms (consumerism, party politics), or 'insured' (but see below) by the state (health, unemployment). In Douglas' terms, organized risk management exemplifies hierarchy, position (C) in the 'grid–group' matrix.

In return for their commitment and loyalty, citizens are rewarded with the 'selective benefits' of social insurance and risk abatement. Modern ordering more generally is articulated along the diagonal between hierarchy (C) and market (A). In social democracies, at least, the hegemony enjoyed by the statist variant is both enabled and circumscribed by a requirement to acknowledge the legitimacy of its marketized and individualistic anti-programme.

The decline, if not the eclipse, of the statist variant of modern ordering has been explained as an effect of a wide-ranging 'post-modernization' (Crook, Pakulski and Waters, 1992: 32–41), as 'disorganization' (Lash and Urry, 1987: 5-8), as a transition from 'Fordism' to 'flexible accumulation' (Harvey, 1989: part 2) and in other ways besides. Some Foucauldian analysts (see Dean, 1996: 213; Barry, Osborne and Rose, 1996b: 4) are suspicious of these general concepts and their use in 'grand genealogies of the present moment' (Barry *et al.*, 1996b: 7). Their arguments raise complex meta-theoretical questions that cannot be considered here, but even if suspicion of 'grand genealogies' is warranted, the attempt to offer a general diagnosis of the times, however provisional and qualified it may have to be, is not a self-evidently foolish enterprise for social theory. The relations between general theoretical statements and the data over which they range need not be conceived in essentialist terms, while the use of theoretical concepts in narrative accounts of social change need not be a symptom of a closet Hegelianism. Foucauldian meta-theory sometimes trades on an exaggerated disjunction between careful attention to micro-level contingencies and the formulation of general theoretical propositions. To return to the case at issue, common themes in accounts of the transformation of advanced societies include the de-legitimation and breakdown of corporatist politics, the increasing globalization of capital markets, the decline of manufacturing industry and the traditional working-class, cultural fragmentation and, significantly here, the fiscal crisis of the state.

These processes threaten the stabilized networks of organized risk management in a number of ways. Welfare state provisions lose their role as elements in corporate decision making and the distribution of selective benefits; economic, social and cultural diversity stretches the capacities of apparatuses of surveillance and control, and a combination of ideological de-legitimation and fiscal stringency threaten a crisis for risk management. Barry, Osborne and Rose (1996b: 11, emphasis added) are correct to the letter in claiming that 'it is a mistake to see neo-liberalism as *simply* a negative response to . . . welfarism or corporatism', but if the 'simply' were deleted, the statement would be a nonsense. If the point is taken seriously that 'programme' and 'anti-programme' direct and shape each other (see discussion above), then it must apply to the relations between welfarism and neo-liberalism, or between organized and neo-liberal regimes of risk management. If mutual shaping and direction is to take place, programme and anti-programme must share enough common ground to be able to recognize each other and to formulate themselves as programme and anti-programme.

So, a critical part of what neo-liberalism 'is' requires it to formulate itself as the anti-programme of welfarism, the correct diagnosis of, and solution to, its congenitally failing character. The impact of fiscal crisis looms large in accounts of the actuarial 'failure' of welfarism. On the whole, state measures for the abatement and control of risks in organized regimes, from old-age pensions to health provision to safety inspections, have been paid from current income, hence the wave of panic around the allegedly escalating costs of an aging population, for example. But of course, and as O'Malley (1996: 194–5) points out, 'welfarism' has always been more of a moral and political programme than an amoral, apolitical form of actuarial calculation. Similarly, the individualized actuarial techniques of a 'prudentialist' neo-liberalism are part of a broader moral and political programme.

Organized risk management, and modern ordering more generally, do not simply disappear as a result of these pressures and critiques. First, there are important differences between the experiences of different advanced societies. The balance between state, individual and employer provision has always varied markedly between, say, the United States, Britain and Japan. Economic and cultural globalization may narrow the range of variation, but will not produce homogeneity in the medium term, at least. Second, even the Anglophone societies that have been at the forefront of 'reform' and 'de-regulation' have found that there are limits to the process. For example, the popularity of public health care in Australia and Britain has made overt attacks on Medicare or the National Health Service too dangerous for most politicians to contemplate.

As organized risk management retreats, states explore ways of shifting costs and responsibilities. That the most attractive way of doing this involves a neo-liberal emphasis on the freedoms and responsibilities of the reflexive individual has been noted by many commentators and discussed above. To repeat one point, the development of neo-liberal risk management involves a transformation of state activity rather than its elimination. To exaggerate, state agencies become information and advice bureaux rather than agencies of regulation and control. There are a number of related reasons why neo-liberal risk management and the

associated hyper-reflexive ordering cannot achieve the degree of hegemonic stabilization that marked the organized/modern model in its
heyday.

Critically, the regime tends to the overproduction and undercontrol of
risks. The provision of advice and information means, precisely, the
'production' and communication of risks in ever greater numbers. To
put it crudely, if you establish an apparatus for the identification of risks,
it will identify as many risks as it can. However, the only mechanisms
available for the control of these newly identified risks are the risk
calculations and lifestyle modifications open to the individual or the
increasingly strained and under resourced controls associated with the
fading organized regime. This is the core of good sense in Beck's claim
that risks are outstripping the processing capacities of society. As
Kasperson and Kasperson (1996: 96) put it, established 'assessment and
management approaches' have a poor fit with the 'ongoing complexification of risk'.

For the educated middle classes of the advanced societies, at least,
risk communications merge with problems of consumption and lifestyle
choice in a general information overload that is more likely to provoke
anxiety and insecurity than a sense of safety and control. This overload
connects with the arbitrariness and necessary incompleteness of even
the most assiduous individual risk calculation. In urging diligence in risk
calculation, Keeny (1996: 128) asks his reader to 'decide how much of
your money it is worth to reduce your risk [of death] by one chance in a
million'. For most readers the precision of the question, and of the
answer it demands, must appear bogus. Later, Keeny (132) explains
how he decided not to spend $200 on a test for colon cancer because (a)
there were better ways of spending the money and (b) the reduction in
the risk of death the test would produce was balanced by the increased
risk of death from driving to the hospital. But why does Keeny stop
there? Why not factor in the risk of switching on the TV, or of assault by
home invaders, or of asteroid strike, from staying at home rather than
driving to the hospital? If there is no rational way to draw the boundaries
around elements of a risk calculation, then the calculations required by
neo-liberal prudentialism become arbitrary.

The subjects of these calculations are imagined as responsible and
calculating prudentialists (O'Malley, 1996: 199), as located at 'A'
(market) in Douglas' 'grid–group' matrix. Of course, there are members
of advanced societies who have the resources to at least attempt to live
this dream of order. For many others, the demand for 'responsibility'
presents as the withdrawal of the resources (material and social) that
support responsibility. Demands for 'rational' calculation present as an

iron shell of constraint rather than as an opportunity. That is, more and more of the subjects of neo-liberalism are closer to position 'B', the structurally constrained isolates than position 'A', the market-oriented autonomous individuals, in Douglas' matrix. As Douglas writes of the 'enterprise culture', it must produce 'a large class of rejects. They are not the low-grade citizens of the bottom echelons of hierarchy, but disfranchised derelicts who cannot be incorporated into the system which excludes for poor performance' (1992: 227).

Neo-liberal risk management constantly threatens to de-legitimize itself because it delivers the risks without the management. Because hyper-reflexive ordering and neo-liberal risk management still require high levels of state activity and expenditure, fiscal crisis becomes a permanent condition. The risk anxiety inherent in the neo-liberal over-production and undercontrol of risk is amplified by the sense of perpetual crisis with its associated uncertainties in employment and the wider sociocultural environment. It follows that hyper-reflexive ordering and neo-liberal risk management must be difficult to stabilize. Berking's (1996) discussion of 'solidary individualism' shows how processes of de-traditionalization and individualization lead to a series of 'paradoxical demands on one's behaviour' (195) that motivate 'post-traditional community formation' (196). In a similar vein, discussing the more restricted issue of consumption anxieties, Warde (1994: 892) reviews the range of 'compensatory mechanisms, processes and institutions' through which individuals develop ways of avoiding choice and anxiety. These solidaristic 'reflexes' cannot be directly traditional because of their elective character, but in their generation of solidarity they are 'neo-traditional'.

In Douglas' terms, the managed tension within modern ordering between 'hierarchy' 'C' and 'market 'A' is increasingly overlaid and disrupted by the diagonal running between 'B', the 'isolates' and 'D' the 'voluntary group'. Neo-traditional ordering and ritualistic risk management become alternatives or supplements to hyper-reflexivity and neo-liberalism. Merging identity with one of Lash's (1994) 'reflexive communities' is an alternative to constant 'choice', anxiety and isolation. One important dimension of the 'complexification of risk' is that any given regime of risk management is now constituted in programme/anti-programme complexes with two other regimes and with the isolates of position 'B' of the 'grid–group' axis. Not only are there three regimes plus isolates, but six pairs of opposites that can be conceived as programme and anti-programme (in the abstract, A-B, A-C, A-D, B-C, B-D, C-D).

In addition to this formal 'complexification', neo-traditionalism and ritualism are difficult to stabilize. Ritualism is associated with collective actors who have an 'interest' in risk production, and both its 'political/ public relations' and 'subpolitical/solidaristic' variants mobilize versions of certainty and safety – as promises for the former and as demands for the latter – that cannot be redeemed in practice. Neo-traditionalism more generally produces local solidarities, whether defined by taste, ethnicity, place or any other marker, that take their significance from a balance of inclusion ('us') and exclusion ('them'). This is one of the oldest of the lessons of sociology, and it points to the constant potential for conflict associated with intense solidarity. That potential is heightened because, from the point of view of the established social and cultural centre arrayed along the 'grid–group' diagonal C-A, the other diagonal B-D manifests a multiply dangerous liminality. Its subjects are outsiders and its groups embody the anti-structure of *communitas*. Its preoccupations with low-probability, high-consequence risks on the boundary of nature and culture undermine the responsible, calculative prudentialism that is the public face of neo-liberalism.

Our present situation is circumscribed, then, by a triangle of regimes of risk management, each of which is partially operative but none of which can be effectively stabilized. Individually and collectively in present circumstances, organized, neo-liberal and ritualized regimes of risk management are each plausibly constructed by their plural anti-programmes as 'congenitally failing operations'. Through different mechanisms, each regime tends to produce more risks than it can abate or control. This circumstance reacts back upon the more general work of 'ordering': the triangle of regimes of risk management nests in a triangle of orderings, none of which can attain the hegemonic status once enjoyed by statist modern ordering. This claim is not offered as a lament: we may have reasons to be grateful that a Mexica-like 'stabilization' of ordering and risk management is improbable in the advanced societies. Again, there may be some reassurance in the suggestion that we have not simply passed from organization to unstructured chaos in risk management. However, the account developed here is also anti-utopian in its implications. We cannot look to either a risk-induced 'hyper-enlightenment' (as in Beck) or a world-saving solidarism (as in some deep-green arguments) to usher in a new age of safety. One possible outcome of our present disorderly orderings of risk may be a spreading awareness that living with risk means living with uncertainty and instability. Regimes of risk management 'produce' risks in order to tame them, but as congenitally failing operations, any stabilities they engender can only be temporary and regional. The ways in which political systems, cultures and social networks engage with these circumstances will be among the defining processes of the next few decades.

REFERENCES

Akrich, M. and Latour, B. (1994) A summary of a convenient vocabulary for the semiotics of human and nonhuman assemblies. In Bijker, W. and Law, J. (eds.), *Shaping Technology/Building Society.* Cambridge, MA: The MIT Press.

Alexander, J. and Smith, P. (1996) Social science and salvation: risk society as mythic discourse. *Zeitschrift für Soziologie*, 25(4), 251–62.

Barry, A., Osborne, T. and Rose, N. (1996b) Introduction. In Barry, A., Osborne, T. and Rose, N. (eds.), (1996a) *Foucault and Political Reason: Liberalism, Neo-liberalism and Rationalities of Government.* University College of London Press.

Barry, A., Osborne, T. and Rose, N. (eds.) (1996a) *Foucault and Political Reason: Liberalism, Neo-Liberalism and Rationalities of Government.* University College of London Press.

Baudrillard, J. (1983) '. . . Or the end of the social.' In *The Shadow of the Silent Majorities.* New York: Semiotexte.

Beck, U. (1992) *Risk Society: Towards a New Modernity.* London: Sage.
   (1994) The reinvention of politics: towards a theory of reflexive modernization. In Beck, U., Giddens, A. and Lash, S., *Reflexive Modernization: Politics, Tradition and Aesthetics in the Modern Social Order.* Cambridge: Polity.
   (1996) Risk society and the provident state. In Lash, S., Szerszynski, B. and Wynne, B. (eds.), *Risk, Environment and Modernity: Towards a New Ecology.* London: Sage.

Berking, H. (1996) Solidary individualism: the moral impact of cultural modernisation in late modernity. In Lash, S., Szerszynski, B. and Wynne, B. (eds.), *Risk, Environment and Modernity: Towards a New Ecology.* London: Sage.

Bernstein, P. (1996) *Against the Gods: the Remarkable Story of Risk.* New York: Wiley.

Burchell, G. (1991) Peculiar interests: civil society and governing 'the system of natural liberty'. In Burchell, G., Gordon, C. and Miller, P. (eds.), *The Foucault Effect: Studies in Governmentality.* Hemel Hempstead: Harvester Wheatsheaf.

Burchell, G., Gordon, C. and Miller, P. (eds.) (1991) *The Foucault Effect: Studies in Governmentality.* Hemel Hempstead: Harvester Wheatsheaf.

Castel, R. (1991) From dangerousness to risk. In Burchell, G., Gordon, C. and Miller, P. (eds.), *The Foucault Effect: Studies in Governmentality.* Hemel Hempstead: Harvester Wheatsheaf.

Clendinnen, I. (1991) *Aztecs.* Cambridge University Press.

Crook, S., Pakulski, J. and Waters, M. (1992) *Postmodernization: Change in Advanced Society.* London: Sage.

Dean, M. (1996) Foucault, government and the enfolding of authority. In Barry, A., Osborne, T. and Rose, N. (eds.), *Foucault and Political Reason: Liberalism, Neo-Liberalism and Rationalities of Government.* University College of London Press.

Douglas, M. (1982) Environments at risk. In Barnes, B. and Edge, D. (eds.), *Science in Context: Readings in the Sociology of Science.* Buckingham: Open University Press.

(1986) *Risk Acceptability According to the Social Sciences.* London: Routledge & Kegan Paul.

(1992) *Risk and Blame: Essays in Cultural Theory.* London: Routledge.

Douglas, M. and Wildavsky, A. (1982) *Risk and Culture: an Essay on the Selection of Technological and Environmental Dangers.* Berkeley, CA: University of California Press.

Foucault, M. (1991) Governmentality. In Burchell, G., Gordon C. and Miller, P. (eds.), *The Foucault Effect: Studies in Governmentality.* Hemel Hempstead: Harvester Wheatsheaf.

Freudenberg, W. (1996) Risky thinking: irrational fears about risk and society. *Annals of the American Academy of Political and Social Science,* 545, 44–53.

Giddens, A. (1991) *Modernity and Self-Identity: Self and Society in the Late Modern Age.* Cambridge: Polity Press.

(1994) Living in a post-traditional society. In Beck, U., Giddens, A. and Lash, S., *Reflexive Modernization: Politics, Tradition and Aesthetics in the Modern Social Order.* Cambridge: Polity Press.

Harvey, D. (1989) *The Condition of Postmodernity.* Oxford: Blackwell.

Hindess, B. (1996) Liberalism, socialism and democracy: variations on a governmental theme. In Barry, A., Osborne, T. and Rose, N. (eds.), *Foucault and Political Reason: Liberalism, Neo-Liberalism and Rationalities of Government.* University College of Press.

Kasperson, R. and Kasperson, J. (1996) The social amplification and attenuation of risk. *Annals of the American Academy of Political and Social Science,* 545, 95–105.

Keeny, R. (1996) The role of values in risk management. *Annals of the American Academy of Political and Social Science,* 545, 126–34.

Kunreuther, H. and Slovic, P. (eds.) (1996) *Challenges in Risk Assessment and Risk Management; Annals of the American Academy of Political and Social Science,* 545 (special issue on risk).

(1996) Science, values and risk. *Annals of the American Academy of Political and Social Science,* 545, 116–25.

Lash, S. (1994) Reflexivity and its doubles: structure, aesthetics, community. In Beck, U., Giddens, A. and Lash, S., *Reflexive Modernization.* Cambridge: Polity Press.

Lash, S. and Urry, J. (1987) *The End of Organized Capitalism.* Cambridge: Polity Press.

Latour, B. (1991) Technology is society made durable. In Law, J. (ed.), *A Sociology of Monsters.* London: Routledge (Sociological Review monograph 38).

(1993) *We have Never Been Modern.* Cambridge, MA: Harvard University Press.

Law, J. (1994) *Organising Modernity.* Oxford: Blackwell.

Luhmann, N. (1989) *Ecological Communication.* Cambridge: Polity Press.

(1993) *Risk: a Sociological Theory.* Berlin: de Gruyter.

Lupton, D. (1994) The great debate about cholesterol: medical controversy and the news media. *Australian and New Zealand Journal of Sociology,* 30(3), 334–9.

Maffesoli, M. (1996) *The Time of the Tribes.* London: Sage.

Malpas, J. and Wickham, G. (1995) Governance and failure: the limits of sociology. *Australian and New Zealand Journal of Sociology*, 31(3), 37–50.

Miller, P. and Rose, N. (1990) Governing economic life. *Economy and Society*, 19(1), 1–31.

O'Malley, P. (1996) Risk and responsibility. In Barry, A., Osborne, T. and Rose, N. (eds.), *Foucault and Political Reason: Liberalism, Neo-Liberalism and Rationalities of Government*. University College of London Press.

Petersen, A. (1996) Risk and the regulated self: the discourse of health promotion as politics of uncertainty. *Australian and New Zealand Journal of Sociology*, 32(1), 44–57.

Pollack, R. (1996) Government risk regulation. *Annals of the American Academy of Political and Social Science*, 545, 25–34.

Szerszynsky, B., Lash, S. and Wynne, B. (1996) Introduction: ecology, realism and the social sciences. In Lash, S., Szerszynski, B. and Wynne. B. (eds.), *Risk, Environment and Modernity: Towards a New Ecology*. London: Sage.

Turner, V. (1995) *The Ritual Process: Structure and Anti-Structure*. New York: Aldine-de Gruyter.

Viscusi, W. and Zeckhauser, R. (1996) Hazard communication: warnings and risk. *Annals of the American Academy of Political and Social Science*, 545, 106–15.

Warde, A. (1994) Consumption, identity-formation and uncertainty. *Sociology*, 28(4), 877–98.

Zeckhauser, R. and Viscusi, W. (1996) The risk management dilemma. *Annals of the American Academy of Political and Social Science*, 545, 144–55.

Index